SARAJEVO DAILY

SARAJEVO DAILY

A City and Its Newspaper Under Siege

TOM GJELTEN

HarperPerennial
A Division of HarperCollins*Publishers*

To my parents

CONTENTS

CONTENTS

A NOTE TO THE READER

This book grew out of my reporting in the former Yugoslavia for National Public Radio from 1991 to 1994. Every scene I describe I either witnessed or had described for me in detail by someone who was present.

I had not visited the region before my editors assigned me there, and I do not speak Serbo-Croatian. I therefore relied on interpreters to assist me in my interviewing. Fortunately, many of the journalists at *Oslobodjenje*, the Sarajevo newspaper that is the focus of this book, are fluent English speakers, as are other Sarajevans I met during the months I spent there. Of the principal characters in this book, I interviewed the following consistently in English: Gordana, Ivo, and Boris Knežević; Kemal Kurspahić; Ljiljana Smajlović; Vladimir and Dubravka Štaka; Džeilana Pećanin; Zlatko Dizdarević; and Mehmed Halilović. All quotations attributed to them are their actual spoken words. All other conversations were conducted through an interpreter.

I refer to the republic of Bosnia-Herzegovina, or Bosnia

for short. The official name, Bosnia *and* Herzegovina, dates from the time when there were two separate regions. If you imagine the republic as a triangle standing on its point, Herzegovina is the lower half of the triangle and the point. Bosnia is the broad upper half. There is no longer a clear border between the regions, although people still identify themselves as coming from eastern Herzegovina (generally Serbs and Muslims) or western Herzegovina (Croats). When I refer in the text to the Herzegovina region, I mean the counties at the southern tip of the republic, on both the eastern and the western sides. By Bosnia, I refer to the entire country.

A word of explanation may also be needed about the terms *nation* and *ethnic*, which are at the heart of the conflict in the former Yugoslavia. *Nation* in this book is not synonymous with *state* but designates a group of people bound by common ethnic origin, religion, or cultural heritage. Serbs, Croats, and Muslims are the three nations of Bosnia. Similarly, *national* means "of or pertaining to a nation." In this sense, I use the term interchangeably with *ethnic*.

When speaking of the religion and associated beliefs or practices, I use the word Islamic. When speaking of the people, I use Muslim. I also distinguish between Serb and Serbian. The first in my usage is an ethnic term, while the second refers to the republic. A Serb may or may not be a Serbian. The Serb army in Bosnia was assisted by the Serbian army from Belgrade.

In writing this book, I have relied on other published works, reports, and articles by colleagues. I have chosen not to break the narrative with footnotes, but in the Notes section I include the citations for assertions that demand attribution.

A GUIDE TO PRONUNCIATION IN SERBO-CROATIAN

c = *ts* as in mats

č = *ch* as in chalk

ć = *ch* as in rich

dž = *j* as in judge

dj = *g* as in forge

j = *y* as in yellow

lj = *li* as in million

nj = *ny* as in canyon

š = *sh* as in shoot

ž = *s* as in measure

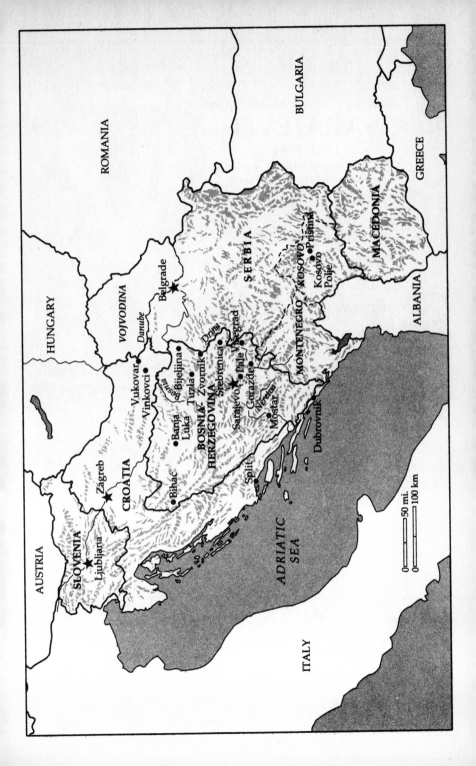

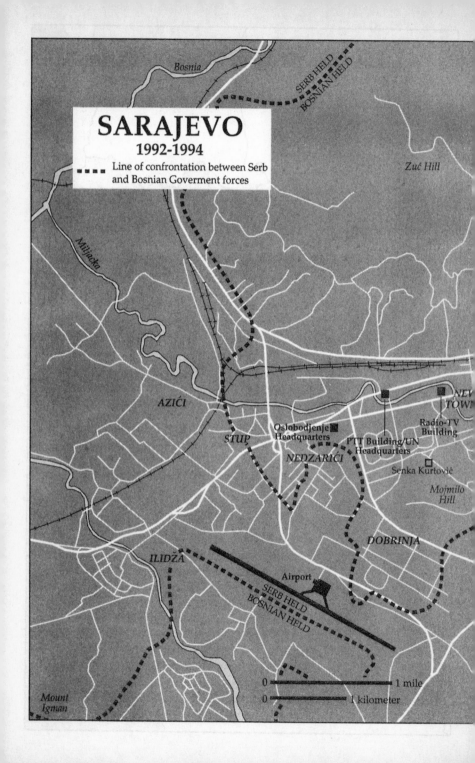

SARAJEVO
1992-1994
- - - - Line of confrontation between Serb
and Bosnian Goverment forces

Bosnia

SERB HELD
BOSNIAN HELD

Zuć Hill

Miljacka

AZIĆI

STUP

Oslobodjenje
Headquarters

NEDZARIĆI

PTT Building/UN
Headquarters

*NEW
TOWN*

Radio-TV
Building

Senka Kurtović

*Mojmilo
Hill*

DOBRINJA

ILIDŽA

Airport

SERB HELD
BOSNIAN HELD

*Mount
Ignan*

0 ————————— 1 mile
0 ————————— 1 kilometer

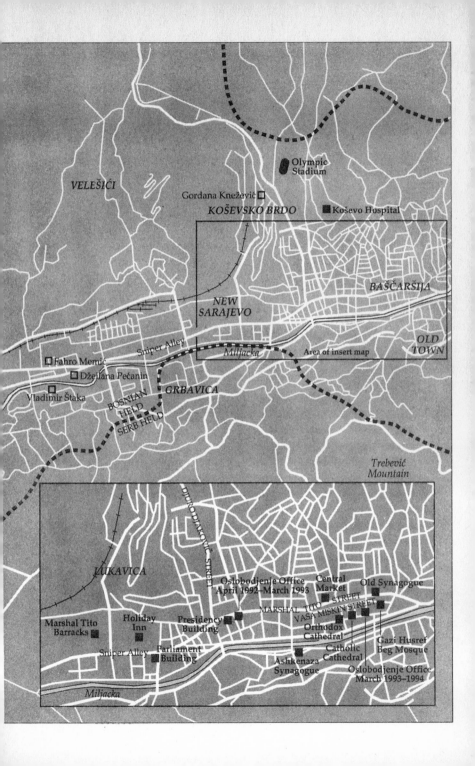

SARAJEVO DAILY

A War over Names

The woman at the government press office had warned me that the entire front side of the Holiday Inn was exposed to gunshots and that only the rear entrance was approachable. But where exactly was it? I drove cautiously around the back, looking for a sign or a doorman or a taxi. My attention was caught instead by a hand-lettered notice taped to a light pole: *Snajper!* Not wanting to linger, I made a quick U-turn in the hotel driveway and sped away to find other lodging.

The Holiday Inn, a mustard-colored cube thirteen stories high and nearly a block wide, sat in what had been the heart of Sarajevo's business district. Built for the 1984 Winter Olympic Games, the 300-room hotel faced the high-rise head-quarters of the Bosnian Parliament. The twin towers of the UNIS trade corporation stood just to the east. But on that summer afternoon in June 1992, the big-city backdrop only made the deserted streets, the burned-out cars, and the crackle of automatic rifle fire around the Holiday Inn all the more eerie, as if war had come to downtown Cleveland.

I had not been to Sarajevo before, and while driving through shell-blasted neighborhoods where pedestrians scurried in terror from one doorway to another, I remembered how peaceful Belgrade and Zagreb had seemed when I visited them a week earlier. Yugoslavia's violent breakup was primarily the result of nationalist demagoguery in the republics of Serbia and Croatia, yet their capitals were intact. Sarajevo, where people of various cultures and confessions had mingled harmoniously for centuries, was probably the city in Yugoslavia least to blame for the country's collapse, but it was under attack, as if the idea of coexistence itself were now marked for destruction.

The Holiday Inn, decorated with memorabilia of the Olympic Games, was where the war had begun, two months earlier. In the early afternoon of April 6, 1992, gunmen holed up in upper-floor rooms rented to leaders of the Serb nationalist party in Bosnia opened fire on a "peace and unity" demonstration across the street. Twenty thousand or more Sarajevans—Bosnian Serbs as well as Muslims and Bosnian Croats—had gathered that day in front of the Parliament Building to show their support for an independent, united Bosnia. Nationalism—the belief that a "people" or "nation" of common ethnic origin or religion need to unite to defend their collective rights—was to the crowd at the Parliament a dangerous, divisive doctrine. They advocated a "citizens' state," based on civil rights and constituted for individuals of all ethnic and religious backgrounds. The Holiday Inn snipers killed four demonstrators and wounded several others.

The Serbian Democratic Party (SDS), headquartered at the Holiday Inn and claiming to speak for the Serb nation in Bosnia, had opposed independence for Bosnia ever since the proposition had been raised six months earlier. Serb leaders argued that Bosnia-Herzegovina, one of six republics making up the former Yugoslavia, as an independent state would be dominated by the Muslims, because they outnumbered the Bosnian Serbs and Bosnian Croats. With backing from the Serbian government in Belgrade, the Bosnian Serb leaders were demanding the establishment of a separate "Serb Republic" on Bosnian territory and the partitioning of Sarajevo into ethnic zones.

But the attack on the peace rally suggested that the war in the former Yugoslavia was no longer the simple conflict between rival ethnic groups that it had been a year earlier, when Serbs in Croatia took up arms against the Croatian government. In Sarajevo, Serbs

The Holiday Inn hotel in Sarajevo stood just 200 yards from the front battle line and bore the scars of siege.   (MARK H. MILSTEIN/ANS)

fought on both sides, with some joining their Muslim and Croat neighbors to oppose the Serb nationalists. This was to be a war over the way people identified themselves and defined their city.

After the April 6 shooting, Sarajevo was bloodied a little more every day. Serb party leaders had distributed automatic weapons to their followers, organized them into paramilitary squads, and assigned them to "defend" particular neighborhoods. The federal Yugoslav army, on orders from Belgrade, clandestinely joined the fighting on the Serb side. Federal army artillery units shelled downtown Sarajevo from nearby hilltops. The Serb nationalists blocked all roads leading into and out of Sarajevo and resolved to keep the city surrounded until the Bosnian government agreed to their demands for a partition.

Over the next two and a half years, the rebel Serb forces through shelling and gunfire would kill more than 9,000 Sarajevans, 1,500 children among them. United Nations troops would bring more than 100,000 tons of food and other humanitarian aid to the encircled city, but the average Sarajevan still lost about twenty-five pounds. By the time the shelling finally ended, in the spring of 1994, 60 percent of the buildings in Sarajevo had been severely damaged or destroyed; a U.N. team estimated it would cost at least $4 billion to restore the city to its prewar condition.

Around the world those who believed in interfaith tolerance and human rights felt common cause with people in Sarajevo who said it was wrong to turn neighbors against one another. Elie Wiesel, Susan Sontag, Bernard-Henri Lévy, and other intellectuals and celebrity activists argued that the battle for an undivided Sarajevo was a struggle of civility versus barbarism. The enlightened Western world, they said, had a stake in the outcome. Wartime sojourners found it impossible not to be moved by the suffering of the civilian population or outraged by the cruelty of the men who fired at the city from their sniper nests and hilltop bunkers. Over and over Serb artillery gunners targeted water lines, food distribution points, and other places where crowds might gather. The aim was to demoralize the population and to force the city's surrender, but Sarajevans resisted. Most of the foreign journalists who spent extended periods of time in besieged Sarajevo found themselves sympathizing instinctively with the people they met there. I know I did.

When I couldn't find the back door to the Holiday Inn, I went to see Gordana and Ivo Knežević, whose names I had been given by a journalist at Radio Belgrade, and I ended up sleeping on a couch in their three-room apartment. Gordana was the deputy editor of *Oslobodjenje,* Sarajevo's leading daily newspaper; Ivo taught philosophy at Sarajevo University. I only had to mention over the telephone their friend Azra to secure Gordana and Ivo's welcome and an invitation to bunk for a night in their living room. The walls were decorated with prints and hangings from Egypt, where Gordana had spent four years with her family as *Oslobodjenje*'s Middle East correspondent. Books were stacked high on a corner desk and lay open on the coffee table, alongside overflowing ashtrays and foreign magazines.

Gordana is a strong-boned woman, about five ten, with square-rimmed glasses and straight brown hair that she pulled back in a ponytail. She wanted to talk about the war in her country. At age forty-one she had worked as a journalist for twenty years and was raising three children; her smoke-hardened voice suggested she had aged beyond her years. Gordana was born a Bosnian Serb. Ivo Knežević, eight years older than his wife, was more reserved. While Gordana leaned forward as we spoke, her arms folded tightly across her waist, Ivo sat serenely back. A handsome man with a gentle face, he had curly brown hair that had receded to his temples, leaving a well-tanned forehead and scalp. When I arrived at the Knežević house, he had been reading the works of the French writer Michel Foucault, on whom he lectured. Ivo is a Bosnian Croat.

Gordana and Ivo Knežević were the first people I met in Sarajevo, and they were in part responsible for my early idea of what was special about Bosnia and its capital city. I had spent weeks in Serbia and Croatia reporting on the Yugoslav war for National Public Radio, and I had grown weary of the national chauvinism and defensiveness I encountered on both sides. Gordana and Ivo were different. They had nothing but scorn for Franjo Tudjman, the president of newly independent Croatia, considering him a foolish and narrow-minded man who had needlessly alarmed and offended Croatia's Serb minority. But they also saw Serbian President Slobodan Milošević as contemptible, a leader prepared to wage war in order to carve a new "Greater Serbia" out of all the Yugoslav lands where Serbs resided. That Gordana happened to be a Serb and Ivo a Croat was irrelevant. "Being almost fifty," Ivo told me, "my biggest disappointment is how I've been forced against my will to be aware of my nationality at all. I can't think as a Croat. It's not the way I'm connected to people. I have human relations, not national or religious relations."

Gordana likewise felt uncomfortable with Serbs who considered their national origin to be the core of their being and who demanded the right to live exclusively among their own kind. "By my family name, I should be a Serb," she conceded, "but I'm a bad Serb. Being brought up in Bosnia, I feel a bit Muslim and a bit Croat as well." Gordana told me that political and social changes in Yugoslavia were "forcing people to choose an identity. We are no longer allowed to act simply as human beings." I could not have expressed it better. At last, I thought, Yugoslavs who thought as I did.

I stayed eight nights at the Knežević apartment, contributing my provisions of Belgrade cheese and salami to the meals of rice and bean soup that Ivo prepared each evening with the help of his thirteen-year-old son, Boris. Six weeks earlier Gordana and Ivo had put Boris's older brother, Igor, and his younger sister, Olga, on the last bus out of Sarajevo, keeping Boris behind at his own request. "I didn't want to leave my friends," he told me. A skinny, black-haired teenager who passed his time with Hemingway novels and heavy metal music, Boris taught me to recognize the hiss of an incoming artillery shell and turn away from the windows before it hit. During that week I also met Kana Kadić, the Muslim lady in the neighboring apartment, who came over almost every night with a plate of cookies or honey cakes in hand. Unusually religious for a Muslim woman in Sarajevo, Kana kept her head covered with a scarf and prayed five times a day, but she cared for her Serb and Croat neighbors as if they were family.

My stay with the Knežević family was my introduction to multicultural Sarajevo. It was not the only city in Yugoslavia where I would find men and women who rejected nationalist thinking and could live comfortably with people of all ancestries, but in Sarajevo that disposition rested on tradition and enjoyed official sanction. The city was founded in the Middle Ages by the Ottoman Turks, who were in the process of conquering Christian lands up and down the Balkan peninsula. In Bosnia the Turks offered feudal landowners the opportunity to retain their property and privileges in return for taking the faith of their new overlords. The nobles who accepted this curious arrangement were the builders of Sarajevo, and the line between Christianity and Islam was therefore blurred in the city from the beginning. Having compromised their own religion so thoroughly, the town fathers were accommodating of others' beliefs. It was developed as a predominately Muslim city, but over time Sarajevo became home also to Orthodox Serbs, Catholic Croats, Sephardic Jews, and Gypsies. So it remained: In 1991 half of the city's 430,000 residents were non-Muslim.

Separate Christian and Muslim communities existed throughout Bosnia, but Sarajevo was a trading center, and its history of interfaith contact is unmatched in the rest of Europe. Mosques, churches, and synagogues were built within yards of one another in the city center, and spiritual leaders routinely acknowledged one another's holy days. Most Sarajevo Christians grew up familiar with Islam, and Sarajevo Muslims often joined their friends at worship services on Christmas Eve or Easter. I heard the story in Sarajevo of an old Muslim man who regularly went to a Catholic church to pray because his legs were weak and he liked sitting in a pew. "It is the house of God," he explained. "God is all-knowing."

The religious and cultural mix in Sarajevo was always volatile, of course. The assassination of the Austrian archduke Franz Ferdinand by a young Serb nationalist in Sarajevo on June 28, 1914, set off a night of fierce anti-Serb riots in the city. Mindful of the danger of intercommunal conflict, city authorities had occasionally tried to mandate harmony, as when they ordered that steeples on Orthodox or Catholic cathedrals be built no higher than the minaret on the main mosque. Attempts to balance the interests of the various national or religious groups peaked during the thirty-five years of Yugoslavia's rule by Josip Broz Tito, the World War II Communist Partisan leader, who treated ethnic tension as a divisive threat that needed to be suppressed at all costs.

Because of Sarajevo's record of relatively peaceful interethnic life, Tito saw it as a model for the rest of Yugoslavia, and, in the period immediately following World War II, he even considered making it the federal capital. Sarajevo lost that campaign but won another three decades later, when it earned the right to host the 1984 Winter Olympic Games. The city's elegant hospitality in 1984 made all Yugoslavia proud. Sarajevans charmed visitors with their friendliness, their sophistication, and their apparent unity. Theirs was one city where Yugoslavia clearly worked. With the collapse of one-party rule in 1989–90, competing nationalist regimes came to power in most Yugoslav republics, but in Sarajevo the Communist injunction against ethnic divisiveness was taken seriously. Formal support for a multiethnic state and society carried over into the post-Communist period in Sarajevo to a greater extent than in other Yugoslav capitals.

One of the best examples of a Sarajevo institution practicing interethnic harmony was the newspaper where Gordana Knežević worked. *Oslobodjenje*, which means "Liberation," was founded in 1943 as an underground organ of Marshal Tito's Communist Partisan movement, whose ranks in Bosnia included Serbs, Muslims, and Croats fighting alongside one another. The staff had rebelled against Communist Party control in the late 1980s, in order to establish their newspaper as a genuinely democratic media enterprise, but they retained the Communists' distaste for nationalist politics. When separate Serb, Croat, and Muslim political parties were formed in advance of the 1990 elections, *Oslobodjenje* criticized them all, throwing its support instead behind parties with pan-national programs. In early 1992, when Serb nationalists sought to block the Bosnian independence drive and demanded that the republic be partitioned along ethnic lines, *Oslobodjenje* aligned itself with the Bosnian government in opposing the Serb campaign. Based in the western Sarajevo suburb of Nedjarići, the *Oslobodjenje* staff reflected the mix of Serbs, Muslims, and Croats in Bosnia as a whole, and Gordana Knežević and other editors wanted it to stay that way.

Oslobodjenje defied the Serb nationalists in the spring of 1992 as had the demonstrators on April 6, and, also as had the demonstrators, the newspaper's ten-story headquarters of gleaming blue glass became a sniper target. A few days after the Holiday Inn shooting, Serb militiamen with high-powered rifles let loose a volley of bullets from a hundred yards. The office of editor in chief Kemal Kurspahić was among the first hit, as though the gunmen knew which windows were his.

Kurspahić was in a conference room, presiding over a meeting of his editorial board. At the sound of shooting, he moved the session to a room on the opposite side of the building. Opening a bottle of whiskey, he poured drinks for everyone and broke the tension with a crack about United Nations "peace" keepers in Sarajevo, who had been dispatched a few weeks earlier in the hope they could reduce tensions.

Kurspahić was the first *Oslobodjenje* editor to be chosen by the newspaper staff rather than the Communist Party. Muslim by name but wholly secular in outlook, he was married to a Serb and, like many Sarajevo Muslims, showed little interest in his own ethnic background. In February and March of 1992, Kurspahić had been one of the Sarajevans who assured foreign visitors that ethnic war would not come to the city. His outgoing manner, a reputation for fairness, and good humor had made him popular with his colleagues. Kurspahić still displayed his wit after the Serb gunmen shot up his office a second time at the end of April and a Sarajevo television crew came to film the damage. "Look what they did to this magnificent piece of art," he said, pointing to an oil painting punctured by a bullet. Turning to face the camera, Kurspahić delivered a mock rebuke to the Nedjarići snipers: "We just can't have this in our neighborhood!"

While Yugoslavia was sliding into civil war, Sarajevo was still known as a place where fears could be laughed away. This was the city that claimed the best films, the finest cuisine, and the most talented rock bands in Yugoslavia, and the residents were desperate to hold on to the good times. A Croatian friend who visited Sarajevo at the height of the 1991 Serb-Croat conflict told me later he was infuriated by the atmosphere of escapist playfulness he found. The bars and discos were full every night, and not a person he met seemed to know or care that war was raging in the Yugoslav republic just fifty miles to the west. In those days nearly every downtown street was lined with sidewalk cafés, and Sarajevans would sit for hours chatting over tiny cups of thick coffee and sticky Turkish sweets.

But by the time I arrived in Sarajevo, the cafés were closed, the streets were empty, and people were cowering in basement shelters. I found a Sarajevo of boarded-up storefronts, shattered windows, and pavements pockmarked with shell craters. It was obvious that it had been an enchanting city. Cobblestone lanes wound through the old Baščaršija (Bazaar) district, past tiny shops, around ancient mosques, and up hillsides. Straddling the banks of the Miljacka River over a length of eight miles, the city was only two miles across at its widest point. Tree-covered mountains rose steeply on the south flank and at the eastern end of the city, providing a verdant background to the red-tiled roofs and white minarets of the skyline. Sarajevans had flocked to those green hills to hike and ski on weekends until the spring of 1992, when the Serb-dominated federal army positioned heavy artillery guns and howitzers along the ridge tops. After that the hills were, as one woman said, "the place from where death comes," and many Sarajevans could not look up from their city without feeling sickened.

Walking through downtown Sarajevo one unnaturally quiet day, I imagined how it had been in peacetime. The restaurant Dalmacija might have been an inviting place before the mortar shell hit the wall above the front entrance, leaving the sign a dangling shred of twisted metal. The big Magros department store on Marshal Tito Street, its name spelled out in large blue letters, would have been like any other of its kind in Yugoslavia, the counters piled high with inexpensive clothing and underwear. But now the windows were all blown out, and the store had been thoroughly trashed.

It seemed as if time stopped the day shooting started. The final moment of the prewar era was frozen on the downtown walls and kiosks, where the same theater bills hung for two years: *Cyrano* with Gerard Depardieu was showing at the local cinemas. The Sarajevo Radio and Television Orchestra was advertising Tchaikovsky's Symphony No. 5 in E minor on April 11 at 8:00 P.M. Another poster said CITIZENS OF SARAJEVO! in red letters across the top; it was a call to gather in front of the Parliament Building on April 6 to show support for a unified Bosnian state. After that date, no more posters were hung.

The big turnout at the April 6 demonstration showed that a significant segment of the Sarajevo population firmly opposed the creation of separate, ethnically based minirepublics in Bosnia. National (ethnic) identities had been weakening in Sarajevo year by year since World War II. In 1991 one of three new marriages in Sarajevo was between partners of different national backgrounds, the highest rate ever registered.* Sarajevans born of such marriages could not be fit neatly into a "national" category and were likely to feel uncomfortable in any republic established primarily for one ethnic group—the state model favored by nationalists. Boris Knežević, with one parent a Serb and the other a Croat, was not sure of his own nationality. "Bosnian . . . I guess" was his answer when asked. Not because his parents were of one ancestry or another but because he was from a place called Bosnia. Implicit in such a view was the idea of a civil state, where the rights of citizenship extend automatically to anyone born in the country, without regard to ethnic or religious background. When Yugoslavia moved toward a multiparty democracy in the late 1980s, liberal reformers favored a system modeled broadly on these lines. In theory, the Bosnian government advocated a civil state, as did most of the staff at *Oslobodjenje* and other leading intellectuals in Sarajevo.

The Serb nationalists (like their counterparts across Eastern Europe and the former Soviet Union) had a radically different notion of democracy and statehood. Given the history of ethnic conflict in the Yugoslav lands, they claimed, the Serbs in Bosnia required constitutional protection not as individuals but as a *nation*. This could be achieved, they argued, only if they had their own state and could live separately from non-Serbs. But their argument was undercut by Sarajevo, with its tradition of tolerance, high rate of interethnic marriage, and example of urban Serbs who favored a unified Bosnian state. Croat nationalists in Bosnia, who also wanted their own ministate, did not bother to contest multiethnic Sarajevo, because Croats made up only about 7 percent of the city's population and were generally content to live in peace with their Sarajevo neighbors. The Serb nationalists could not afford to abandon a claim to Sarajevo, however; almost 120,000 Serbs lived in the five municipal districts that formed the core urban area.

The unique circumstances in Sarajevo meant that the Bosnian war had a more ideological character in the capital than in the northern and eastern parts of the country, where Serbs simply attacked

*According to the Bosnian government's Institute for Statistics, 18.6 percent of marriages recorded in the period 1981–1991 in Bosnia-Herzegovina were between partners of different nationalities. The proportion was 29.2 percent in urban municipalities, versus 9.5 percent in nonurban areas. Sarajevo reported the highest intermarriage rate, with 34.1 percent in 1991, up from 30.1 percent in 1981.

Muslims in order to seize their land. Serb leaders responded to the Sarajevo challenge by arguing that interethnic harmony was a myth promoted mainly by the Muslims, whose political party dominated the Bosnian government. The Muslim national party officially advocated an undivided Sarajevo, but the Serb nationalists said the Muslims' commitment to coexistence was meaningless because they outnumbered the Serbs and therefore had nothing to fear from them. "Don't talk to us about multiethnicity," a Bosnian Serb official told a reporter from *The Washington Post*, "because in Sarajevo that means the domination of a single culture."

As for people in Sarajevo and elsewhere who called themselves Bosnians—whether pro-government Serbs such as Gordana Knežević or offspring of mixed marriages, such as her son Boris—the Serb nationalists simply declared them nonexistent. "We in Bosnia have never considered ourselves other than Serbs, Croats, and Muslims," claimed Radovan Karadžić, president of the Serbian Democratic Party, in a column published in the *Financial Times* in London a year after the war began. "There is no Bosnian patriotism," he wrote. "There is no Bosnian nation. There is just a common home for three peoples." Karadžić's argument was undercut by the intermarriage data, but he was laying out the reality he intended to *create*. To the extent that people in Bosnia or Sarajevo did not define themselves in ways that suited the nationalist agenda, the Serb side was determined to redefine them. It was an effort that had begun before the war started. In the weeks preceding the national census of 1991, the Serb nationalist party put up posters all over Sarajevo asking residents of Serb ancestry to mark their nationality "Serb" and not "Yugoslav," as many had done in previous census tallies.

Given their goal of realigning human relations in Sarajevo, it was fitting that the man the Serb nationalists chose to lead their party was a practicing psychiatrist. Dr. Radovan Karadžić had always yearned for fame and fortune outside his professional world, although he had mostly come up short. Before becoming a politician in 1990, Karadžić had served eleven months in a Sarajevo prison for embezzlement. Leading the Serb nationalist party in Sarajevo gave him the public exposure he had long sought, however, and he excelled at it. "The Muslims are trying to create an Islamic state here," Karadžić told visiting reporters, "but we Serbs are not going to let them." Less than two years earlier, Karadžić had told a Belgrade magazine that Bosnian Serbs had no reason to distrust their Muslim neighbors, but those who knew him well were not surprised that he changed his tune when circumstances dictated.

The first step in the Serb nationalist strategy for Sarajevo was to expose the ethnic tensions that the Muslims and their government allies were allegedly concealing. If the unacknowledged conflicts proved deep enough, Sarajevo would separate on its own as soon as the fault lines were revealed. In March 1992, as the international community prepared to recognize Bosnia as an independent state, Karadžić and his fellow party leaders urged Serbs in Sarajevo to abandon their city.

To the shock and disappointment of their friends, some Sarajevo Serbs immediately packed up their cars and left. A few were simply alarmed at the prospect of war and wanted to escape before it hit; indeed, Muslim and Croat residents were among those who fled at the first signs of trouble. But there were also Serbs who did not like their Muslim neighbors and did not want to live in a Muslim-ruled Bosnia. At *Oslobodjenje*, about a fourth of the Serb employees departed, including several journalists, reporter Ljubo Grković among them. "A lot of people think Sarajevo was this ideal place," Grković told me a year later in Belgrade, "but it wasn't. It was all a farce. We were angry and jealous of each other; we just weren't supposed to talk about it." Given the Serb exodus, foreign journalists who had been impressed by Sarajevo's apparent cohesiveness were forced to reconsider their initial judgment.

From his relocated party headquarters in Pale, a village in the hills overlooking Sarajevo, Radovan Karadžić attempted to make the most of the population movements, describing them as natural in the aftermath of Communism's collapse in Yugoslavia. "Tito threw us together," he said. "We were like oil and water. While he shook us, we stayed together. Once we were left alone, we separated."

In the Serb-controlled countryside, however, the main shift in the early months of the Bosnian war involved Muslims and Croats being forced out of their villages at the point of Serb guns. Inside Sarajevo the ethnic rearrangement was far from complete. Even in the face of war, thousands of Serbs chose to remain in the city, including most of the Serb editors and reporters at *Oslobodjenje*. Many Sarajevo Serbs did not want to give up their apartments or had nowhere else to go. Others saw no reason to flee, or they wanted to live in a diverse society with a civic culture and believed the chances of establishing such a system were better in cosmopolitan Sarajevo, even under a Muslim-dominated government, than in Pale or Belgrade. The more urbane and educated they were, the less likely Serbs in Sarajevo were to take the nationalists' side. There would indeed be a fight to save the city's soul.

When it became clear Sarajevo was not dividing on its own accord, the Serb nationalists moved to the second phase of their strategy: They encouraged the partition process by deliberately provoking ethnic conflict. The Serb nationalist media ceaselessly depicted the Bosnian government as an Islamic fundamentalist regime, determined to force Muslim rules and customs on the Serb population. The brutality with which the war was fought suggested that the Serb aim was as much to sow hatred as to capture territory. Around Sarajevo the shelling seemed to be coordinated to promote a physical division of the city. Settlements with an especially high proportion of Muslim residents suffered the most, while Serb army commanders ordered their artillery units to spare neighborhoods with large concentrations of Serbs. The idea was evidently to show Muslim and Serb residents that their destinies in Sarajevo were not shared after all.

With the Serb nationalists intent on bombing Sarajevo into submission, resistance was simply a matter of continuing to keep prewar ways alive. At an *Oslobodjenje* staff meeting in late April 1992, Kemal Kurspahić appealed to his journalists to join him in making the newspaper a symbol of Sarajevo's character and persevering spirit. "I cannot guarantee you will be alive when this war is over," Kurspahić told them, "nor can you expect awards or promotions just for staying. But I will make you this promise: As long as Sarajevo exists, we will continue to publish this newspaper."

The *Oslobodjenje* headquarters, however, was hit repeatedly— first by sniper fire, then by antiaircraft rounds, and finally by grenades and artillery shells. Kurspahić was at work on the day in May 1992 when Serb forces in Nedjarići brought in a tank and opened fire on the *Oslobodjenje* building. When the first shell hit, he heard a loud explosion and then a screech "like a cat when you kick it," as though the glass and aluminum structure could feel its ribs being broken. The shelling continued from that day on, tearing the building apart floor by floor, office by office, until it collapsed five months later. *Oslobodjenje* operations were moved to underground rooms originally built as atomic bomb shelters.

Over the next two years, incredibly, the paper managed to produce an edition every single day, although on two occasions ferocious shelling prevented it from being distributed. When electricity was cut, editors located a generator and begged diesel fuel from U.N. peacekeepers or bought it on the black market. When newsprint stocks ran out, *Oslobodjenje* was printed on paper meant for advertising flyers or packaging. It shrank from twenty-four broadsheet pages to eight tabloid pages (two or three of which were taken up by death notices), and the press run fell from 60,000 to 3,500, but the paper kept coming out. Under war conditions, *Oslobodjenje* took on an importance in Sarajevo that newspapers rarely know. It provided information in a city starved for it, and it survived as a relic of prewar life in a city desperate to remember normal times.

Under bombardment Sarajevo slid steadily toward something like a postmodern Stone Age. First to go was the public transportation system, then the telephones, water, gas, and electricity. Relief agencies brought in enough food to keep the population alive, but for fuel people had to chop down trees in the city parks, burn their furniture, and scavenge the hillsides, directly under the big Serb guns. I witnessed the process of degradation during seven visits while the city was under siege. I eventually located the rear entrance to the Holiday Inn and stayed at the hotel most of the time thereafter. I always spent a few nights with the Knežević family, however, as I had on my first visit, and, for several weeks in the summer of 1993, I rented a two-room flat in a west Sarajevo high-rise building. Observing my neighbors go about their daily routines, I saw how physically and emotionally exhausting the work of survival could be. Month by month the web of civility that held the city together frayed.

One morning in July 1993 I was awakened by angry wailing in the courtyard below my eighth-floor window. Looking down, I saw a boy standing in a shallow pit, next to a partially dug up tree stump. A man was sitting on the stump, as if to claim it, but the boy also wanted it, and he was in a tearful fury. I had watched people from the neighborhood taking turns at the stump for three days, hacking off bits of wood to be burned in their kitchen stoves. The boy's father must have sent him to the stump early that morning with instructions to hold it, because the boy stood his ground as though the survival of his whole family depended on him. Still, the man refused to move. A passerby stopped in response to the boy's anguished cries; only then did the man on the stump say anything. He waved his hand dismissively at the boy and, pointing to the stump, said something loudly to the passerby, who moved on then without intervening. There was little to quarrel over. The main portion of the stump was already cut off; this was a fight over the underground part. Several hours of chopping, however, could still yield enough wood chips to fill a large plastic bag. Three other stumps nearby had already been dug up and the holes in the earth refilled.

They had been big trees. The barren lot behind my building must have been a shaded and leafy garden before the people of the neighborhood took to it with their saws and axes. They had had no choice. The only bread to be eaten was that baked at home over a wood fire. What water could still be collected was contaminated and needed to be boiled. And now the search for chips and twigs left a neatly dressed man and a boy in sneakers facing each other meanly over a hole in the ground. The boy's unrelenting whine soon attracted a small crowd. A discussion ensued, and somehow the dispute was resolved. By afternoon the last of the stump had been cut up and taken away.

The conditions of siege slowly created in Sarajevo the strife that Serb nationalists had claimed from the beginning. Muslims were increasingly convinced that as the principal victims of the war they deserved special attention. Non-Muslim residents came under pressure to prove their patriotism even while being expected to endorse the official claim that Serbs and Croats were treated fairly. In March 1993 Ivo Knežević was made information minister in the Bosnian government. Although he supported the government in its confrontation with the Serb nationalists, he felt at times that his real cabinet role was to be the Loyal Croat, and he was not pleased by the assignment. Gordana was also concerned at the weakening of democratic values in her city, as were colleagues at her newspaper and other Sarajevans who believed in a state based on civil rights. But she and other editors felt that dissent and political opposition were out of place as long as Bosnia remained at war. Under the circumstances, *Oslobodjenje* occasionally reverted to the uncritical reporting habits it had displayed during the Communist era.

In February 1994, after a 120-mm mortar shell killed sixty-eight people at Sarajevo's main downtown market, the Serb forces agreed to withdraw their heavy weapons from around the city as part of a ceasefire negotiated by the British commander of U.N. forces in Bosnia, Lt. Gen. Sir Michael Rose. A month later Rose opened a U.N.-controlled crossroads outside Sarajevo, enabling limited traffic to move to and from the city for the first time in more than two years. By late spring electricity, water, and gas services were largely restored under U.N. supervision.

Visiting Sarajevo in June 1994, I finally saw for myself what the city had been like before the war. Couples were strolling arm in arm along the Miljacka River embankment, just as in postcard scenes. I found old men sitting on a bench in front of the Gazi Husref Beg mosque, in desultory conversation such as old men would have been in any Balkan capital. For the first time I heard trolley car bells and the whine of motor scooters on Marshal Tito Street. The sidewalk cafés in the Turkish bazaar district were once again packed with coffee drinkers. I was impressed by how quickly Sarajevans seemed to be bouncing back to normal. Before the war they had refused to face the horror that was coming their way. It occurred to me that their surprisingly quick recovery was the flip side of that attitude: Now people seemed to be pretending that the war had never happened.

What I could not see was how profoundly Sarajevo had *changed*. By the spring of 1994, as much as half of the prewar population had managed to get out of the city, including a majority of the Serbs and Jews and many Muslims and Croats who had financial resources or international connections. A slightly smaller number of people, almost all of them Muslims, had meanwhile arrived from small towns and villages in eastern Bosnia, where the Serb nationalists had been "cleaning" their territory by killing or expelling the non-Serb population. Residents who had stayed throughout the war complained that they no longer felt entirely comfortable in their city, that many of the people downtown were newcomers to Sarajevo, conspicuous with their conservative dress and country ways.

The demographic shift in Sarajevo strengthened the position of the main Muslim political party, which had dominated the Bosnian government since the 1990 elections. Ruling party membership was becoming a prerequisite for appointment to leadership positions in government-related institutions, just as it had been in the Communist times. Independent enterprises, such as *Oslobodjenje*, found themselves in danger of being marginalized, and some Sarajevans were debating whether their government could still be considered democratic.

The social and political changes were also beginning to trouble people around the world for whom Sarajevo had come to stand as a symbol of enlightenment values under assault. By June 1994 some were ready to admit defeat. "I'm not sure we should stay here any longer," said Radha Kumar, the Sarajevo representative of the Helsinki Citizens Assembly. She had come to the city three months earlier as part of her organization's program to promote democratic values in post-Communist countries. But by June she was feeling discouraged. "I fear it's moving inexorably toward a dictatorship here," she said. "No matter how much people want democracy, I'm afraid it's going to be almost impossible to have it."

The concern over antidemocratic tendencies in Sarajevo surfaced just as some Western media analysts were reassessing the performance of foreign news organizations in reporting the Bosnian war. Critics charged that correspondents had overstated the Bosnian government's commitment to pluralism while romanticizing prewar life in Sarajevo and "demonizing" the Serb nationalist side. The conflict in Bosnia, it was alleged, had generated a "propaganda war" between the two sides, and the Muslims and their allies had simply proved more adept than the Serbs at manipulating the press. If so, the world was getting a distorted version of the Sarajevo story. The anecdotes that disillusioned peace activists brought back from the city only added to the controversy; perhaps it was time for those of us who had described the Sarajevo struggle in moral terms to rethink our sympathies.

The problem with such analyses was that they skipped too quickly over intervening events and came too hastily to the conclusion. Missing was the long view of what had happened in Sarajevo: As Communist authority collapsed, the values of civil society and a democratic state began taking root in Sarajevo but soon came under fierce assault. Serb nationalists set out to divide the city by force and establish ethnically pure zones where civil rights would not apply. The ensuing struggle was one in which the rest of the world had a stake, because the principle of interethnic coexistence with which Sarajevo was associated will be endangered again somewhere else. Particular features of the Bosnian war—that it was fought in the aftermath of Communist rule and in a land where Muslims formed the largest share of the population—make the Sarajevo experience all the more relevant when Cold War–era security institutions are being refashioned and militant Islam is a growing political force. But to make clear the import and lesson in the Sarajevo story, it must be told with fullness and precision.

I focus on *Oslobodjenje* and the people who worked there, although their wartime achievements were not unique. Consider the doctors and nurses who returned day after day to Koševo Hospital, the Sarajevo firemen, and the utility workers who braved land mines and sniper fire to repair downed power lines. The unimaginable became ordinary in besieged Sarajevo, and heroes abounded. But it was through the *Oslobodjenje* workers that I came to know Sarajevo. They were journalists like me, but with a duty to inform a confused and frightened community. I admired the ideals for which their enterprise stood, and in the story of their daily newspaper I found the whole Sarajevo saga. The values of harmony and tolerance would stand or fall with the struggle of the *Oslobodjenje* staff to stay together and remain true to their tradition.

Their lives for me defined the daily Sarajevo ordeal. Like everyone else, they lugged canisters of water up the stairs in darkened apartment buildings, stood in line for packages of donated macaroni, went for months without a bath, and were frightened every time they went outside. They were enraged at the failure of the international community to save their city, they quarreled, they saw family members die, they despaired, and they carried on.

1

Bloodlines

Sarajevo on the first Saturday of April 1992 was about to learn its fate, and its people were waiting to see what they should do. European Community foreign ministers intended to recognize Bosnia-Herzegovina as an independent state at a meeting in Luxembourg on the coming Monday, April 6, in the hope that doing so would reduce the likelihood of civil war in the republic, one of four remaining in the Yugoslav federation after Croatia and Slovenia seceded. But Radovan Karadžić and other Serb nationalist leaders had been preparing to lead a Serb uprising in Bosnia, and they were warning that international recognition of the Muslim-dominated republic would be the spark that would set them off. Every flight out of town was fully booked that weekend, and there were long lines at all open gas stations. Police set up checkpoints around the city and nervously stopped passing vehicles to search for weapons. Yet many Sarajevans went on with their normal Saturday business—washing cars, cleaning their flats, and shopping. The prospect of an interethnic war was simply too awful to contemplate in a city where Serbs, Muslims, and Croats lived in the same apartment buildings, worked and socialized together, and even married each other.

Oslobodjenje reporter Senka Kurtović was due to see her boyfriend, Dragan Alorić, that Saturday evening. Dragan hosted a popular Saturday night interview and music program on Radio Sarajevo, and Senka liked to sit in the studio with him during the broadcast. Although he was a Serb and she was not, their national backgrounds had never been an issue between them. Like other Sarajevans in their twenties, Senka and Dragan spent many of their evenings in bright and noisy downtown cafés where an MTV-defined pop culture dominated and where men who blustered in early 1992 about the rights of their "nation" were ridiculed. In Senka and Dragan's café circle, talking like a nationalist got you branded a *papak*, "hoof" in Serbo-Croatian, suggesting you belong in a barnyard.

In the Yugoslav census a year earlier, Senka had done her part to protest her country's obsession with ethnic identity, a result of which was the requirement that all Yugoslavs had to declare a nationality. Senka was of mixed ancestry and saw no reason to place herself in any ethnic category. When a census taker asked the nationality question, Senka didn't know how to respond. As she pondered, the census worker commented that with her short blond hair and rosy red cheeks Senka reminded him of a girl he once knew in Holland. "That'll do. Put that down," she said, and Senka was officially registered as Dutch. Among friends Senka said she felt "more Croat than anything," but that was only because she had grown up on Croatia's Dalmatian coast and sometimes went to church with her Catholic Croat acquaintances. Her father was actually a Bosnian Muslim, and her "Croat" mother was half-Jewish. Senka assumed that her boyfriend, despite his Orthodox Serb family background, felt as she did on matters of nationality. Dragan had often told her that names and religion meant nothing to him, and she had believed him.

For his show on Saturday, April 4, Dragan had suggested that Senka participate in an on-the-air discussion with other studio guests about the upcoming commemoration of Sarajevo's liberation from German occupation on April 6, 1945. Senka was herself a granddaughter of Yugoslav Partisan fighters and had written about the liberation day anniversary for *Oslobodjenje*'s "City Chronicle" section. After her segment ended and the other guests left, Senka waited quietly in the studio for Dragan to finish the program. She noticed he was unusually reserved. The early morning news bulletins brought reports of Serb paramilitary squads clashing with Bosnian police in the southwest and northeast of the republic and erecting street barricades in Ilidža, a suburb to the west of Sarajevo; Dragan seemed bothered by what he heard.

During a music break he turned to Senka and said, "You shouldn't go out today. Something serious is going to happen." She asked him to explain, but he would say only that anyone smart should leave the city. She could see Dragan was holding something back, and it made her angry, but Senka couldn't get him to elaborate. When the program was over, Dragan drove her home in silence. It would be the last time they were together.

At six-thirty Sunday morning, an *Oslobodjenje* duty editor called Senka to say he needed her at the paper. There were signs it could be a big news day, he said. For the third consecutive morning, about 90 percent of the *Oslobodjenje* delivery drivers had failed to show up for work and offered no excuse for their absence. All were Serbs. More ominously, there were reports that many Serb members of the Sarajevo police force had left their posts the day before, taking weapons and equipment with them. Mindful of Dragan's strange behavior and cryptic warning of the night before, Senka went to work nervous.

Around midday, demonstrators for peace were to march from Dobrinja—the suburb where Senka lived—to the city center, about six miles away. Dobrinja was on the outskirts of the city, adjacent to the airport. It was a new residential development, built during the construction boom that had preceded the 1984 Winter Olympic Games. Many of the residents were young professionals like Senka, and they were of all nationalities. The march was to be a demonstration against nationalism and the apartheid notions of those who wanted to see Bosnia divided. Senka had to settle for watching it on television in the *Oslobodjenje* newsroom. The marchers headed down Proleterske Brigade, a broad avenue running through the ethnically mixed New Sarajevo neighborhood. As they walked, people sang and shouted, "We can live together!" In the high-rise apartment buildings that flanked the street, residents watched from open windows, cheering and waving. By the time the march reached the Bosnian Parliament Building, several thousand people were in the streets, chanting "*Bosna!* Bosnia!"

The rally annoyed gunmen who were watching from the heavily Serb neighborhood of Grbavica on the other side of the Miljacka River. As the crowd milled in front of the building, rifle shots were fired over the people's heads. A group of demonstrators then moved onto a bridge. They were headed toward barricades that had been erected by armed Serb nationalists the night before. There was another burst of gunfire, this time aimed directly at the people. Several demonstrators were hit, among them a university student named Suada Dilberović, who died of her wounds a few hours later.

Television Sarajevo carried live reports from the scene, and at *Oslobodjenje* Senka and other workers huddled around the newsroom set. Senka's assignment was to take notes from the television coverage, check the information against radio reports, and stay in telephone contact with correspondents downtown. One woman interviewed held her blood-smeared hands up before the camera and said, "This is from that girl killed on the bridge! We were yelling, 'Killers! Killers!' at them, but they just kept on shooting." She described the gunmen as being masked and said some wore army uniforms. The building from which the shots were fired was known to be occupied by Serb militiamen.

After the shooting the demonstrators forced their way into the Parliament Building, where an informal People's Assembly was declared in the packed parliamentary chamber. It soon turned into a wild but inspiring open forum, with speaker after speaker standing before the roaring crowd to call for peace and attacking all nationally oriented politicians, whether Serb, Croat, or Muslim. A banner was hung from a wall with the slogan "Down with nationalists, chauvinists, Nazis, and fascists!" About 2,000 people remained at the Parliament overnight, singing folk songs outside the front doors. Senka stayed at the *Oslobodjenje* building, monitoring late developments and writing into the early morning. Residents in the Old Town neighborhood reported hearing explosions after midnight, and fires were burning around the airport.

The next day stores, schools, and offices were closed because of the liberation holiday. News of the dramatic scene at the Parliament Building spread quickly, and thousands more people came to show solidarity with the demonstrators. Busloads of coal miners in blue overalls and tin helmets arrived from central Bosnia. Many in the crowd were old Communists, and some carried huge portraits of Tito, whose efforts to keep Yugoslavia together looked increasingly laudable in hindsight. "Tito is ours! We are Tito's!" they chanted, reviving an old propaganda slogan. By midday the plaza in front of the Parliament was packed with people. The sky was overcast and the temperature cool for an April day.

Gordana Knežević came to the rally on Monday as much to be

there with the people as to watch it as a journalist. Her sister Dubravka was also there, with her two children. The size of the crowd lent a slightly festive air to the gathering, and for a few hours it remained peaceful, with speeches and music on a stage in front of the building. During a lull in the activity, Dubravka walked over to visit her father, who lived nearby, leaving her children with friends. Gordana went to the *Oslobodjenje* office to work on a column for the next day's paper. "A new Bosnia is being born," she wrote.

Shortly after 1:00 P.M., gunshots rang out around the building. Džeilana Pećanin was standing with a friend near the edge of the plaza when she heard a "poof" and saw a little burst of dirt fly up from the grass a few feet away. "Was that a bullet?" she asked. No, her friend said. But it was, and, when more shots followed a few minutes later, they ran. With thousands packed into the plaza area, however, many people were forced to scramble for cover behind shrubs or just lie on the ground, behind their friends.

The gunfire came from upper floors of the Holiday Inn, across the street from the Parliament. Several of the windows were open, and armed men could be seen looking out, their rifles pointed at the crowd. More snipers were on the roof, and they were also shooting. Within minutes several people lay wounded and bleeding in the plaza and the street next to it. There was no question who was responsible. The Holiday Inn was under the control of the Serbian Democratic Party; its leader, Radovan Karadžić; and his pack of bodyguards.

After their initial panic people caught in the plaza by the shooting were collectively enraged. They surged across the street and toward the hotel, ready to find and disarm the gunmen. They were led by members of the Bosnian Interior Ministry's Special Forces Unit, which was supposed to provide security at the Parliament rally. The Bosnian policemen charged into the hotel lobby, shooting their guns in the air. Terrified guests and hotel workers vaulted over the reception counter or hid in the stairwells. Some demonstrators rushed in behind the police, breaking windows as they went, while the policemen proceeded on a door-smashing room-by-room search for the snipers. The police eventually found and arrested six men, among them one of Karadžić's bodyguards. As the gunmen were marched out the front entrance to a waiting police van, people outside the hotel screamed at them, "Garbage!"

Television Sarajevo was still broadcasting live from the scene, and viewers around the city could follow the Holiday Inn action.

Gordana's sister watched from their father's apartment, which was on the opposite side of the hotel, a block north of the Parliament. She dashed back, only to find that everyone, including her children, had scattered. She located them later at the home of friends. Gordana, Senka, and other *Oslobodjenje* staff watched in horrified silence at the newspaper office. Soldiers and civilians attached to the U.N. Protection Force in Sarajevo gathered around their televisions, wondering what the violence would mean for their peacekeeping mission. Watching at home, people who had not imagined such things in their city glimpsed what lay ahead.

Sarajevans later considered the Holiday Inn shooting the official start of the war: It violated the city's sense of itself. On Monday evening a Sarajevo television anchor summed up the news by concluding, "We were shot at all day long by those who have no idea what Sarajevo is and what Bosnia-Herzegovina is." In truth, it was not so much that the Serb gunmen at the Holiday Inn didn't know what Sarajevo and Bosnia represented but that they challenged the official story. The Serb nationalists had their own idea of Bosnian history and the lessons to be drawn from it. To fight an ethnoreligious war in a land where everyone shares the same Slavic blood and almost no one goes to church is a challenge. The Serb nationalist program required that people in Bosnia be reminded constantly of what set them apart, and that meant talking about the past.

Creating Ethnic Identities

Analysts of Bosnian politics noted that the republic's 1990 multiparty elections, the first since the rise and fall of Communism in Yugoslavia, resembled an ethnic census as much as a contest of rival ideologies. The three national parties—one for the Serbs, one for the Croats, and one for the Muslims—captured more than 80 percent of the vote among them, so the election results indicated little beyond who lived where. The election-as-census pattern should not have been altogether surprising, however, because the converse was also true: Population tallies in Bosnia had for five centuries carried strong political connotations. "Ethnic" identity in Bosnia generally reflects loyalty to a particular religious and political heritage rather than a blood connection to one or another tribe.

Most of the ancestors of the people who fought one another in Bosnia in the twentieth century were Slavs who came to the region fourteen centuries earlier from the area that is now Poland and

Ukraine. In that migrating mass were two tribes called the Serbs and the Croats. According to historical accounts, the tribal leaders headed their people in different directions once they crossed the Danube River, settling finally in the vicinity of the lands now named Serbia and Croatia. There were undoubtedly other tribes as well, less powerful than the Serbs and Croats and long since forgotten. One seventh-century Armenian manuscript refers to twenty-five Slavic peoples in the territory of the Byzantine Empire. The Slav tribes organized separately in family and village groupings, but the people were all agriculturalists, they spoke a common language, and they prayed to the same pagan gods at the same times of year. Within a few hundred years, the tribes had intermingled to such an extent that the boundaries between their territories were no longer easily discernible. The "Serbs" and "Croats" living in Bosnia today have no sure way of knowing whether they are actually descended from the original Serb or Croat tribespeople.

Serb and Croat national identities developed in the South Slav (or Yugoslav, *yug* meaning "south") lands largely because separate Serb and Croat kingdoms became established in the region during the Middle Ages, supported in turn by the Byzantine and Holy Roman empires and thus identified respectively with the Eastern Orthodox and Roman Catholic churches. The Slavs in Bosnia who later called themselves Serbs or Croats were actually signaling their church affiliation and their political allegiance to either the Serbian-Byzantine or the Croatian-Roman tradition. There was also a medieval Bosnian kingdom, but it was not connected to a powerful empire, and its unique church-state tradition was wiped out when the Ottoman Turks invaded and converted much of the Christian population to Islam. In 1993 some Muslim Slavs in Bosnia began calling themselves Bosniacs, after the inhabitants of the old kingdom, in the same way Orthodox and Catholic Slavs had named themselves after the Serbian and Croatian states. The Muslims needed to counter charges that they were only a religious group and not a genuine "nation" like the Serbs and Croats. The Bosniac usage came too late in the game, however, to make much of an impression.

The construction of separate national identities among people who were ethnically indistinguishable was the root cause of communal hatred in Yugoslavia and ultimately led to the country's fragmentation. Bosnia, where the various South Slav nationalities mixed and sometimes collided, was the republic that had most to fear from ethnic conflict. It was also the place where national divisiveness was resisted most energetically. Of the Yugoslav nationalities, the Muslim Slavs of Bosnia had the least to gain from the exaggeration of national differences for political purposes and were the least responsible for it. It was in Bosnia that citizens argued most forcefully that religion should not be a basis for political organization. Those Serbs (and Croats) in Bosnia who supported the government during the 1992 war often referred to themselves as "Bosnians of the Orthodox (or Roman Catholic) faith," in order to show that church affiliation need not be equated with nationality. But the link between religious and ethnic identity, artificial though it may have been, had developed over many centuries and was too strong to be easily severed.

Medieval Kingdoms

The Slavs who came south broke into competing national blocs largely because the land to which they migrated was already divided between rival empires. Two hundred years before the Slavs arrived on the Balkan peninsula, the two sons of the Roman Emperor Theodosius had split his dominions, and the dividing line ran right down the middle of the territory that the Slavs settled. The eastern half, based in Constantinople (today Istanbul), evolved into the Byzantine Empire. The western half, based in Rome, was lost to the barbarians and then reclaimed by Charlemagne and other Frankish kings. To the east the Greek language and heritage dominated, with a strong Oriental influence. Latin remained the official language on the Roman side. Christianity diverged as well, with an Eastern Orthodox church developing in Constantinople and Catholicism in Rome. The ethnic identity that Slav peasants ultimately adopted depended on which side of the great religious and cultural divide they found themselves or were assigned by their rulers. Bosnia was in the middle, so the national development of the Bosnian Slavs was especially convoluted.

Byzantine and Roman rulers alike saw the Balkan Slavs as people to be brought into their orbits and subjugated. Croats who settled along the Adriatic coast recognized Charlemagne as their sovereign by the end of the eighth century and accepted Roman Christianity and culture. For about two hundred years Croat princes were allowed to have their own kingdom, ruling parts of what became Croatia and Bosnia-Herzegovina until the king of Hungary claimed the Croat throne in the eleventh century.

The Byzantine side, however, had the conquering and proselytizing edge. Byzantine emperors dispatched missionaries throughout the Balkan lands to convert the Slavs to the Eastern version of Christianity and tie them to Constantinople. The Byzantine missionaries worked in the vernacular language and even developed a new phonetic alphabet so that the Gospels could be written in Slavonic. (With the later addition of Greek characters, the Byzantine alphabet evolved into Cyrillic, the script favored by Serbs to this day.) By teaching in the language of the people, Orthodox priests were better able to establish a popular church than were the Catholics. Another Constantinople advantage was that the Byzantine state and church functioned virtually as a single entity, while the imperial and ecclesiastical worlds were more separated on the Western side. Even after Pope Leo III crowned Charlemagne as the first Holy Roman emperor in 800, the relation between the Roman church and the Frankish rulers was tenuous. In contrast, the supreme church authority in Constantinople was the emperor himself.

Byzantine rule was also enhanced by the clever patronage of subordinate empires. Serb tribal chieftains, for example, were allowed to have a kingdom of their own. It lasted for two centuries and comprised at its zenith what is now Albania, northern Greece, Macedonia, Montenegro, southern Serbia, and parts of Bosnia-Herzegovina. In the thirteenth century, the Byzantine emperor even approved the establishment of an independent Serbian Orthodox church under the direct authority of the Serbian king.

Without their associated churches, the miniempires in the Byzantine-ruled lands might not have lasted. In the modern sense the medieval kingdoms in the Balkan area were not states at all but alliances of powerful feudal landowners around a central leader. With the defection of one or two nobles, the kingdoms could collapse as the landowners cut new deals with the adversaries of their former potentate. The territories ruled by the rival dynasties consequently shifted and overlapped; a single village could be under Croat or Bulgar dominion one century and Serb the next. The peoples so ruled were in all likelihood from varied tribal or ethnic backgrounds, and being subject for a time to a Serbian king was hardly enough to make anyone feel Serbian. But the Serbian church became synonymous with the Serbian state and kept the political tradition alive even when the state did not exist. The church fathers canonized the early Serbian kings regardless of how despotic their rules had been, and the kings' names were recited in the Serbian church liturgy for centuries.

At the outer reaches of the empire, however, the churches were naturally weaker. Slav peasants viewed religion as a practical matter, focusing on worldly welfare, and it was not uncommon to switch from one faith to another with each change of ruling power. Nowhere was this more evident than in Bosnia, a mountainous land that bordered both halves of the old Roman Empire and passed between Eastern and Western rule many times. Neither Roman Catholicism nor Eastern Orthodoxy gained a firm foothold as long as Croat-Hungarian and Serb-Byzantine rulers were contesting the territory. Furthermore, missionary work was handicapped by the rough terrain; Slav peasants in Bosnia remained heathen long after their neighbors in the Serb and Croat lands had become Christians, and the faith of those who did convert was generally weak.

In the absence of a strong Orthodox or Catholic presence in the region, a nonaligned Christian church was able to develop in Bosnia, identified mainly with the feudal ruling class. Little is known of the native Bosnian church. Some historians believe that it came under the influence of the Bogomil sect, which originated in Bulgaria. The Bogomils were dualists, believing God alone to be good and all earthly things evil; that included emperors, kings, popes, and all the hierarchs whose rivalries had made Bosnia a land of endless border conflicts. The activities of the heretics in Bosnia alarmed church leaders in Rome, and they persuaded the Hungarian kings to impose Catholic authority over the Bosnian diocese by force. Powerful Bosnian nobles led a resistance revolt, expelled Catholicism from the country, and embraced the heretics, thereby consolidating Bosnian church independence.

With a religious boundary separating it from the Croat and Serb lands on either side, Bosnia was able to stand as a separate state for more than 200 years. Among the medieval Slavic kingdoms, Bosnia was unique in two ways: First, it was the only Balkan state not identified with a tribe or ethnic group, taking its name from a river instead. The Bosnian Slavs were of unknown tribal origin. They were bound by their residence in a particular location, but their rulers made no apparent effort to persuade them as Bosniacs that they were a single nation with a common ancestry, as the Serb and Croat chieftains did. Second, medieval Bosnia was alone in being relatively free from imperial entanglements, at least in its early history.

When Serb nationalists started a war in 1992 to thwart the Bosnian independence drive, they shunned all references to the medieval Bosnian state and denied any meaning to its existence. Those Bosnians who worked for their republic's independence, meanwhile, looked to the old kingdom for inspiration and would have liked to reinstate it. They wanted to revive the tradition of nonalignment and go back to the time when Bosnians identified themselves by the region where they lived rather than the people from whom they were descended.

But a regional consciousness is easily lost, and a small state without an imperial master is a state without a protector. The Kingdom of Bosnia was doomed.

The Ottoman Conquest

Turkish armies set foot on Balkan soil for the first time in the late fourteenth century and marched steadily on, eventually conquering all the Slav lands. On June 28, 1389, the Ottoman Turks under Sultan Murad defeated a combined force of Serbs, Bosniacs, and Albanians at Kosovo Polje (the Field of Blackbirds). Although Serb leaders would continue their resistance to the Ottoman invasion for years to come, the Kosovo Polje battle was the turning point. Seventy years later the Turks overran Bosnia, after the Catholic powers ignored a final desperate plea for help from the Bosnian king.

For the next four centuries the entire occupied Balkan area was merged into a single administrative zone, with no trace of the old Slavic states. By the standards of medieval Europe, Ottoman rule would be relatively tolerant. If people resisted the Turkish invaders, they faced the possibility of massacre, but if they submitted they had the option of retaining their Christian religion and a degree of local autonomy. Forced conversions were rare, and there was little that compared with the excesses of the Catholic Counter-Reformation or the Inquisition, at least in the early years of the Ottoman occupation. The conquered Slavs generally kept their Christianity, with the notable exception of those living in Bosnia, where most of the people willingly accepted Turkish rule and eventually converted to Islam. Thus were produced the Bosnian Muslims, a Slavic-speaking Islamicized population of wholly European ancestry who would complicate national politics in the Yugoslav lands for centuries to come.

The conversion did not come en masse, nor did it happen overnight. Twenty-five years after Bosnia fell to the Turks, fewer than 20 percent of the population were yet declared Muslim. The rate was climbing each year, however, and would do so for another two centuries. The reasons for the widespread adoption of Islam in Bosnia when no comparable conversion took place in the other Ottoman-occupied lands (with the exception of non-Slavic Albania) had to do with unique local circumstances. Because of its weak foundation and lack of outside support, the independent Bosnian church could not sustain itself long. Many Bosnians found it easy to take up a new faith, having already been exposed to Orthodoxy, Catholicism, and neo-Bogomilism. Finally, the people of Bosnia had suffered long and hard living in a contested no-man's-land, and they were ready for peace. The last Bosnian king told the pope that the new Ottoman rulers won the favor of Bosnian peasants simply by treating them well and offering them the promise of a better life.

Islamicization was also more extensive in Bosnia than in other Ottoman-ruled lands because Bosnia lay at the edge of the empire, where the occupiers were willing to offer special conversion incentives in order to keep the population as loyal and trustworthy as possible. Bosnian nobles were more likely to hold on to their property and privileges if they took the Islamic faith; they could lose them if they refused. Not surprisingly, the bulk of the feudal class in Bosnia went over to the Turkish side. This development was important, because it meant that later Serb-Muslim tensions had the character of a social class conflict, with Serb peasants revolting against Muslim landowners.

Within 200 years of the conquest, about three-quarters of the Bosnian population were Muslims, and the character of the country had undergone a major change. Turkish influences were evident in language, cuisine, arts, and architecture. A new capital, Sarajevo (the Field around the Castle), was built in the narrow valley of the Miljacka River. The old Bosnia was gone forever.

But not the old Serbia. Paradoxically, the Ottoman conquest actually laid the groundwork for a Serbian national revival four centuries later. First, it provided the raw material for heroic national myths and legends. Second, it set up a church-based governing structure, thereby preserving the most important Serbian institution just as the Serbian kingdom was beginning to disintegrate. Had it not been for the Ottomans, medieval Serbia might well have slid into terminal decay.

The Kosovo Polje defeat took on an ironic significance as the most important event in Serbian national history. In its commemoration through epic poetry, the battle symbolized the martyrdom of the Serbian state and the source of all Serb misfortunes that were to follow. The leader of the Serb army at Kosovo, Prince Lazar, became a Serbian saint. When Slobodan Milošević launched his nationalist power grab in 1987, it was to Kosovo Polje (near the city of Priština, in the Serbian province of Kosovo) that he first journeyed. In the Serbian mind, the Kosovo battle showed the Serbs to be heroic protectors of Christian Europe against the encroaching forces of Islam. (Never mind that many Serb chieftains promptly went over to the Turkish side and later supplied troops for Ottoman battles against Christian armies in Hungarian-ruled lands.) Kosovo provided a loss for future Serb fighters to avenge and an enemy—the Muslim Turks—for the whole Serb nation to hate.

The Serb national cause also benefited from the Ottoman system of governance. Under Ottoman rule each religious community or *millet* was left to the charge of its own church leaders, who acted as agents of the Ottoman administration in collecting taxes and keeping order. It was this system that enabled Orthodox, Roman Catholic, and Jewish communities to flourish in Sarajevo and other Bosnian cities. Moreover, by grouping the subject peoples into self-governing religious communities, the Ottoman rulers perpetuated the church-state links of the Byzantine era. Religion was not simply a matter of individual belief and practice: It became the basis of communal political organization and group identity. The pattern endured for centuries, deepening religious divisions by giving them an additional political and "national" dimension. The Ottoman *millet* system helps explain why the first political parties to emerge in Yugoslavia after the collapse of Communism were set up along religious (national) lines: The people were long accustomed to organizing themselves that way.

The *millet* arrangement was particularly significant for the Serbian Orthodox church, whose fortunes in Bosnia actually improved under the Turks. Before the Ottoman conquest the Serbian kings had lost Bosnia, and Catholicism was winning adherents away from Eastern Orthodoxy. But under Ottoman rule the Serbian church in Bosnia became a protected institution and was able to begin slowly rebuilding. By the end of the Ottoman period, Orthodox Christians in Bosnia had actually drawn even in number with the Muslims. A big boost came when Ottoman officials resettled ethnic Vlach herdsmen (native to Romania) along the edge of Ottoman territory in unpopulated parts of northwestern Bosnia. The Vlachs, whom the Ottomans considered politically reliable, had been Christianized by Orthodox missionaries.

Along with the Vlachs, some ethnic Croats living in northwestern Bosnia also practiced the Orthodox faith. Descendants of the old Serb tribe, in fact, probably constituted a fairly small proportion of the Orthodox believers in northwestern Bosnia. And yet, after the Bosnian war broke out in 1992, it was in northwestern Bosnia that Serb nationalism took its most extreme form. The development of a deeply felt Serb identity in a population that was not of Serb tribal origin was the extraordinary achievement of the Serbian Orthodox church. With its liturgical commemoration of Serbian kings and warriors, the church slowly built a national consciousness among its communicants, persuading them they were not just Orthodox but Serb, no matter what their ancestors may have been. Serbian priests, in fact, had little theological training and were generally not spiritual advisers to their congregations. Theirs was a political church that functioned primarily to venerate Serbian national heroes, to preserve the memory of the old Serbian state, and to prepare for its second coming.

Nineteenth-century Thinking

The Bosnian war that began in 1992 had modern aspects, inasmuch as it was fought as a contest of media images, with U.N. forces and international relief workers squarely in the middle. But with its origins in nationalist thought, especially on the Serb side, the war came straight out of the previous century. The Serbian national revival occurred in the early 1800s, and the aspirations expressed by Serbian leaders in the years immediately following were the same ideas that inspired Serb nationalists in Bosnia in the 1990s.

Ottoman rule in the Balkans in the early 1800s was crumbling from corruption, decay, and economic decline. When Habsburg armies attempted to penetrate Ottoman territory, Serbian church leaders offered assistance. Tensions between the rural working class and the increasingly cruel Ottoman overlords were also building, and in 1804 Serb peasants broke out in open revolt. The Turks eventually suppressed the uprising and exacted a heavy revenge on the rebels, but two years later Serb peasants led a second revolt, and this time it culminated in the establishment of a free Serbian state, the first in more than 350 years. The borders were the Danube River to the north (at the edge of Belgrade) and Greece to the south. Bosnia remained under Ottoman rule.

The mid–nineteenth century saw an explosion of national passion in newly independent Serbia and across Europe. Serbian leaders, inspired by the rebirth of their national state, were seized by visions of territorial expansion, and they broadened their national claims. Everyone who belonged to the Serbian Orthodox church had already been defined officially as "Serb," but the national category was widened further to include all Slavs who spoke the Serbian dialect of the Serbo-Croatian language. By this definition, virtually all of Bosnia, including Sarajevo, could be considered Serbian national territory.

In 1844 the Serbian interior minister, Ilija Garašanin, wrote a memorandum, entitled "An Outline," that was the first proposal for the creation of a new Greater Serbia incorporating all territory where "Serbs" lived. "Serbia cannot limit itself to its current borders," Garašanin wrote, "but should strive to attract to itself all of the Serb peoples who surround it." His envisioned state would be huge, modeled after the medieval Serbian kingdom at its maximum extent, and would include within its current borders the Montenegrins, the Macedonians, and the Bosnian Muslims. "Serbia must make sure that it is the natural protector of all the Turkish [Muslim] Slavs," Garašanin advised, "and that the other Slavs will relinquish this right."

The Bosnian Muslims could hardly be comforted by Serbian offers to "protect" them. Serbian national literature at the time was heavy with exhortations to Muslim Slavs to abandon the faith of their occupiers and return to their Christian roots. "So tear down the minarets and mosques! Also kindle the Serb yule logs and paint our Easter eggs," wrote Petar Petrović-Njegoš in the classic Serbian epic *The Mountain Wreath*, published in 1847.

The slogans, diatribes, and proposals of the nineteenth-century Serb nationalists reemerged virtually line for line 150 years later in the threats and declarations of Slobodan Milošević, Radovan Karadžić, and other Serb leaders during the Bosnian war. They called again for a Greater Serbia, declared Bosnia to be Serbian territory, and demanded that the Bosnian Muslims accept Serbian domination. The behavior of Croat nationalists mirrored that of the Serbs. Their militia forces came into the Bosnian war in 1993 with the idea of securing a portion of Bosnian territory in order to establish a Greater Croatia. Like the Serb nationalists, the Croats were carrying out a program proposed more than a hundred years earlier; in the Croat case, it was by men such as Ante Starčević, who argued in the 1860s that all South Slavs were in reality Croats. Starčević and his disciples imagined a Croatia stretching all the way to the border with Bulgaria.

Caught between the rival Slav nationalisms in the nineteenth century (and for a hundred years thereafter) were the Bosnian Muslims, viewed as ex-Serbs in Belgrade and as ex-Croats in Zagreb. The vast majority of Bosnian Muslims, however, saw themselves neither as Serbs nor as Croats but only as Bosnian Slavs who practiced the Islamic religion. They were not caught up in the nationalist fever that swept Europe in the nineteenth century, largely because they had no sense of an exclusive ethnic identity and had never had a national state of their own, except for medieval Bosnia, and that was Christian. During the Ottoman period the Bosnian Muslims were called Turks in the same way Orthodox Christians became known as Serbs and the Catholics as Croats. But the parallel didn't hold: The Bosnian Muslims did not see themselves as being attached to the Turkish state as Orthodox Christians were to Serbia or Catholics to Croatia. Few Bosnian Muslims ever learned the Turkish language, and they were always careful to distinguish themselves from the Turkish-born Ottoman officials around them. Some Bosnian Muslims even joined in the anti-Ottoman uprisings.

By the end of the nineteenth century, the Bosnian Muslims found themselves alone. Although they were Slavs like the Serbs and Croats and spoke the same language, the Muslims had broken from their Christian brothers by adopting the faith of the Turkish occupiers. But by then turning away from the Turks, the Bosnian Muslims were left without allies or compatriots. Some joined the Croat national movement, declaring themselves Croats "of the Islamic faith," and a few called themselves Islamicized Serbs and supported the Serbian state struggle, but most stayed aloof from both sides. After the Ottoman rulers surrendered Bosnia-Herzegovina to the Habsburg Empire in 1878, the Bosnian Muslims accepted the new Austrian occupiers of their land with the same equanimity they had shown toward the Ottoman Turks. "I believe there has never been a people so lonely as the Bosnian Muslims," wrote the Bosnian novelist Meša Selimović in 1970. "Where would their road lead them?" he asked. "The answer is nowhere. They faced a tragic dead end."

Interethnic Conflict

One frequently debated question about the 1992 Bosnian war was whether it was an extension of the 1991 Serb-Croat war or was entirely separate from it. The answer was not obvious. On the one hand, the war was fueled by longstanding, competing Serbian and Croatian claims to Bosnian territory, with Muslims caught in between. "This is a war between Serbs and Croats that will be fought down to the last Muslim," a Bosnian army commander in Mostar told me in August

1992. In northwestern Bosnia, in eastern Bosnia, and around Sarajevo, however, the war was largely between Serbs and Muslims themselves, and it was a carryover of violence that had erupted in previous decades.

Serb nationalists were disappointed that Bosnia-Herzegovina had been turned over to Austro-Hungarian rule by the Congress of Berlin in 1878, and the "liberation" of Bosnia became a top Serbian priority. Although there were also Muslims in the ranks of the anti-Habsburg movement, many Serb nationalists were contemptuous of the Muslims for their acceptance of foreign rule, and Serb-Muslim tensions were rising. The 1914 assassination in Sarajevo of the Habsburg crown prince, Franz Ferdinand, provoked a wave of anti-Serb violence across Bosnia, for which Muslims were largely responsible. During World War I, Serbian army guerrillas carried out attacks on Muslim landowners, whom they regarded as Habsburg agents. The guerrilla fighters called themselves *Chetniks* after Serbian irregulars who had fought the Turks in the previous century. Serb nationalists warned ominously of what the Muslims could expect at the end of the war. "As soon as our army crosses the Drina [the river separating Bosnia from Serbia]," a leading Serbian politician said, "it will give the Turks [i.e., the Muslims] twenty-four hours, or perhaps forty-eight, to return to the faith of their forefathers, and then slay those who refuse."

The collapse of the Habsburg and Ottoman empires at the end of the war made possible the formation of an independent South Slav state, the first Yugoslavia, in 1918. The organization of the state required a compromise between Serbian and Croatian leaders, both of whom had to give up dreams of separate states for their own peoples, and Serb-Croat rivalries undermined the federation almost from the start. Serbian nationalism was undiminished, and Serb animosity toward Muslims continued, with occasional reports of whole Muslim families killed at the hands of Chetnik vigilantes. In a sentiment typical of the period, one Serb nationalist warned in 1926 that a "social de-Islamicization" of the Bosnian population was required, ideally through intermarriage with Serbs. If that wasn't enough, "there remains only one solution; short, clear, and inexorable. The singer of folk songs has foretold it and sung about it; he sings about it even today. We shall not repeat it here, because we all know it." He was evidently speaking of mass murder. The folk songs to which he referred were sung again by Serb nationalists in 1992, as they "cleansed" the Drina River valley of Muslims, killing thousands in the process.

Muslim leaders in Bosnia finally began to organize politically. In 1918 a Yugoslav Muslim Organization (YMO) had been formed to defend Muslim interests in the new Yugoslav federation. The movement was a forerunner of the Muslim party that won the 1990 elections in Bosnia under the leadership of Alija Izetbegović. Leaders of the YMO insisted that they were not Muslim nationalists, had no interest in the creation of a separate Muslim state, and had decided to organize politically only after surging Serbian Orthodox and Croatian Catholic nationalism left them no choice. "We were the victims of religious fanaticism and were therefore forced to group ourselves on the religious basis, too," a YMO spokesman explained. Far from being separatist, the Bosnian Muslims were strong supporters of the 1918 Yugoslav state, seeing it as one in which the Serb-Croat tug-of-war over Bosnian territory might finally be relaxed.

Alija Izetbegović, a devout Muslim, advocated a multiethnic state as his country's first democratically elected president.

(MARK H. MILSTEIN/ANS)

Serb and Croat nationalists, however, were not relenting in their demands that Bosnian Muslims declare themselves to be either Serb or Croat; "Muslim" was still not recognized as a separate national category. In 1939 the rival Serbian and Croatian claims on Bosnian territory were finally resolved in a *Sporazum* (Understanding), negotiated between the Yugoslav prime minister, Dragiša Cvetković, and the Croat opposition leader, Vladko Maček. Bosnia would be split, with Croat-dominated areas going to Croatia and the rest to Serbia. When Maček asked what should be done about the Bosnian Muslims, Cvetković reportedly said, "Let's pretend they're not there." The agreement would be recalled fifty-two years later, in March 1991, when Croatian President Franjo Tudjman and Slobodan Milošević met in the town of Karadjordjevo in Serbia to plan the division of Bosnia between them. The discussion went nowhere; the Serb-Croat war broke out two months later.

The 1939 "Understanding" was not implemented either. One month after it was signed, World War II began with the German invasion of Poland. In April 1941 a Nazi-allied independent Croat state was declared under the leadership of Ante Pavelić, a founder of the fascist Croat *Ustashe* (Insurgent) movement. To complicate the ethnic question all the more, Pavelić argued that Croats were originally Germanic Goths and not Slavs at all. He showed his devotion to the Nazi cause of racial purity by ordering that a portion of the Serbs living on Croatian land be killed, along with all the Jews and Gypsies. Those Serbs spared execution would be expelled or forced to convert to Catholicism. Muslims would not be treated so harshly; if they could produce convincing evidence of their Aryan ancestry, they would be left alone.

Backed by German Nazi and Italian forces, the Ustashe set out to attack the Serb population throughout the new Croatian state, which they defined to include all of Bosnia-Herzegovina. Serb women and children were usually spared, but not always, and many were placed in Ustashe detention camps. Almost immediately Serbs in Bosnia and Croatia began organizing to defend themselves. The army of the (exiled) Yugoslav government was reorganized as a new Chetnik movement in the Bosnian mountains under the command of Colonel Draža Mihailović. Led by right-wing Serb nationalists, the Chetniks took as their slogan "Serbs above all." The Croatian-born Communist Josip Broz Tito, meanwhile, organized an anti-Ustashe, anti-Nazi Partisan movement. Serbs also dominated Partisan ranks, but the movement included fighters of all nationalities. Tito himself was of

Croat-Slovene ancestry and had fought in World War I as an Austrian soldier.

Once again Bosnian Muslims found themselves in the middle. When Ustashe and German Nazi forces moved into their territory, some Muslims joined rather than resisted. An all-Muslim Nazi SS brigade was organized and carried out murderous attacks against Serb civilians in Bosnia. Relatively few Bosnian Muslims, however, shared the Ustashe genocidal vision, and most Muslim cooperation with the Ustashe was of the same passive character evident in earlier collaboration with the Ottoman Turks and the Austrians. When Tito's Partisans marched west across the breadth of Bosnia in the summer of 1942, many Muslim volunteers joined them along the way. Some may have wanted only to be on the winning side, but others were attracted by the Partisans' multinational structure and antinationalist program, which were elements rarely evident in Yugoslav politics and ones the Muslims had learned to appreciate. By the time the Partisan march reached Bihać, in the far northwest corner, Muslim Partisans outnumbered Muslim Ustashe fighters.

The conflict soon developed into a three-sided civil war, among the Croat-led Ustashe forces, the Serbian Chetniks, and the Partisans. The Chetnik-Partisan alliance against the Ustashe, Nazi, and Italian fascist forces did not last long. The Chetniks angered the Partisans by choosing to attack civilian targets rather than well-armed Axis troops, and the Partisans in Bosnia eventually saw the Chetniks as their principal adversaries. The Partisans regarded the Chetniks as undisciplined, long-haired, hate-filled brigands. A Partisan historian observed that during the short period of Chetnik-Partisan collaboration in the early months of the war, "one of the big differences between [Partisans and Chetniks] was that the Chetniks reeked of brandy."

In the manner of their World War I predecessors, the Serbian Chetniks soon went after Bosnian Muslim civilians, even though only a tiny minority of the Muslim population had taken part in crimes against the Serb people. In a declaration that echoed the statements of nineteenth-century Serb nationalists and presaged those of Bosnian Serb leaders in 1992, Colonel Mihailović defined the Chetnik war aims in December 1941 as including the creation of an "ethnically clean" Greater Serbia free from "national minorities and non-national elements" throughout its territory, which was envisaged as including Bosnia.

The chief Chetnik ideologist, Stevan Moljević, wrote Mihailović in February 1942 that it was time to "start cleaning the land of all non-Serb elements. The guilty ones should be immediately punished," he wrote, "and the rest should be given an open road— Croats to Croatia, and Muslims to Turkey and Albania." A year later a Chetnik commander in the Drina River valley wrote Mihailović that all the Muslim villages in his assigned area were "completely burnt down. All the property is destroyed, except for the cattle, hay and wheat. During the operation," he reported, "we performed the complete extermination of the Muslim population." Over the course of World War II, in fact, the Serbian Chetnik forces were responsible for the slaughter of thousands of Bosnian Muslims, principally in the Drina valley, as well as large numbers of Croat civilians.

For their part, vengeance-seeking Partisans murdered thousands of Chetniks and Croat Ustashe fighters and their family members in the final months. By the end of the war, about one million Yugoslavs were dead, the vast majority killed by their own countrymen. Most of the fighting took place in Bosnia-Herzegovina. Serbs accounted for more than half the total war dead in Yugoslavia, although, according to the most careful demographic investigations, Bosnian Muslims died in greater numbers proportionate to their share of the population.

Titoism

Tito and his Communist Party set out after the war to remake Yugoslavia. Having seen the cost of fratricidal hatred, Tito was determined to fashion a country that would never again be torn apart by nationalist conflict, and he promised a new era of "brotherhood and unity." His efforts fell far short of achieving that goal, although Tito was more successful in this regard than his detractors would later claim.

In 1943 Tito and his fellow Partisans had declared the formation of a Yugoslav federation. Five of the six republics were linked by name to their lead national groups, Macedonia being a new creation. Bosnia was the sixth, established over the vigorous objection of many Serb and Croat leaders within the new government. Officially, it was to be mixed in its national design; in Tito's words, "neither Serb nor Croat nor Muslim, but Serb and Croat and Muslim." As a unique case, Bosnia's survival was linked to the destiny of the larger federation, to Tito himself, and to his idea of how Yugoslavia could work.

Unfortunately, the plan Tito devised for Yugoslavia was mod-

eled after the Soviet Union, and it was equally flawed. Tito claimed
the practice of Communism would eventually produce a socialist
"Yugoslav" consciousness in which narrow national attachments
would be swept away by feelings of fraternity. In characteristically
Stalinist fashion, he assumed this transformation could be carried out
if necessary by police state force: He would end nationalist thinking
in Yugoslavia simply by making it illegal. But by blocking the free
work of democratic institutions, Tito inhibited the growth of the civic
culture Yugoslavia needed if its people were to begin thinking of
themselves as citizens and not as members of rival national groups.
The dozens of "Brotherhood and Unity" highways, railroads, and
bridges Tito christened around Yugoslavia reduced the phrase to a
forgettable cliché.

By the early 1960s Tito realized that socialism and state authority
alone were not eradicating the old nationalisms, and he changed
strategies. Rather than suppressing the nationalist forces, he started
trying to balance them against one another, giving the republics more
authority and allowing small measures of national expression. Albanians and Hungarians in the Serbian provinces of Kosovo and Voj-
vodina won some autonomy, and the Macedonians were given their
own Orthodox church (although it was unrecognized by the Orthodox hierarchy outside Yugoslavia). The Bosnian Muslims were recognized as constituting a separate nationality. They had finally concluded that, regardless of how they actually felt, they would have to
act as a "nation" in the Yugoslav framework if they wanted to defend
their interests politically.

Tito tried to manage his country like some grand puppeteer, but
the strings became increasingly tangled. Having given Croatian leaders more room to maneuver, he cracked down on them when they
went too far. Among those he ordered arrested was the future Croatian president, Franjo Tudjman, who had served in the Partisan army
but had then become an outspoken Croat nationalist and historian. In
a clumsy effort to be impartial, Tito followed the repression in
Croatia with a move against liberals in Serbia. No one was satisfied.

The Yugoslav federation began to weaken soon after Tito's death
in 1980. Serb national leaders had accepted an internal border arrangement in Yugoslavia that left almost 2 million Serbs outside
Serbia only because Serbs dominated the Communist Party, the federal army and security forces, and the organs of the central government. With Tito's decentralizing reforms gradually weakening those
Belgrade-based institutions, Serb nationalists were outraged. Social

and economic conditions in Yugoslavia worsened, meanwhile, but there were no ready outlets for popular discontent. Political elites in Serbia, Croatia, and Slovenia, anxious to deflect anger from themselves, encouraged people to blame their Yugoslav neighbors for their troubles, just as they had done in the past. Nationalist leaders began denouncing Tito's declarations of Yugoslav brotherhood as "a big lie." By 1990 Tito's portraits had vanished from all public buildings in Croatia. In Serbia the 5,000-dinar note bearing his image was withdrawn from circulation, and statues of Tito were taken down in the main squares of cities that bore his name.

Only in Bosnia were the Tito pictures left hanging on office walls. Patriotic Bosnians were not naive in their assessment of Tito, but they knew that, without the supporting structure of his Yugoslav federation, Bosnia's separate existence was in jeopardy. Once unleashed, Serb and Croat nationalist fervor had historically focused on Bosnia first. Bosnian Muslims, meanwhile, saw Tito as a man who had protected their interests. In a survey taken in 1990, with the federation already on the road to collapse, Bosnian Muslims were found to be more highly attached to the idea of Yugoslavia than any other ethnic group in the country. If nothing else, Tito's Yugoslavia had left them alone, which was as much as they had ever wanted.

By the time the Bosnian war started in 1992, Serb nationalists were ready to take as much of Bosnian territory as they could grab, and they said the Muslims were entitled to no more than what Serbs relinquished claim to. When asked in August 1993 why he was offering the Muslims such a small piece of territory, Radovan Karadžić told a television interviewer that Muslims didn't deserve more because they were "a religious group, not a nation," effectively withdrawing from the Muslims the status Tito had given them and the security that went with it.

. . . April 6, 1992

Most of the Serb gunmen arrested at the Holiday Inn on Monday afternoon were quickly released, in exchange for the freedom of several hundred teenage cadets who had been taken hostage at the Sarajevo police academy by Serb nationalist militiamen. The bodyguard to Radovan Karadžić was kept under arrest for a few days, although he was let go after Karadžić threatened to order a massive shelling of Sarajevo if he were not freed. By late Monday afternoon, most of the

Radovan Karadžić, a Sarajevo psychiatrist and amateur poet, presided over a "Serb Republic" in Bosnia, organized for Serbs alone.
(MARK H. MILSTEIN)

demonstrators at the Parliament Building across from the hotel were gone.

A day earlier the Bosnian government had released a statement addressed to the Muslims, Serbs, Croats, and other peoples of Bosnia-Herzegovina: "This country is the property of all of you," it said, "and you all should defend it together." The two Serb nationalist members of the Bosnian collective presidency, Biljana Plavšić and Nikola Koljević, resigned their positions on Monday, however, and they and other Bosnian Serb leaders declared the existence of a new "Serb Republic of Bosnia-Herzegovina." Sporadic sniper fire was reported all around Sarajevo that afternoon. Several people were wounded in fighting around the headquarters of Television Sarajevo.

Senka Kurtović left the *Oslobodjenje* building exhausted on Monday night and returned alone to her apartment in Dobrinja. Her Serb boyfriend, Dragan Alorić, had secretly been working with the Serb nationalist party (SDS), which was already distributing weapons to its members and ordering them to prepare for war. Two days later Senka saw Dragan on television, acting as a spokesman for the SDS "war presidency" in Ilidža. He later went to work as a television news announcer at a Serb-controlled station in Pale, outside Sarajevo. Dragan began his broadcast each night by saying, "Good evening, my dear Serb people," and holding up his right fist with the thumb and first two fingers raised. When they pray, Serbian Orthodox Christians cross themselves with those three fingers, and the sign signaled Serb solidarity.

2

A Time of Change

The *Oslobodjenje* front page on April 7, 1992, carried a triple
headline:

MASS CRIME OVER THE CITY

PEOPLE ASK FOR GOVERNMENT CHANGE

EUROPE RECOGNIZES BOSNIA

A short report from Brussels correspondent Ljiljana Smajlović on the European Community recognition vote led the
paper, but the rest of the front page was taken up with stories
about the events at the Parliament and around the city on
Monday. A mortar shell had hit the stone roof of the sixteenth-century Gazi Husref Beg mosque in the Old Town.
Gun battles between Serb nationalist militiamen and volunteer Sarajevo defenders raged all night on the edge of the city.
Three hundred people (most of them coal miners from central
Bosnia) went to the main hospital to donate blood. Kemal
Kurspahić had a front-page commentary, and Gordana Kne-

žević had a brief story inside the paper about the peace demonstration and the Holiday Inn shooting, plus a commentary of her own.

The articles on page 1 were all printed in Cyrillic script. Latin lettering was used on the page 2 stories, and the alternation continued through the paper. The next day it would be reversed, with the front page in Latin. The style, which dated from the paper's founding, mostly had to do with politics. Sarajevans were so accustomed to reading both scripts that they didn't even notice the difference as they went from one story to the next. By alternating between the alphabet used by Serbs and the one preferred by Croats, *Oslobodjenje* was showing perfect evenhandedness toward both sides, and that was what counted.

When the war in Bosnia erupted, *Oslobodjenje* was one of the institutions still loyal to the "brotherhood" ideal of the Tito period. For most of its history the newspaper had been the organ of the Socialist Alliance of Working People, a Communist Party organization in Bosnia, and the *Oslobodjenje* journalists had officially been "social-political workers." The Party had appointed the editors and dictated the newspaper's editorial line, one element of which had been the carefully balanced attention to rival ethnic interests in Bosnia. As Communist power weakened, *Oslobodjenje* was able to follow its own course, as were other Party-related institutions. Most of the *Oslobodjenje* staff favored maintaining the Titoist commitment to interethnic cooperation, but with democratic reforms.

Many ex-Party leaders, however, broke with the "unity" line during the post-Communist period and opted instead for exclusivist, ethnically based political movements. By separating from this trend, *Oslobodjenje* was isolating itself from much of the old Party power apparatus. The newspaper would find the adjustment to the post-Communist period difficult and challenging.

Kemal Kurspahić and Ljiljana Smajlović

During Tito's time the national conflict in Yugoslavia was considered such a delicate matter that movie producers had to pair every scene in which the bad guy was a Croat with one in which a Serb was the villain. When a leading public citizen who happened to be a Muslim was arrested for a crime, an important Serb or Croat was certain to be accused of something shortly thereafter, even if the charge had to be trumped up. As a Party paper, *Oslobodjenje* dutifully followed the custom. Reporter Djuro Kozar, a Serb, was assigned a story in the late 1970s about a Serbian Orthodox priest who was convicted of "inflaming national hatred" in his village after he led a party in the singing of World War II Chetnik songs that celebrated the killing of Muslims. *Oslobodjenje*'s editors followed Kozar's story a few weeks later with an article alleging that a Muslim imam (prayer leader) in a town nearby was also stirring up nationalist passion among his people. "It was completely blown up and unfair," Kozar said later of the charge against the imam. "He hadn't done anything."

As the Communist grip on Yugoslavia loosened, *Oslobodjenje*'s professional standards rose. By the time Kemal Kurspahić took over as editor in 1988, the newspaper was no longer publishing contrived stories for the sake of showing balance. But Kurspahić respected the paper's tradition of not taking sides, and he found modern ways of remaining true to it. When the Belgrade-based Tanjug wire service (pro-Serb) and the Zagreb-based HINA agency (pro-Croat) sent out conflicting stories about the same event during the 1991 Serb-Croat war, Kurspahić had *Oslobodjenje* run both versions, just as it used two alphabets. He showed the same consideration in his careful efforts to maintain an ethnically mixed staff. His deputy editor and his politics editor in 1991 were Serbs, as were several of his senior reporters and columnists. His foreign editor was a Croat, while his main news desk editor was a Muslim, as was a majority of the rest of the staff. Bosnia's population at the time was categorized as 44 percent Muslim, 31 percent Serb, 17 percent Croat, and 8 percent "Yugoslav" or "other."

Having taken charge of *Oslobodjenje* just as Communist rule was breaking down in Yugoslavia, Kurspahić was proud of the way he kept his newspaper together. "Some of my staff served the old regime, some were policemen, some were anti-this or pro-that, but I managed to use them all," he told me one day in 1992, sitting up in his chair with his arms folded high across his chest. He had a round, pink face, a gray mustache, and brown eyes that shone with the pride of someone who has come a long way and enjoys basking in the thought of his accomplishment.

The newspaper was his whole professional life. His parents separated when he was three years old, and Kemal spent much of his childhood on his own; in his words, he was "a good candidate to be a street kid." Instead, he became a sports news stringer for *Oslobodjenje* at the age of fifteen. He walked with some difficulty, the result of having fallen off a horse at age six and hiding the injury from his mother for fear of what she would say. A lack of exercise thereafter

Editor in chief Kemal Kurspahić led a drive to free
Oslobodjenje from Communist Party control and establish its political independence. (*OSLOBODJENJE*)

and a fondness for drink and good food had left him at forty-six with
a paunch to match his thinning hair, although his manner was unfail-
ingly gallant. No *Oslobodjenje* journalist I met, including those who
left the newspaper in anger, ever disputed his decency or the fairness
of his leadership.

Although Kurspahić worked hard to turn his paper away from its
old Party-organ tendencies, he later looked back on the Communist
era with some nostalgia. He kept a picture of Marshal Tito on the wall
behind his desk in his wartime office downtown. "It was there when
I moved in, and I decided to leave it up," he explained when I asked
him about it. "Personally, I appreciate many things he did. We can
see what happened after he died, how hard it was to keep the country
together. Of course he was authoritarian, but those were Yugoslavia's best years." Even after many in Sarajevo dismissed such notions as naive, Kurspahić clung to an old-fashioned faith that conflict
could be avoided within his newspaper if only he worked hard

enough to keep everyone happy. In early 1992 he was still one of Sarajevo's optimists, promising foreign visitors that the city would not come apart because the tradition of communal life was unbreakable.

When he finally realized that war was coming and that multiethnic enterprises such as his would be targeted simply for what they represented, Kurspahić reacted angrily. "On the very anniversary of its [World War II] liberation," he wrote in his April 7, 1992, column, "the Nazis are shooting at Sarajevo once again." But Kurspahić's wartime commentaries never had the hard edge of other *Oslobodjenje* writers'. He had put his faith in conciliation and lost, and for Kurspahić the outbreak of war was a personal defeat from which he would never recover.

Brussels correspondent Ljiljana Smajlović, a Serb, had once been Kemal's most favored reporter; their political and journalistic views were similar. But Smajlović foresaw the horrors coming to Sarajevo, fled to Brussels before they hit, and began to detach herself from her town, her newspaper, and her colleagues. Her April 7 story about the European Community's recognition of Bosnia had the flat tone of a wire-service report from a foreign news agency. There was no hint of whether she considered the action a triumph for the Bosnian government or a slap in the face for the Bosnian Serbs.

Before moving to Brussels, Smajlović had edited the politics section at *Oslobodjenje.* In those days she had written commentaries on the dangers of nationalism, often playing the door-slamming, argumentative idealist to Kemal the compromiser. Petite in build, with a thin, pretty face and a pale complexion, Ljiljana had a high-pitched, childlike voice and often arched her eyebrows as she spoke, as though she were straining to give power to her words. When the Serb, Croat, and Muslim national parties made their appearance in Sarajevo, Ljiljana urged that the paper make clear its opposition to all of them. Her ex-husband and the father of her son was a Muslim, and the Serb nationalist vision of a partitioned Sarajevo was never one Ljiljana shared. But her willingness to fight had gradually worn down. Her own mother became a supporter of the Serb party, and when Ljiljana saw a confrontation between the Serb nationalists and the rest of Sarajevo looming, she stepped back from the front line of opinion slinging. She could not bring herself to write articles suggesting that her mother was on the enemy side.

Ljiljana stayed in Brussels after the outbreak of the war, reporting on European and international news related to Bosnia. But, by the

Ljiljana Smajlović was a star reporter and editor at *Oslobodjenje*, but left the newspaper during wartime and moved to Belgrade.   (*OSLOBODJENJE*)

end of the summer, the *Oslobodjenje* paychecks had stopped coming, and in November 1992 Ljiljana cut her ties with the paper and moved with her nine-year-old son to Belgrade, where she went to work for *Vreme*, a weekly opposition newsmagazine. "I can choose to stay out of this war and not take the side of my people," she told me, referring to the Bosnian Serbs, "but I cannot fight against them, and that's what staying at *Oslobodjenje* would have meant."

From Communism to Nationalism

Ljiljana Smajlović came to *Oslobodjenje* straight out of college in 1978. By her own description, she was a Communist editor's dream, eager and ideological. At age twenty-two Ljiljana was already a committed Party member and may have been the only reporter at *Oslobodjenje* who actually saw her work as serving some abstract Party cause. "I wrote stories about the way things should have been, not the way they really were," she said later. She became an immediate star and was assigned to cover the Communist Party itself.

Ljiljana's politics came directly from her parents, both of whom were Communist Partisans in World War II. Her mother, Danica, was sixteen years old and just starting high school when the Croatian Ustashe launched its drive to wipe out the Serb population. Danica's whole family joined the Partisan movement, along with almost everyone else in the country village where she lived. Although many girls in the Partisans became nurses or communications workers, Danica was given a gun and became a combatant. Under the Partisans' strict discipline, family members were assigned to different units, and she soon lost touch with her father and brothers, one of whom died in combat. During one campaign Danica became sick with typhus. Word of her illness eventually reached her father, and he set out to join his daughter, only to be killed by Ustashe forces before he could find her. Telling me the story fifty years later, Danica began to cry.

She met Ljiljana's father, Mirko Ugrica, after the war at a Belgrade military academy. After rising to the rank of lieutenant colonel in the Yugoslav army, Danica Ugrica was eventually posted to Algeria, where Ljiljana began secondary school. Ljiljana looked up to her parents and felt so strongly about Communist heroes that the 1968 death in a plane crash of Soviet cosmonaut Yuri Gagarin sent her into tears, to the great amusement of her Algiers schoolmates. Like the children of other dedicated Yugoslav Communists, Ljiljana was taught not to think about her ethnic origin; her mother marked 0 on official documents in the space where nationality was to be noted. National traditions were given so little attention in the Ugrica household that Ljiljana was sixteen years old before she learned that her father was from a Serb family, just like her mother. Knowing only that he had been born in Croatia, she had assumed he was a Croat. Ljiljana learned English as an exchange student in San Francisco, and, with her French from Algeria, she came to *Oslobodjenje* as one of the best-educated and most widely traveled reporters on the staff.

At the time *Oslobodjenje* was still a regime newspaper, and the Bosnian regime was especially rigid. Bosnia was the Yugoslav republic with the greatest potential for conflict, and to Stalinist minds that meant Communist Party rule had to be especially dogmatic. *Oslobodjenje* journalism, not surprisingly, was not exactly courageous. The lead story on March 3, 1965, began as follows:

The Fourth Congress of the Communist Party of Bosnia and Herzegovina opened yesterday in the main hall of Djuro Djaković Workers' University in Sarajevo. About 130,000 members of the Communist Party of Bosnia and Herzegovina are represented by 750 delegates, including members of the Central Committee.

In a pattern characteristic of journalism throughout the East Bloc, to express something meaningful a reporter had to write in coded language, which could be understood only by other Party insiders and perhaps only by the individual for whom the message was intended. *Oslobodjenje* reporters themselves operated politically, supporting allies and undermining their enemies, or they allowed themselves to be used by others in the system, to the extent of permitting their bylines to run over articles submitted by someone outside the paper.

The newspaper opened up only in the middle 1980s, pushed by Ljiljana Smajlović, Kemal Kurspahić, Gordana Knežević, and other young reporters and editors who saw their chance as Communist power slipped away. The year 1987 was critical for the country, and for the newspaper. After having been propped up for years by Western governments anxious to support a nonaligned Communist alternative, the Yugoslav economy was beginning to crumble. In March and April workers rose in unprecedented protest against decreasing wages and increasing inflation, with more than a hundred strikes being called around the country and 20,000 workers walking off the job. The unrest caught Communist authorities off guard, and their political vulnerability was suddenly made evident. New allegations of corruption in high Party circles surfaced weekly, and newspapers in Yugoslavia learned that they could dig for dirt and not be stopped by anyone in power. The biggest Party scandal of all was in Bosnia, an illicit bond scheme involving the huge Agrokomerc agriculture conglomerate and its director, a prominent Muslim politician named Fikret Abdić. *Oslobodjenje* reporter Emir Habul was on the breaking edge of the story. "It was a heady time for us," Ljiljana recalled. "We had been apologists for the system, and suddenly we found out we had a profession after all. We were real journalists."

The erosion of Communist Party authority, however, was not simply the work of a crusading press. Behind the scenes key figures within the Party had realized that the system was in a terminal crisis, and by 1987 they were moving to direct its collapse in such a way that they would emerge on top. Chief among them was Slobodan Milošević, head of the League of Communists in Serbia. Although he was every inch a product of the Party machine, Milošević was clever enough to know when he had to separate himself from the apparatus (or appear to) and even to inspire populist revolt. The revelations in the news media of mismanagement and corruption among the bureaucratic elite in Yugoslavia came in part because Milošević and his allies were quietly encouraging the reporting of such stories.

Milošević was the first Communist leader in Yugoslavia to understand the importance of the news media in shaping popular thought. As the Party boss in Serbia, he acted swiftly to bring the state television network under his control; he then used the medium to his great political advantage. He spoke directly to the people in simple words, eschewing the convoluted language of his predecessors. In one brilliant move Milošević ordered live television coverage of a 1987 meeting of his own Central Committee, where his allies attacked his rivals, calling them crooks and enemies of the Serb people. Never before had people in Yugoslavia seen what went on behind closed doors at Party sessions, and the entire country stopped what it was doing to watch the spectacle. By making the debate public, Milošević stripped his Party rivals of the mystique of authority that had helped keep them in power. When Milošević himself spoke, he addressed the people at home rather than the Central Committee. Before they knew what was happening, the Central Committee members had become irrelevant to the political process. Within three months Milošević's chief rival was ousted from the Serbian presidency, and Milošević was taking over.

But if Milošević were to secure his base in Serbia and build a system around him, he needed a new dogma to replace the old one, and it had to be powerful enough to mobilize the country in a time of rising discontent and cynicism. The ideology he chose was the one that had proven its potency over two centuries: Serb nationalism. Tito had largely silenced the Serb nationalists while he was in power, but they had survived as a force both inside and outside the Communist Party, particularly among Serbian intellectuals, who had always seen themselves as the guardians of the national culture. In 1986 the Serbian Academy of Arts and Sciences had published a memorandum arguing that Tito's Yugoslavia had been damaging to the interests of the Serb people because it had left them divided among three republics. The memorandum called particular attention to the plight of Serbs in the semiautonomous province of Kosovo, where they were allegedly suffering at the hands of the ethnic Albanian majority. In a restatement of the 1844 Greater Serbia "Outline" of Ilija Garašanin, the memorandum declared: "The establishment of the full national and cultural integrity of the Serb nation, irrespective of the republic and province in which it finds itself, is its historic and democratic right."

As a Communist conservative, Milošević had repressed Serb nationalism when ordered to do so, and the League of Communists in Serbia under his chairmanship formally (though not publicly) condemned the academy memorandum when it appeared. But with Communist authority waning, Milošević shrewdly changed his position on nationalist expression. In April 1987 he traveled to a meeting of Communist delegates in Kosovo Polje, the site of the epic Serb defeat by the Ottoman Turks in 1389. When several thousand Serbs showed up, Milošević offered to meet with them, staying up all night to hear them complain about their Albanian neighbors. In a concluding speech to the throng, he suggested that they start standing up for their interests, just as their Serb ancestors had done. "Nobody, either now or in the future, has the right to beat you," he said to their roaring satisfaction. Serbian analysts and journalists say it was only at that meeting in Kosovo that Milošević realized what a powerful political force he would have at his disposal if he gave full rein to Serb chauvinism.

The province of Kosovo was the place to begin. The medieval Serbian kingdom had been centered in Kosovo, and to patriotic Serbs that meant the region belonged to them forever, no matter who might be living there. With the Turkish conquest Serbs had fled and Islamicized Albanians had moved in, but after World War I Kosovo became part of the first Yugoslav state, and Serbs set out to recolonize the region. They never attained a majority, however, and in the 1960s and 1970s the Serb share of the population in Kosovo declined further, dropping to just 13 percent by 1981. Kosovo was by far the poorest and least developed area in Yugoslavia, and much of the Serb outmigration was for economic reasons, judging by the high number of professionals and skilled workers who left. Serb nationalists, however, claimed the Kosovo Serbs were being chased out by Albanians who wanted the province all to themselves. The evidence was dubious and in some cases fabricated, but for Serbs raised on the epic of Prince Lazar, the prospect of losing Kosovo was a stirring call to action.

Upon his return to Belgrade in April 1987, Milošević provoked a split in the Communist leadership by demanding the Party stand unequivocally on the Serb side against the Kosovo Albanians, whom he treated as alien intruders, even though they were full Serbian citizens. "What we are discussing here can no longer be called politics," Milošević said. "It is a question of our fatherland." He directed his media to exploit the Kosovo issue to the limit, and they complied, publicizing wild and unfounded stories about how Albanians were raping Serb women in Kosovo and committing "genocide" against the Serb population there. The Serbian Orthodox church lent its full support to the campaign of slander. With an eye on the upcoming six hundredth anniversary of the 1389 Battle of Kosovo Polje, Milošević raised the Kosovo question constantly, calling on the Serb people to help him take back their historic lands, to "stop the terror in Kosovo and unite Serbia." At the same time he encouraged a general national paranoia, soberly informing his people that "Serbia's enemies outside the country are plotting against it." He said the Tito regime had worked for the benefit of Croats, Hungarians, and Albanians in Yugoslavia but always against Serbs.

With his new line of argument, Milošević was breaking with the traditional Communist teaching that workers should be defended without regard for their nationality. He was also rejecting the idea of federal Yugoslavia and beginning to work toward the goal of a Greater Serbia that would incorporate Bosnia, parts of Croatia, and all other areas where Serbs lived. By 1988 Milošević had become the most popular and powerful figure in Serbia since Tito, skillfully coalescing three sentiments: anti-Communist anger, Serb national passion, and economic discontent. Milošević told his people they were justified in feeling fed up with their Party leaders; then he supplied the reason: Communism cheated the Serbs. Framing it that way Milošević awakened the dormant force of nationalism. Serbian workers, upset by their falling incomes, were encouraged to scapegoat Albanians or Croats or Slovenes. With Milošević everything fit together and made sense.

In Sarajevo, Ljiljana Smajlović didn't buy the Milošević analysis, but her mother did. Danica Ugrica had gradually become disenchanted with Communism. "I've taken a long, hard look at that system," she once told her daughter, "and I'm convinced it's the worst in the world." But, having spent her formative years in a rigid military organization and her professional life serving a dictatorship with no room for individual expression, she was accustomed to authoritarian leadership. "Milošević came along, and my mother fell for him," Ljiljana told me. "She swallowed it completely." Ljiljana, who was still a member of the Communist Party, tried to persuade her mother that Milošević was a demagogue and not to be trusted, but it made no difference. She told Danica that Milošević's mother-in-law had betrayed clandestine members of the Communist Party to the Nazis during the war. But that was the wrong argument to use with Danica Ugrica. "She was damn right to do it," Danica said.

An Independent Newspaper

Kemal Kurspahić took over as *Oslobodjenje* editor in chief in December 1988, just as Milošević was at his peak of power and influence. The paper was still officially under Communist control, but by then the Party was so weakened by scandals and exposés that the leadership made no effort to impose an editor as it had always done before. The newspaper staff voted on candidates, and the Party simply accepted their choice. Kemal had the support of most of the leading reporters, including Ljiljana Smajlović and Gordana Knežević, who voted from Cairo, where she had gone as correspondent a year earlier. Kurspahić himself had just returned from serving four years as the New York correspondent, and he told his colleagues he wanted to transform *Oslobodjenje* from a Party organ into something closer to newspapers he had read in the United States.

His top priority was to give personality to his writers and accommodate a variety of viewpoints. *Oslobodjenje* had been a mouthpiece of the Communist Party for so long that it read the same from front to back. Kurspahić introduced a front-page column titled *U Žiži* (In Focus), written each day by a different reporter, editor, or guest commentator, and he set aside the second page for opinion articles and letters to the editor. He also introduced color printing and a separate insert section, much like those he had seen in American newspapers. On Mondays and Tuesdays the paper came with a sports news supplement; a world section was included on Wednesdays, a weekend section on Thursdays, a television guide on Fridays, an arts and culture supplement on Saturday, and a week in review section on Sunday.

In 1989 *Oslobodjenje* was named the best newspaper in Yugoslavia in a poll of professional journalists. Circulation rose to 60,000, making it the third most widely read newspaper in the country, just behind the leading dailies in Belgrade and Zagreb. Its only competition in Sarajevo was an afternoon newspaper, *Večernje Novine,* which it easily outranked. Staff members earned salaries above the Sarajevo average, with reporters paid the equivalent of about $1,000 a month and editors substantially more. Full-time bureaus were maintained in Bonn, Moscow, New York, and Cairo, with part-time bureaus in four other foreign cities. The high-rise office tower that served as the paper's Sarajevo headquarters was among the most modern buildings in the city and included a day-care center, a café and restaurant, and a movie theater.

Kurspahić placed a high value on experience abroad and competence in foreign languages, and he made Ljiljana Smajlović one of his top editors. In 1989 she won a fellowship to spend six months at the Cleveland *Plain Dealer*. The opportunity came at a key time, just as she and her newspaper were refiguring what journalism meant in Sarajevo. In the United States she found that newspaper standards and expectations were entirely different from what she was accustomed to in Yugoslavia, where ideological correctness was valued above accuracy and reliability. "I had a certain contempt for the facts before that," she told me.

On her return to Sarajevo, Smajlović saw her paper in a new light. "It looked terrible," she said. "We were running anything we got. Nothing was checked." In Sarajevo journalists were under no obligation to confirm the reliability of a piece of information passed on to them; if it proved untrue, the source was blamed, not the reporter. One of the first stories that came across her desk after she returned was a highly opinionated article from reporter Ljubo Grković, saying Serbs in Bosnia needed a political party of their own. Smajlović killed it. "You're here to report," she told Grković, "not write editorials."

At the time political parties were all the talk. The collapse of Communist regimes across Eastern Europe in the fall of 1989 had brought immediate repercussions in Yugoslavia. The Communist parties in Croatia and Slovenia came out in favor of a multiparty system and free elections. The Yugoslavia-wide League of Communists followed soon after, and within weeks new parties were organized across the country. In January 1990 Kurspahić ordered the slogan "We swear ourselves to you, Comrade Tito" removed from the upper-left-hand corner of the front page and had it replaced with an ad for a Slovenian refrigerator company. In an *U Žiži* commentary, Kurspahić wrote that the Tito legacy "does not depend on our oath to him, but on whether we follow his road."

Kurspahić was the first editor in chief in Yugoslavia to make such a move, and it impressed his peers. "How did you do that? Who did you ask?" a Belgrade editor wondered the next day.

"No one," Kurspahić answered. "If I had asked, I couldn't have done it."

In April 1990 Kurspahić sent his senior reporter Vlado Mrkić, a Serb, to investigate the Serb-Albanian conflict in Kosovo. It was an obvious assignment. Although he was fifty years old and the father of four children, Mrkić enjoyed nothing more than going off alone in his white VW Golf to dig up a story. Tall and thin, with tousled white hair and black-rimmed glasses that sat crookedly on his face, Mrkić had a reporter's knack of blending into a new environment unnoticed. He came from a humble background, and his appearance suggested it. His shoes were unpolished, his clothes plain and rumpled, and his manner quiet. In Kosovo he was trusted immediately by Serbs because he was one of them and by Albanians because he was polite and respectful, unlike many Serbs they encountered.

Mrkić was not a nationalist, although he was fully conscious of his Serb identity, having suffered grievously for it at the beginning of his life. He was born in 1940 in Mostar, the son of a poor locksmith. Traditionally the seat of government for the Herzegovina region, Mostar had a sizable Serb population before World War II, but when the Independent State of Croatia was declared in 1941, Mostar lay unfortunately within its borders. Ustashe forces immediately began rounding up local Serbs. When Vlado was barely a year old, Ustashe troops took his father away, and he never came back. Mrkić later learned they had lined his father up with other Serbs on the bank of the Neretva River and shot him dead. Soon after that Vlado and his older brother were themselves sent to an Ustashe-run concentration camp. His brother became ill at the camp and died shortly after being released. After the war Vlado and his mother moved to Bijeljina, in the far northeast corner of Bosnia, where his mother found work in a tobacco factory. They were poor, and their lives were hard.

Similar experiences left some Serbs in Bosnia convinced that they would be safe only if they lived among other Serbs in a Serb-controlled state. Mrkić, however, turned inward. He was too smart and too cautious to put his destiny into the hands of others, whether Communists or nationalist demagogues who claimed to speak for the interests of the Serb people. Although he joined the Party as a young journalist and even served briefly as a Party secretary at *Oslobodjenje* shortly after going to work there in 1967, he said later that he did it only for his own security. He worked for one year as a desk editor at the paper, but he found the position unsatisfying and soon returned to reporting.

Mrkić had a style all his own. At *Oslobodjenje,* as at every Party-guided newspaper in the country, controversy had to be avoided. Mrkić learned to write elegant and compelling stories that were full of imagery but came to no conclusion. "If you were a painter, you'd have been an impressionist," Gordana Knežević once told him. She didn't mean it as a compliment, but Mrkić didn't mind. He believed in writing what he saw, heard, smelled, and felt and leaving the analysis to others.

In Kosovo, Mrkić attended the funeral of two young Albanian men killed by Serb policemen during a demonstration near the railway station in their country town of Glogovac:

> On the street, first by the fence and then on the sidewalk and then along its whole length, thousands and thousands of people from Glogovac and surrounding villages came and just stood. The silence was so strong that only the ravens in the trees could be heard. I approached a man in a miner's helmet standing at the gate [to the City Hall]. He said: "My name is Aslan Spahja. I have worked as a metallurgist in Feronikl [factory] for 27 years. . . . Here you can see workers, students, and intellectuals from this region. We asked for equality and democracy; we got bullets."

Mrkić made a point in Glogovac of tracking down a local Serb family, one of six in the town. The father told Mrkić they were leaving Kosovo and moving back to Serbia, an item Mrkić put high in his story. He also quoted the Serb father, however, as saying he and his family had no problem with their Albanian neighbors. Mrkić ended his description of the funeral with an open-ended observation:

> While we were standing to let the mourners pass, a fighter jet swooped very low over our heads, and the earth was shaken. Did the appearance of this uninvited guest at the funeral of young Albanians in Glogovac and the roar that followed announce some horrible events that will soon shake this country?

Mrkić wrote as if he were a curious correspondent from a foreign land. His stories struck a chord with many Sarajevans, who saw the Kosovo conflict as troubling but not of obvious concern to themselves.

Ethnic Politics

The developments in Kosovo were, however, soon to have implications for Bosnia. Under a new Serbian constitution approved in September 1990, Kosovo lost its semiautonomous status and was put under Belgrade's direct control; Slobodan Milošević made clear he regarded the plight of all Serbs as his personal business. His new constitution gave Serbia the right to intervene in any Yugoslav republic where Serbs lived. Its enactment was arguably the event most directly responsible for the breakup of Yugoslavia.

Croatia was Milošević's next concern, but Bosnia was already in his sights, as it had always been for Serb nationalists. Milošević began actively interfering in local Bosnian affairs, encouraging the leaders of Serb-dominated counties to look to him and to Serbia for protection. Pro-Milošević media began a campaign aimed at stirring up anti-Muslim feelings among the Bosnian Serbs. An article in the Belgrade newspaper *Politika*, effectively a Milošević organ, reported that the Serbian security service had found that the outmigration of Serbs from Bosnia-Herzegovina was in response to interethnic tensions in the republic.

If true at all, the claim was vastly overstated. Serbs in Bosnia lived mostly in rural areas, and demographic studies showed that the movement of Serbs to Belgrade fit the classic rural-to-urban migration pattern that occurs in every country during modernization. The Serbian propaganda about Bosnia and Kosovo, in fact, ran along parallel lines: Belgrade nationalists had long claimed both areas were "Serbian," and the Milošević regime was now trying to portray Serb inhabitants in the regions as endangered by the non-Serb majority, manufacturing or exaggerating evidence to support its case as needed.

In Bosnia, Serb supporters of Milošević highlighted the nascent Muslim political movement, portraying it as an Islamic threat to Serb interests. The development of a Muslim political party in Bosnia in 1990 in fact was partly related to an Islamic religious revival in the country, but it was primarily a response to Serb and Croat aggressiveness. Serbs in Bosnia were never able to show that they suffered persecution because of their nationality or had any reason to fear their Muslim neighbors.

Muslim leaders had been organizing their people informally ever since Tito relaxed controls on national expression in the late 1960s, although their efforts were initially faltering. Some had argued that

Bosnia should be declared "a state of the Muslim nation," just as Serbia and Croatia had been constituted as states of their dominant peoples. But the proposal went nowhere, because the Muslims were not strong enough or committed enough to push it. In 1971 Muslims in Bosnia barely outnumbered Serbs, 40 percent to 37 percent, and they still lacked a strong national identity. Mosques were generally empty during the 1960s and 1970s, and many Muslim parents in Bosnia gave their children Serb names. Unlike the Serb and Croat "nations" in Yugoslavia, the Bosnian Muslims had always seen their identity in religious rather than national terms; as their religiosity weakened, so did their group consciousness. A Bosnian Muslim national movement finally came to life in the 1980s only because some Muslims rediscovered religion and others recognized a need to organize in the face of growing Serb and Croat nationalism.

The worldwide Islamic renaissance of the late 1970s had extended to Bosnia, and some Muslims had begun focusing on the need for a "spiritual" defense of their people. The most prominent was Alija Izetbegović, a Sarajevo lawyer and businessman long active in Muslim affairs. In 1970 Izetbegović had written a fifty-page "Islamic Declaration," outlining "the vision of a democratic and humanistic social order" for the whole Muslim world. The overall tone and message were moderate, but in one widely quoted (and misinterpreted, he says) line, Izetbegović wrote, "There can be neither peace nor coexistence between the Islamic faith and non-Islamic social and political institutions." The statement suggested that he looked favorably on states that were organized on the basis of Islamic law, such as Saudi Arabia. In 1983 Communist authorities imprisoned Izetbegović for supporting "counterrevolutionary" activity.

The declaration was reissued in 1990, and Serb nationalists cited it constantly during the Bosnian war, saying it proved Izetbegović was determined to turn Bosnia itself into a fundamentalist state. (The Serbs conveniently ignored passages in the declaration that showed Izetbegović to be a moderate, such as where he called for "understanding and cooperation" between Christianity and Islam or observed that Judaism and Islam share a common culture so interwoven that "a distinction between Islamic and Jewish elements . . . is impossible to make with certainty.") Izetbegović, who was released from prison in 1988, never explained precisely what the political implications of his declaration were, but he insisted that the document was not meant to apply to a multiethnic country such as Yugoslavia, where Muslims would always be a minority. In fact, it contained no reference either to Yugoslavia or to Bosnia-Herzegovina, and the Bosnian Muslim party that Izetbegović helped found in 1990 did not propose a political program remotely Islamic in content or separatist in aim.

Izetbegović may personally have been comfortable with the idea of an Islamic state, but the secular wing of his party was firmly against it. (Tension between the clerical and secular branches of the Bosnian Muslim movement would resurface during the Bosnian war, as Muslim politicians debated the character of the future Bosnian state.) Once he became a politician, Izetbegović dropped most references to Islam in his public pronouncements, focusing instead on the danger that Serb nationalism would present to the Bosnian Muslims if they remained unorganized. The more Slobodan Milošević rallied Serbs to stand up against their non-Serb neighbors, whether in Kosovo, Croatia, or Bosnia, the more Muslims rallied in support of their own political leadership.

In Croatia nationalism was also astir. The movement that had been pushed underground by the Tito regime in the early 1970s resurfaced with a vengeance in the late 1980s, prompted in part by the revival of Serb nationalism but also by the prospect of an end to Communist rule and the opportunity to reestablish an independent Croatian state. In 1990 Franjo Tudjman emerged as the leader of a new party called the Croatian Democratic Union. Tudjman trumpeted Croat national symbols and celebrated the republic's short and Nazi-tainted World War II independent state tradition. In the process he alarmed the minority Serb population, for whom independent Croatia stood for only one thing: the murder of Serbs. Tudjman and his allies pushed for a completely independent Croatian state, with full sovereignty over its entire territory, including the Serb-populated areas. Not surprisingly, they met with fierce resistance.

A vicious circle was evident: By encouraging nationalism among Serbs, Slobodan Milošević had alarmed Muslims and Croats, who responded with national movements of their own, which served in turn to reinforce old Serb prejudices. Soon after the formation of the Croat nationalist party, pro-Milošević leaders of the Serb community in Croatia announced they were organizing their own Serbian Democratic Party (SDS). A few months later a Bosnia branch was established under the same name and with the same goals as the Serb party in Croatia.

The SDS structure in Bosnia took shape slowly, however. The Muslims were doing nothing to the Bosnian Serbs that was comparable to what the Croat nationalists were doing in Croatia. There was a secessionist drive in Croatia that, if unchallenged, would result in Croatian Serbs being left on the other side of an international border from Mother Serbia, but no such movement was yet evident in Bosnia. The Bosnian branch of the Serbian Democratic Party, in fact, was initially organized only in those areas bordering Croatia. Officials of SDS even had difficulty finding someone to lead their party in Sarajevo. The party presidency was offered to several leading Sarajevo Serbs, only to have them all turn it down.

The call was finally accepted by Radovan Karadžić, a jovial forty-four-year-old Sarajevo psychiatrist well known and liked around town but until then not taken seriously as a man of politics. If anything, Karadžić was seen as a bit of an oddball, having dabbled in everything from chicken farming to poetry in a fruitless quest for wealth and glory. At the time he joined the SDS, he was serving as psychiatrist for the Sarajevo soccer club, whose team had fallen into a humiliating slump. Karadžić had been hired to instill "a winning attitude" in the players and was trying to use group hypnosis with them. Oblivious to the disdain players felt for him, Karadžić maneuvered to be included in team photos and pestered the *Oslobodjenje* reporter who covered the soccer club to write stories about his work with them. He was a tall, bulky man with an enormous shock of gray hair that swooped across his forehead and curled over his ears, making him look scruffy no matter how smartly he tried to dress.

Those who had known him as a university student in Sarajevo suspected Karadžić of having been a police informer. In 1968 he had joined the student protest movement that was sweeping Europe. Communist Party authorities in Bosnia cracked down hard on the movement, arresting several student leaders and stripping others of their scholarships and jobs; Karadžić himself faced possible expulsion from medical school. Married at the time, with two children to support, he was vulnerable to police pressures. When he suddenly found an apartment and then received a well-paying university sinecure, his friends started to wonder. After two occasions when students were arrested on the basis of information they believed to have come from him, Karadžić was ostracized from the movement.

When he became an adult, Karadžić's thirst for recognition found expression in his drive to become a famous poet. He was known well enough to get his work included in government-subsidized anthologies of Bosnian poetry, though without acclaim. A critic in the mid-1980s gently noted that Karadžić was "not very successful" with his poetry and that he was threatened "by a tendency of verbal narcissism." Karadžić himself regarded his poetry as no less than brilliant, however, and told the chief psychiatrist at the mental health clinic where he worked that he was destined to become "one of the three most important poets writing in the Serbian language," a claim that foreshadowed the egotistic impulse he displayed during the Bosnian war.

In 1985 Karadžić was convicted in a Sarajevo court of the misuse of public funds and sent to prison. At the time he was having a large house built in the village of Pale, outside Sarajevo, where he would later establish his party headquarters. Bills for the project were allegedly paid by Momčilo Krajišnik, the director of a state conglomerate, who was sentenced to prison along with Karadžić. Both men were later released on the order of a prominent Serb judge in Sarajevo. Krajišnik himself would become a leading Serb nationalist politician and later speaker of the parliamentary assembly of the self-declared Serb Republic in Bosnia.

The appointment of Karadžić to the SDS presidency surprised many of his friends and acquaintances, who had not known him to be a Serb nationalist. Some Sarajevans concluded he agreed to the appointment only because he was indebted to the Bosnian Serb political leadership for financing his Pale venture and then getting him out of prison. Just three months before taking over the Serb party presidency, he had joined a newly formed Green Party in Bosnia, declaring in a speech at a party forum that "Bolshevism is bad, but nationalism is even worse." Some at the forum recalled that the main Karadžić contribution had been a proposal to label food packages according to standards of healthiness.

A Short-lived Democracy

The Constitutional Court of Bosnia-Herzegovina declared in June 1990 that the republic could legally have ethnically oriented political parties, and preparations began immediately for free elections in November. Five main parties would compete: the Serbian Democratic Party (SDS), the Croatian Democratic Union (HDZ), the Party of Democratic Action (SDA), representing Muslims; the Social Democratic Party (SDP), composed mostly of former Communists; and the Alliance of Reform Forces, which advocated a Yugoslavia-wide program of democratic change and free-market reforms.

Two days after the formal establishment of a multiparty system,

Oslobodjenje and the former Communist Party severed all their remaining ties by mutual agreement. The editorial board dropped the line in the masthead that identified the newspaper with the Socialist Alliance of Working People and put a new definition in its place: "An Independent Bosnia-Herzegovinian Daily." In an accompanying statement titled *"Oslobodjenje* and Pluralism," the editors detailed their commitment to nonpartisan reporting, their new "reform orientation," and their tightened editorial standards. The staff were genuinely excited about the prospect of their newspaper playing its proper democratic role. "During the election campaign," the editors promised, *"Oslobodjenje* will report objectively about the parties' meetings and make it possible for all the parties to represent their ideas equally."

But the *Oslobodjenje* editors and reporters were soon to find out that the political parties did not see the newspaper in a uniform way. Of the three national parties, only the Muslim SDA was unequivocally committed to the existence of Bosnia as a single republic within its current borders. The Serb and (to a lesser extent) Croat national parties were indirectly controlled by politicians outside Bosnia who had publicly questioned the republic's right to exist. Because it had been identified with Bosnia from its inception, *Oslobodjenje* was seen by the SDA as a potential ally and by the other two ethnic parties as unsympathetic. "As soon as we opened up space on the opinion page, Muslim writers gobbled it up," Ljiljana Smajlović said. The HDZ, meanwhile, was distinctly cool, and the Serbs refused to cooperate at all. "I wanted them very much, but they wouldn't even let us interview them," she said. For the SDS ideologues, contributing to the *Oslobodjenje* opinion page would lend legitimacy to the concept of a multiethnic Bosnian state, and it would mean supporting an enterprise that demonstrated pluralism at work. Serb nationalists found those ideas abhorrent.

To the extent that the newspaper had a political leaning of its own, it was against all three ethnic parties. In their June declaration the editors had addressed their readers individually as "citizens" of Bosnia rather than collectively as "peoples," a choice of words that implicitly challenged the notion that Bosnian society should be organized into national blocs. The party sympathies of most of the newspaper staff lay with the Reformists and the Social Democrats.

To the unpleasant surprise of many Sarajevans and *Oslobodjenje* journalists, the Serb, Croat, and Muslim parties together captured 80 percent of the Bosnian vote in the November elections. The Social

Democrats and Reformists took only 31 of the 240 seats in the Bosnian Parliament. The massive vote for the ethnic parties (the election-as-census pattern) was later interpreted by some foreign analysts as an indication of the depth of national divisions in Bosnia and a sign that conflict was inevitable. But surveys showed that fear of the prospect of an interethnic civil war was the critical issue in the election. Many voters concluded that the danger of conflict would be lessened when the three ethnic groups were represented politically, with their leaders working out a modus vivendi among themselves.

Such an assumption worked to the benefit of all three national parties, and in this regard the SDS, SDA, and HDZ leaders were one another's allies in the election. In the final days before the vote, Radovan Karadžić, Alija Izetbegović, and Stjepan Kljuić of the Croat party even appeared at a joint press conference to show their readiness to work together. Each of their parties' poll standings shot up after that event. Muslim voters in particular rallied to the SDA. Many were convinced that the Bosnian Serbs and Croats would vote en masse for their respective parties and that Muslims would be left politically weakened if they did not do the same. It was, after all, the first multiparty election Bosnian voters had experienced, and many people, especially in rural areas, lacked a sophisticated understanding of how democracies work.

Positions in the new government were carefully apportioned along ethnic lines. The Muslims took the largest share of the vote, and their party got the dominant position in the government. Three members of the seven-member collective presidency would be Muslims, and SDA leader Alija Izetbegović was made president of the presidency. The post of prime minister was reserved for an HDZ Croat, and the Parliament speakership was given to Momčilo Krajišnik, the SDS Serb businessman who five years earlier had gone to prison with Radovan Karadžić. The ex-Communists, having run Bosnia for nearly fifty years, were almost entirely shoved aside, except for those who had been transformed into nationalists.

Of the three ethnic parties, the Serb SDS was most determined to divide all government functions and public offices on an ethnic basis, with the Muslims most resistant. The Serbs wanted the principle extended to the division of territory, with the creation of separate Serb, Muslim, and Croat cantons in Bosnia, an idea to which the Muslims were vigorously opposed. The Croat HDZ was somewhere in the middle. Politically, it was allied with the Muslims against the Serbs, and party leader Kljuić favored a united Bosnia. But his Zagreb overlord, Franjo Tudjman, made clear he wanted to see Bosnia divided the way the Serbs suggested.

As an enterprise where ethnic identity was not supposed to matter, *Oslobodjenje* was without a powerful political ally in the new government, and it soon found itself in jeopardy. As a concession to the Serbs, the Muslim SDA agreed to support the reorganization of all media outlets in Bosnia on an ethnic basis, with the directors and editors of radio, television, and publicly owned newspapers chosen by the national parties. Although *Oslobodjenje* had declared itself independent, its legal status was unclear. The Communist organization that had previously published it no longer existed. In theory the newspaper belonged to the employees, but the government would argue that it was still subject to public control. The government proposal would have allowed the Serb party to choose the newspaper manager, while the Muslim party could appoint the editor in chief. It would have meant an end to the newspaper's principled stand against nationalism and the installation of reporters who answered to party bosses rather than to their editors. A hiring quota would have been established, with positions designated for members of particular ethnic groups. Although he was a Muslim, Kemal Kurspahić would undoubtedly have been replaced as editor by someone politically closer to the SDA leadership. The media proposal showed the extent to which Bosnia was still under the influence of a Communist-era mind-set; the plan seemed perfectly reasonable to the politicians who drafted it.

As the Bosnian Parliament considered the reorganization proposal, Kurspahić assembled his staff to survey their reactions. Ljiljana Smajlović said that letting the ethnic parties divvy up the *Oslobodjenje* positions would bring "complete professional stagnation" at the newspaper. Fahro Memić, a news desk editor (and a Muslim) objected to the proposal on the ground that *Oslobodjenje* was "the only genuinely Yugoslav paper, free from Muslim and Croat and Serb national influences." His colleague on the news desk, Zlatko Dizdarević (also a Muslim), said the partition of *Oslobodjenje* would mean "the beginning of the destruction of Bosnia-Herzegovina."

One of the last to speak was Miroslav Janković, Kurspahić's deputy and the top Serb editor at the paper. He seemed nervous during the meeting, pacing back and forth and walking out of the room several times, only to return a few minutes later. In preceding months Janković had moved closer to a Serb nationalist perspective, and in general he supported the SDS program, but he also recognized that

Oslobodjenje had become a good and profitable newspaper, and he didn't want to see it ruined, if only because ruin would jeopardize his own well-paying job there. Finally, Janković stood and read a short statement he had written.

"*Oslobodjenje*," he said, "can defend itself because it rests on two strong pillars: First, an editorial policy insuring that the news is reported factually and that commentators are free to express their own views; such an editorial policy can no longer be found anywhere else in Yugoslavia. Second, a remarkably good commercial orientation, making this newspaper one of the most successful businesses in the city." With the statement Janković was announcing his opposition to the takeover plan. He had heard through Serb friends that if Karadžić and other SDS leaders were to appoint a newspaper manager, they would simply order the paper decapitalized and drive it into the ground.

Kurspahić published an account of the meeting the next day under the headline "*Oslobodjenje* in a Time of Change." A month later he stepped up his campaign to keep his paper out of the hands of the nationalists by calling for a demonstration of public support in front of the Parliament Building. Thousands of Sarajevans showed up in the first public rally in the city against ethnic partition plans of any sort. Although the Parliament nevertheless approved the proposal, implementation was left pending while *Oslobodjenje* appealed the law. Kurspahić, who had a university law degree, argued his paper's case on his own in front of the Constitutional Court in Sarajevo.

"Why would the appointment of editors by democratically elected representatives of the people harm press freedom?" a judge asked him.

"It wouldn't harm it," Kurspahić answered. "It would destroy it. It would mean party control over the media," he said, "and five decades of Communist rule have shown us what that brings."

In September 1991 the court ruled in *Oslobodjenje*'s favor. The united stand by *Oslobodjenje* reporters and editors against the proposal to make them answerable to the ethnic parties was the newspaper's first triumph as an institution defending democratic values in the face of encroaching nationalism. There would not be many others. Yugoslavia was heading toward a cataclysm.

War in Croatia

The conflict began in Croatia, where nationalists moved hastily to assert their authority over the Serb minority. In the summer and fall of 1990, Serbs in the *Krajina* (Border) area of Croatia violently seized control of roads and villages in the region, declaring their territory to be autonomous. The following spring Croatian security forces tried unsuccessfully to bring Serb communities throughout the republic back under their control, and heavy fighting erupted shortly after Croatia declared its independence at the end of June.

When the war started *Oslobodjenje* reporter Vlado Mrkić got the call to cover it. Over the next months he made several reporting trips to Croatia in his white Golf, often alone. One story in July was about ten Croatian National Guardsmen killed while battling Serbs from a nearby village. Mrkić began with an account of the Croat funeral in the town of Vinkovci.

> Night was setting in. The crowd around the square held burning candles. Around 9 p.m., the coffins of the dead Guardsmen were brought and placed on stands prepared for them. Women hugged the coffins, crying out and calling the names of their loved ones. . . .
>
> After a few minutes, the priest began to speak. ". . . Their last deed in life was defending the Fatherland. God rewards such supreme sacrifice with eternity," he said.

The next day Mrkić went to the Serb village of Mirkovci, where the Croat fighters had been killed. He talked his way through a Croat checkpoint near the front line and proceeded on foot along a mined street. His story continued with the Serb viewpoint:

> In a café, I spoke with members of the village defense. Two were in police uniforms; one named Gradimir Keravica was dressed in civilian clothes. . . . He told his story.
>
> "We are already at war. Any negotiation to have a common life with the Croats is out of the question. Our goal is to live in Serbia. The borders of Serbia must be moved. . . . We are proud of what we are doing, and we don't want the Ustashe government here. We would rather die."
>
> When I returned to Vinkovci, the Croat Guardsmen asked me what the Chetniks were doing. We were sitting on the grass under

the maple trees, talking. "They will not get an inch of Croatian soil," one said. "We would rather die."

I believed I had heard something similar back in Mirkovci.

By striking a balance between the Croat and Serb sides, Mrkić was following the nonpartisan pattern he had demonstrated in his Kosovo reporting. In other Croatian war stories, Mrkić wrote of burning houses, of refugees trudging down highways, and of children crying for their lost parents. But he always stopped short of assigning blame. As Mrkić's Kosovo stories had been, these reports were appreciated by those Sarajevans who related to the war in Croatia as if it were none of their business. Some readers, however, were left wondering what was really going on in Croatia and whether the war Mrkić described so poignantly might also come to Bosnia.

There were disturbing parallels. The Serb party in Bosnia was moving to take total control of the areas it dominated politically, just as the Serbs in Croatia had done. Leaders of SDS had set up a Serb "assembly" and Serb "executive council" in the northwest Bosnian city of Banja Luka and were governing the region as though Serbs alone lived there and it were part of Serbia rather than Bosnia. In November 1990, just before the Bosnian election, Serb deputies from Croatia and Bosnia had met in Belgrade to declare their support for a Greater Serbia. "We rely on Serbia's constitution," said an SDS spokesman from Bosnia, referring to the provision by which Serbs living outside the republic were guaranteed protection. "We tie all our hope to Mother Serbia."

The Serb nationalists were presenting *Oslobodjenje* with a new challenge. If the newspaper continued to be identified directly with Bosnia, it would be on a collision course with the Serbs who were determined to break the republic apart. The changing circumstances were particularly troublesome to Ljiljana Smajlović. She could oppose all three ethnic parties in Bosnia equally, but when the Serb nationalists emerged as the principal adversary, she became uncomfortable. In the 1990 elections her mother had voted for the Serb party, and in the federal Yugoslav census held in April 1991, her mother had declared herself Serb for the first time in her life.

Traveling with Vlado Mrkić in the Croatian war zone, Ljiljana realized she could not keep it up any longer. When Croatian officials told them that the Serbs had burned a nearby Croat village named Ćelije, Ljiljana was skeptical of the claim, thinking it propaganda. She and Vlado went to investigate, along with Jana Schneider, an American photographer with whom they were traveling. At the village edge they were stopped by a Serb militia commander who initially told them reporters were not welcome in the area but then relented and allowed Ljiljana and Jana to continue. Vlado had to stay back. The two women discovered that the Croatian official had not exaggerated. Half of the houses in Ćelije had been burned, and cattle were wandering the deserted streets. They found a dog tied to a post, dying of thirst. Entering a schoolhouse, Ljiljana found a message scrawled in Cyrillic on the blackboard: "This is for 1941, you Ustashe. If you ever return, we'll slit your throats."

Ljiljana was horrified by what she saw in Ćelije, and stunned by her own reaction: She was not able to write about it. "I didn't want the story in *Oslobodjenje,*" she recalled later. "I knew what should have been written, and if it had been a Serb village burned by the Croats, I would have done it. I could have written two pages on that dog alone. But because it was Serbs who did it, I couldn't." She was secretly pleased that Vlado had not been allowed to enter the village, because she knew he would have described exactly what he saw, no matter who was responsible. She told him in general what she had seen but offered no details. Vlado suggested she use the quotation from the schoolroom blackboard in the story they were jointly writing that day, but Ljiljana lied and said she couldn't recall the exact words. In the account of their travels that day, Ljiljana included only a couple of paragraphs about the Ćelije scene, buried deep in the story.

The experience was a turning point for Ljiljana. "When I realized the way I felt," she told me, "I saw this was a war in which I was myself involved. I understood that I was not outside it." Returning to Sarajevo, she told Kemal Kurspahić of her reaction and tried to convince him that it meant *Oslobodjenje* would never be able to report objectively about Yugoslavia's breakup. When her old friend Gordana Knežević arrived back in Sarajevo that August after the end of her Cairo posting, Ljiljana told her the story. Neither Gordana nor Kemal, however, saw the Ćelije incident as proving anything except that Ljiljana had failed as a journalist. In the autumn she moved to Brussels.

3

For or Against Bosnia

In August 1991 Gordana and Ivo Knežević and their three children returned to Sarajevo from Cairo with armloads of souvenirs, new clothes, cartons of books, and photo albums of family outings among the pyramids and at the beach. On a kitchen wall in their three-room Sarajevo apartment, Gordana hung a calendar from the private school in Cairo where her sons, Boris and Igor, had studied. It would be a reminder of the "four years of paradise" she had lived as *Oslobodjenje*'s correspondent in the Middle East. Because Gordana worked out of her Cairo flat, reporting responsibilities did not conflict with home life. The newspaper paid her $3,000 a month, enough to support her family comfortably. Ivo was free to read philosophy, write his master's thesis, and do the family cooking.

While they were in Egypt, however, Gordana and Ivo had missed the most important developments in Yugoslavia since World War II. When they left Sarajevo in 1987, Communist authority was still unchallenged in Bosnia, and *Oslobodjenje* was still a Party organ. By the time they returned, the mighty League of Communists had shriveled to the status of a minor opposition party, and *Oslobodjenje* had become a genuinely independent newspaper. Nationalists dominated the political scene across Yugoslavia, and an interethnic war had broken out in Croatia. In Bosnia the democratically elected government was headed for a confrontation with Serb separatists.

Gordana found her *Oslobodjenje* colleagues struggling bravely to learn a new way of journalism but disoriented by the pace of change and the awesome complexity of the professional challenges they faced. Bosnian President Alija Izetbegović was paralyzed by indecision, desperate to avoid civil war but without a clue of how it could be done. The Serb nationalists alone knew exactly what they wanted and how to get it, with Serbia's help. Their goal was a new Greater Serbia state, incorporating every part of Bosnia where Serbs lived. In the coming months Western European governments would attempt to mediate in Bosnia, but their efforts would fail, largely from a lack of resolve. Serb forces armed by the Milošević regime in Belgrade would attack Sarajevo and seize two-thirds of Bosnian territory. After trying for a time to maintain their independent media profile, most *Oslobodjenje* journalists would conclude that their newspaper's fate was tied to Bosnia's and put the defense of their state above all other aims.

Gordana didn't see all this immediately, but before long she and Ivo were troubled by what they encountered in Sarajevo. Paradoxically, there seemed to be less room for civilized debate under the conditions of democracy than there had been in the old days, when an argument about Tito or Khrushchev would have enlivened a smoky conversation over a bottle of brandy in someone's living room and then ended harmlessly. Gordana discovered that the social atmosphere in Sarajevo had changed after Slobodan Milošević came to power in Serbia. "If I said I didn't like Milošević, people wouldn't come to my house anymore," she told me. "There was a kind of fever on the Serb side." Her uncle's wife refused to speak with her after an argument over Milošević, even though they had been close for many years, and a similar rupture occurred with a cousin. "Each day," Gordana said, "I noticed that someone else was infected with this strange Serb feeling."

On returning to the paper, Gordana replaced Ljiljana Smajlović as politics editor, because Ljiljana was about to leave for Brussels. Her first move was to ask for interviews with the leaders of each of the three national parties: Alija Izetbegović of the Muslim SDA, Stjepan Kljuić of the Croat HDZ, and Radovan Karadžić of the Serb SDS. Izetbegović and Kljuić agreed immediately. Karadžić refused to give her an appointment.

Sliding Toward War

Gordana assumed the Serb SDS still considered itself one parliamentary party among the several in Bosnia, responsible to the body politic at large. She soon realized this was not so. By the fall of 1991, Slobodan Milošević and his allies in Bosnia had set up separate Serb governing structures in self-declared "Autonomous Regions" in Bosnia under their political control. The Serb nationalists were establishing their own media and saw no need to cooperate with *Oslobodjenje*, a newspaper they considered hostile to their interests. With the goal of establishing a Greater Serbia, Serb party leaders were already planning a complete military takeover of all Serb-populated regions in Bosnia.

Transcripts of taped telephone conversations and other documents obtained from official sources by Belgrade dissidents indicated that Milošević had personally authorized the delivery of arms and ammunition to local SDS chapters in Bosnia, turning the party into an illegal paramilitary force. The Serb-dominated federal Yugoslav army, which had already come to the aid of Serb irregulars in the Croatian war, also had a key role in the military occupation of Bosnia-Herzegovina, although its full extent would not be seen until the war was under way. In public, army officers claimed that they were interested only in preventing an outbreak of civil war in Bosnia; privately, they were assisting the Serb side in war preparations.

In January 1991 the Yugoslav army had ordered the disbandment of all remaining civilian "Territorial Defense" units set up by Tito twenty years earlier. With Yugoslavia in danger of splintering, the army commanders argued, a disarming of the militias was necessary to block the emergence of republican armies and other "illegal armed forces." In Croatia and Slovenia leaders resisted or ignored the order, but Alija Izetbegović complied, instructing municipal governments in parts of Bosnia under his party's control to cooperate in the disarmament.

The army, however, double-crossed Izetbegović, making little or no effort to disband Territorial Defense units in Serb-dominated municipalities of Bosnia and even aiding secretly in their reinforcement. The ties between the Yugoslav army and the SDS paramilitary forces were revealed in correspondence found at a federal army barracks in Sarajevo after it was abandoned in June 1992. In one case a federal army commander ordered in writing that thousands of rounds of ammunition, hundreds of mortar shells, and 420 M75 hand grenades be forwarded to a Serb Territorial Defense unit in the northwest Bosnian town of Bosanski Petrovac a full year after the TD units had been ordered disbanded.

The decision by Izetbegović to allow the federal army to disarm his Territorial Defense units was one of several instances in which he took army commanders at their word when they said they would remain neutral in the Yugoslav conflict. On each occasion his judgment was publicly questioned by members of his Muslim party. Izetbegović was already sixty-five when he became president of Bosnia and had no experience in government. Bosnian Muslims had long seen him as a leader of their religious community, exemplary in his faith, but Izetbegović sometimes seemed out of place in the marbled corridors of power.

A short man with a grim, wearied expression, bushy eyebrows, and sea blue eyes, he had an air of pain about him that may have come from the five years he spent in prison in the 1980s. Even critics conceded his basic decency, but his supporters worried that he was naive, as evidenced by his willingness to cooperate with the Yugoslav army. Nevertheless, Izetbegović was determined to do whatever he could to avoid an armed confrontation with the Serb nationalist forces in Bosnia. The trust he placed in the federal Yugoslav army in fact reflected his hope that Yugoslavia itself could be preserved, for its division into rival Serb and Croat states would surely spell trouble for Bosnia and its Muslim people, as had been seen before.

Izetbegović spent most of 1991 working desperately to find a formula under which Yugoslavia could stay together. He proposed a variety of compromises, only to see them all rejected by one republic or another. By the fall of 1991, Slovenia had established full sovereignty over its territory, Serbia and Croatia were at war, and Macedonia was moving steadily toward independence, but Alija Izetbegović was still trying to persuade the world community not to recognize the seceding Yugoslav republics as independent states. (The insistence with which Izetbegović worked to maintain a united Yugoslavia is perhaps the best evidence that he was not scheming to establish an Islamic fundamentalist state; Muslims constituted only about a tenth of the federation's population as a whole.)

Given the irreconcilable positions of the Serb and Croat nationalists, however, Yugoslavia was a lost cause. As Izetbegović came to the
realization that European governments would not force Croatia and
Slovenia to return to the Yugoslav fold, he had to face the question of
Bosnia's own status in the federation. With Croatia gone, "Yugoslavia" would be dominated by Serbia. Croat-dominated municipalities in Bosnia were threatening to secede unless the Bosnian government declared full independence from Belgrade. But Serb nationalists
in Bosnia considered their territory part of "Serbia" already and were
prepared to go to war rather than be separated from their motherland.
Whether Bosnia declared independence or not, the republic was destined to be torn apart, and the Serb- and Croat-dominated regions
could both be lost if Izetbegović were not careful. He stalled as long as
he could but decided in the end that the prospect of being stuck in a
Serb-dominated rump federation was unacceptable given the nationalist leadership in Belgrade. "We don't want to be in this Yugoslavia,"
Izetbegović said in October 1991, as the Bosnian Parliament considered a sovereignty declaration.

The Serb nationalist reaction was instantaneous. Radovan Karadžić warned that the Bosnian leadership was leading the republic "into
a hell in which the Muslims will perhaps perish." Foreign journalists
visiting his Sarajevo headquarters were treated to a stream of anti-
Muslim invective. "The Muslims are trying to dominate Bosnia,"
Karadžić said. "They want to create an Islamic state here, but we Serbs
are not going to let them. You cannot force Christians to live in a Muslim state. It's just like Lebanon. We do not want to live under Oriental
despotism."

Karadžić himself did not believe what he was saying. The script
he followed in his press interviews was the Serb nationalist propaganda line, but Karadžić had had an entirely different analysis of
Bosnian Muslim thinking when he spoke to the Belgrade magazine
NIN in June 1990, one week after he was appointed SDS president:

> In Serbia, the media are wrongly speaking of the dangers of funda-
> mentalism in Bosnia. . . . The situation is quite different. . . . Our
> Bosnian Muslims are Slavs, of our same blood and language, who
> have chosen the European life along with their Muslim faith. In my
> estimation, it is not necessary that the Serbs once again defend
> Christian Europe in the fight against Islam. We Serbs are closer to
> our Muslims than we are to that Europe. . . .

Nothing in the Muslim political program had changed in the fifteen months following the *NIN* interview; Alija Izetbegović had shown he was the moderate he had claimed to be all along. By fabricating an Islamic fundamentalist threat, Karadžić was evidently hoping to influence European Community governments that were considering what action to take should Bosnia formally declare its independence. In mid-December the EC decided to recognize all breakaway Yugoslav republics, provided several criteria were met. Four days later the Bosnian government formally applied for recognition. The EC asked only that a popular referendum be held to determine whether a majority of Bosnian citizens wanted independence; the Bosnian Parliament scheduled a vote for the end of February.

Karadžić responded to the December declaration with another warning to the Bosnian Muslims that they could soon face a terrible assault. If the Bosnian government continued its efforts to gain independence, he threatened, "one nation will disappear." The stage was set for war, but no EC government took action that indicated it understood the dangers facing Bosnia. Nor did any government seem troubled by the consolidation of Serb political and military control over a widening swath of Bosnian territory.

The Bosnian government itself seemed unsure of where it was heading. Izetbegović brushed off the Karadžić threat, but a series of attacks on Muslim monuments in SDS-controlled territory soon suggested the Serb warnings were to be taken seriously. Two weeks before the February 1992 referendum vote, the Ferhadija mosque in Banja Luka, built in the sixteenth century and designated as a UNESCO historic monument, was damaged by a bomb blast. Still anxious to avoid open conflict with the Serbs, Izetbegović said the bombing was the work of "extremists" and urged Bosnian Muslims to remain calm. "Please don't blame the Serb people for this," he said.

Partisan or Patriotic?

In the *Oslobodjenje* newsroom, Kemal Kurspahić was doing his best in the fall of 1991 to keep his staff together in the face of rising ethnic tensions in the republic. His determination was evident in his choice of Gordana Knežević to follow Ljiljana Smajlović as political editor. By replacing one Serb journalist with another, Kurspahić was demonstrating his faith in the multiethnic way of life and work. It required cool leadership on his part; among the Serb and Muslim and Croat journalists who surrounded him were many strong personalities. A less assured editor could easily have lost control of his staff.

Kurspahić and his colleagues had faced one momentous struggle after another. First, they successfully confronted Communist authority. Next, they challenged the ethnic parties' attempt to seize control of the newspaper. But then came the Serb defiance of Sarajevo authority, the bellicose rhetoric, and the pressures from Croat nationalists. War was coming, and *Oslobodjenje*'s fledgling status as a newspaper representing democratic values was in peril. The question was whether it would slide back into its old role as an organ of the ruling party, hold heroically to its independent course, or settle somewhere in between.

Arriving from Cairo, Gordana Knežević brought fresh energy to the embattled paper. As the daughter of an outspoken ex-Partisan, she had learned early to think critically, and working as a foreign correspondent had added to her confidence. She initially saw herself as a journalist rather than an activist and believed *Oslobodjenje* should remain politically independent. But the more she learned of the Serb nationalists, the more she became convinced that they represented the single greatest threat to the establishment of democracy in Bosnia. If her newspaper were to support democratic values, she reasoned, it might be necessary to abandon nonpartisanship and challenge the Serb party directly. She concluded that some of her colleagues were too evenhanded in their treatment of the three ethnic parties. "I was the first one at the paper to say, 'They're not all the same,' " Gordana told me. "I couldn't pretend there were no differences between the parties."

Gordana's editorial judgment soon became evident on page 2, the newspaper's opinion page. Kemal and Ljiljana had published any opinion piece that was well written and thoughtfully argued, and Ljiljana had gone out of her way to solicit Serb nationalist writers to balance the Muslim and Croat perspectives in the paper. "I felt they were going too far," Gordana said. "I had another idea of press freedom. I felt we had a responsibility as people to uphold human rights and not give space to every article that came in." Gordana's views immediately brought her into conflict with some other Serbs at the paper, notably deputy editor Miroslav Janković, who was taking an increasingly nationalist line. Janković was upset when an *Oslobodjenje* headline declared, VUKOVAR HAS FALLEN! after Serb forces flattened and overran the city in eastern Croatia in November 1991. "It

Gordana Knežević, a Serb who fervently supported the Bosnian cause, became *Oslobodjenje*'s deputy editor in May 1992.

(© 1994 ANNIE LEIBOVITZ/CONTACT PRESS IMAGES)

didn't fall, it was liberated," Janković claimed at an editorial board meeting the next morning.

Kemal's inclination had been to accommodate Janković, but Gordana had no qualms about challenging him, perhaps because she was herself a Serb. When Kemal went on a trip to Tokyo in December and left Janković in charge of the paper, the disagreements sharpened. Miroslav often went home early. Gordana stayed late and without asking approved the publication of commentaries attacking the Serb nationalists and defending Muslim or Bosnian government positions. When Miroslav saw the articles, he invariably was enraged. "You're responsible for this rubbish!" he yelled at Gordana one morning, waving an open newspaper in her face. "I don't want to see any more of this Ustashe stuff in the paper!"

The conflict over the newspaper's political line intensified in the period leading up to the referendum vote on Bosnian independence, which was scheduled for the weekend of February 29–March 1. Serb SDS members had walked out of the Parliament session when the referendum plan was adopted, and the Serb party resolved to ignore the vote entirely. An SDS-organized Assembly of Serb People in Bosnia-Herzegovina declared in a session in Sarajevo in January that the referendum would be illegal and that "the Serb people" no longer acknowledged the Bosnian state as a legal entity.

Oslobodjenje did not explicitly take a stand on the referendum, but as politics editor Gordana gave heavy coverage to the Izetbegović government's viewpoint. Page 3 was devoted every day to referendum campaign news. A few articles critical of the referendum plan were published, but the lead story each day came from a government-sponsored daily press conference where a series of speakers presented the case for Bosnian independence. Some editors at *Oslobodjenje,* Muslims as well as Serbs, questioned whether the newspaper should be offering space each day for government propagandists, but Gordana insisted they had a right to make their case.

"My opinion was that the government shouldn't have to buy advertising space," she told me. "A lot of people at the paper wanted to eat me up over this. There was this attitude that we should always be against the state, that it's bound to harm you, and that you should oppose anything that comes from it. But I didn't have this a priori prejudice." Gordana went so far as to speak at one of the pro-referendum press conferences, although she restricted her public comments to media issues.

One day a Serb driver at the newspaper refused to take Gordana to the government press center for the daily news conference, so angered was he by her pro-referendum position. "You're just a driver," she told him. "It's not for you to decide whether I go." But he refused to move. Gordana was furious and asked Kemal to have the driver fired, but he urged her to forget it. With other Serbs at the paper, however, disputes could not be so easily dismissed. Ljiljana Smajlović, who returned from Brussels for a few days in February to attend her father's funeral, was upset to see how polarized Sarajevo had become between the Serb nationalists and those who opposed them. Ljiljana thought Gordana had placed *Oslobodjenje* too far over on one side of the referendum debate, and she told her so.

The dispute strained their friendship. Gordana and Ljiljana had known each other for years, worked together closely at *Oslobodjenje* in the 1980s, and stayed in regular touch even when Gordana moved to Cairo. They shared a common background, as Serbs, Partisans' daughters, and ex-Communist journalists who had fought the system from within. But Ljiljana claimed that by going to Cairo just as

Oslobodjenje was breaking its Party ties, Gordana had missed an important turning point in the paper's evolution and fallen out of step with its thinking. She argued that Gordana's willingness to help the Bosnian government promote the referendum vote reflected old Communist-era tendencies. "Gordana was four years behind time," Ljiljana told me later. "While she was gone, we learned new reflexes and came of age as a newspaper. Then she came back from Cairo and picked up where we'd been when she left. *Oslobodjenje* has a long tradition of being used to promote a political cause," Ljiljana said, "and Gordana was keeping that up."

Not surprisingly, Gordana had an entirely different analysis of their disagreement. In her view it was Ljiljana who had lost touch with developments when she moved to Brussels just as the Serb SDS was transforming itself from a political party into an armed separatist movement. By arguing that the Serb opponents of Bosnian independence should get the same consideration given the elected government, Ljiljana was acting, in Gordana's judgment, as though Bosnia were still in the midst of a freewheeling election campaign and not on the verge of war. Recalling that Ljiljana had been unwilling to report all she had seen on her trip to Ćelije in Croatia six months earlier, Gordana figured Ljiljana was in no position to criticize *Oslobodjenje* for being partial.

Voting in the referendum on Bosnian independence lasted two days. By the time polls closed on Sunday, March 1, 64 percent of the electorate had participated, with 99 percent backing the independence declaration. No exact breakdown of the vote along national lines was possible, but from the returns it was clear that the vast majority of Serbs in Bosnia boycotted the referendum, on the instructions of the Serb leadership. Some non-Serbs presumably stayed away as well, frightened by the warnings of Radovan Karadžić, who predicted that the ratification of independence would provoke a civil war in Bosnia so bloody that "Northern Ireland would seem like a holiday place by comparison." The extent to which Serbs in Bosnia genuinely opposed independence cannot be known. Because the Serb leadership called for a boycott, there was no way to express one's preference secretly on referendum day. Simply showing up at a polling station meant defying local authorities. In some SDS-controlled towns, authorities did not even allow the vote to take place.

In Sarajevo the referendum was marred when gunmen opened fire on a Serb wedding party that was marching down a street in the mainly Muslim Baščaršija neighborhood, carrying a Serbian flag. The bridegroom's father was killed, and an Orthodox priest walking with him was wounded. President Izetbegović immediately issued a statement condemning the murder, calling it "a shot at all Bosnia," and the mayor of the Old Town, Selim Hadžibajrić, apologized and expressed his condolences to the family of the victim.

Serb party leaders ignored the apologies. Their reaction to the incident contrasted sharply to the Izetbegović response to the Banja Luka mosque bombing two weeks earlier. Whereas Izetbegović had asked Muslims not to blame Serb people as a whole for the attack, Radovan Karadžić urged Bosnian Serbs to conclude from the Old Town killing that they could no longer trust their Muslim neighbors. "This murder," he said, "shows what would happen to us in an independent Bosnia." While the Bosnian government was anxious to avoid a violent confrontation, the Serb leadership tacitly encouraged one. "I would like people to keep peace and to control themselves," Karadžić said, "but I am afraid it is too late for such a demand." By midnight Sunday heavily armed Serb militants had set up barricades on streets throughout the city, blocking all traffic into and out of town. The gunmen wore ski masks to conceal their identities and carried automatic rifles, machine guns, and antitank weapons. The speed with which the men appeared, the efficiency with which they sealed off the city, and the size of their arsenal suggested the blockade was carefully orchestrated. After a few days Serb party leaders ordered the blockades removed.

In its coverage of the wedding march killing and its aftermath, *Oslobodjenje* looked again like the Party organ of old. During the Communist period incidents that could provoke controversy or spark national conflict were often alluded to rather than described directly, and so was this crime. No separate, straightforward account of the shooting appeared in the paper, only oblique references. "According to the [SDS party] statement," a reporter wrote, "the main reason [for the barricades] was Sunday's tragedy in Baščaršija, when a civilian of Serb nationality was killed."

The article that caused an uproar among Serb nationalists, however, was a commentary on the Baščaršija incident coauthored by Gordana Knežević and her Muslim colleague Rasim Ćerimagić. They suggested that the wedding party was deliberately asking for trouble by marching with a Serbian flag through a Muslim neighborhood on referendum day. "There was nothing spontaneous about this," they wrote. "Never before have weddings that took place in New Sarajevo been celebrated in Baščaršija." The column prompted angry phone calls and letters from Serb residents who saw it as insensitive. At an *Oslobodjenje* editorial board meeting the next day, Miroslav Janković blew his top, calling the column "the most shameless thing this newspaper has published in fifty years."

The controversies over the referendum coverage and the wedding commentary raised questions about *Oslobodjenje*'s adherence to the editorial principles to which its board had committed the newspaper in June 1990. "Our first duty," the board said at that time, "is objectivity, professionalism, and nonpartisanship. This means that the editorial staff must offer the readers the facts and arguments on all sides. . . . The journalists' duty is to offer as complete a picture of the events as possible in their daily news reports, without putting in their own emotions."

The man who wrote the June 1990 declaration, *Oslobodjenje* editor in chief Kemal Kurspahić, later told me he saw no contradiction between the declaration and what his paper was publishing in March 1992. He pointed out that the paper maintained the separation between news reports and commentaries, and that in the news pages *Oslobodjenje* still reported what Serb politicians said and did. The Knežević-Ćerimagić wedding march commentary was clearly labeled as an opinion column rather than a news story. He was not troubled that Gordana had limited the expression of Serb nationalist viewpoints in the paper. "We stood for Bosnia," Kemal said. "As long as the SDS was a parliamentary party, I thought we should cover them as we would any other party. But as a newspaper we were against the idea of Greater Serbia and against the forced partition of the country." That stance, however, meant the newspaper was placing itself squarely in opposition to the expressed wishes of the majority of the Serb population in Bosnia.

Indeed, the dispute over *Oslobodjenje* news coverage and commentaries in the weeks before the outbreak of war had less to do with issues of journalism than with the question of Bosnia's future. Virtually all the editors and reporters would have liked their paper to be more like *Le Monde* or the *New York Times*, but they were not yet sure how they could emulate such models, given what *Oslobodjenje* had been through and what it was facing. Miroslav, Kemal, Gordana, and Rasim disagreed over what should become of their republic, and their feelings were strong enough that they were willing to fight within their newspaper for what they believed. At such moments questions of professionalism were secondary to those of patriotism, whether Serb or Bosnian. Ljiljana Smajlović raised serious questions about the paper's standards, but only from the safety of her perch in Brussels, where she had fled when she realized she was herself in danger of losing her objectivity.

The Call to Separate

In the weeks following the referendum, the prospect of a peaceful settlement of the conflict between the Bosnian government and the SDS nationalists dimmed. The European Community was sponsoring negotiations over a design for an independent Bosnia that would be acceptable to all sides, but the talks were not productive. The SDS Assembly of Serb People of Bosnia-Herzegovina declared itself opposed to any EC plan that would leave Serbs answerable to a central Bosnian government, no matter how weak its powers. One Serb deputy said the EC's delivery of an independent Bosnia would represent "the birth of a Muslim bastard on the land of our grandfathers."

In March 1992 EC mediators persuaded the Serb, Muslim, and Croat party leaders to accept a "new constitutional structure" that would have redefined Bosnia as a state composed of three ethnically based units whose territorial boundaries would be drawn on the basis of economic and geographic as well as demographic criteria. But the key issues were still unresolved. The document did not say whether Bosnia-Herzegovina would remain within Yugoslavia or be independent of it, nor was there agreement on a territorial map. The canton boundaries suggested by the Serb side, in fact, bore no resemblance whatsoever to those being tentatively proposed by the EC mediators. Conveniently ignoring the discrepancy, the Serb leaders declared that the EC outline legitimized their "Serb Republic" in Bosnia. But the Muslims and Croats said they had not agreed to that, and they repudiated the accord two weeks later.

Alija Izetbegović and other Bosnian government leaders were frustrated by what they saw as naiveté on the part of the EC negotiators. It appeared to Izetbegović that the Europeans did not recognize that a partition of Bosnia along ethnic lines could not be achieved without a massive and impractical displacement of the population. Hundreds of thousands of Muslims lived in those parts of Bosnia that the Serb nationalists had already defined as Serbian land. Any attempt to isolate the Muslims and Serbs from each other, Izetbegović pointed out, would be "like trying to separate cornmeal from flour after they were stirred in the same bowl." But pronouncements by Serb leaders about the impossibility of continued coexistence suggested that such a division was precisely what they favored. The "Serb Republic" was already being established on the basis of apartheidlike principles, with governing structures oriented exclusively to the Serb population. The Serb media were each day becoming more anti-Muslim in tone. But the EC mediators kept suggesting the creation of ethnically oriented "cantons" in Bosnia, as though they were proposing another Switzerland rather than another South Africa. Izetbegović and other Bosnian government officials continued the EC negotiations only because they saw no alternative.

Serb nationalist leaders, meanwhile, were already encouraging their people to separate from their non-Serb neighbors. They met with limited success in Sarajevo, where the crude nationalist rhetoric offended many educated Serbs. While the Serb party included a few urban intellectuals and university professors in its ranks, much of the SDS leadership in Bosnia came from outside Sarajevo or had a tainted past, as was the case with Karadžić and his deputy and former criminal codefendant Momčilo Krajišnik. Endorsements from more *Oslobodjenje* Serbs would have helped. Ljubo Grković, whose reporting assignment was to cover the local electric utility, had gone to work as chief of staff to Radovan Karadžić, but he was the only *Oslobodjenje* journalist directly associated with the Serb party. The most prominent Serb journalist with nationalist leanings was deputy editor Miroslav Janković. Both Grković and Janković would leave the paper within a few weeks of the outbreak of war, Grković joining Karadžić in Pale and Janković moving to Belgrade. The nationalists had hoped for more notable defections.

One SDS intellectual phoned Aco Štaka, a veteran *Oslobodjenje* film critic and essayist who had recently retired. "A new wind is blowing among the Serbs in Bosnia," he told Štaka. "You should come with us, and be a part of it." Štaka was known in Yugoslavia as a man of integrity who had long been a thorn in the side of Communist editors, and his alignment with the SDS would have enhanced the party's standing. But he brushed the SDS caller off with an obscenity.

After Aco Štaka snubbed them, the SDS didn't even bother to contact his twenty-nine-year-old son, Vladimir, a reporter in the paper's cultural section. "Nationalism is a disease that runs through the family," Vladimir told me later in Sarajevo, "and we didn't have it. In our house, we talked about François Truffaut, not Kosovo Polje." He contrasted his own upbringing with that of his friend Duško, who worked as a photographer for the *Oslobodjenje* weekend supplement and had been best man at Vladimir's wedding a year earlier. Like Vladimir, Duško was cultured, fluent in English, and well traveled. But his Serb father was obsessed with the old Serbian battle tales and the need for Serb solidarity. Around Vladimir and other friends, Duško regularly made fun of his father for "talking that Serb crap" over dinner.

With such a family background, however, Duško was one of the Sarajevo Serbs who would find it difficult to ignore the call to arms once it became clear that war was coming and that there would be a separate Serb side. In early 1992 Duško "flipped out in a Serb way," in Vladimir's words, and took up the nationalist cause with zeal. He warned an old Muslim friend that he was prepared to kill him if called to do so, and he told Vladimir that he had a hand grenade stashed under the front seat of his car for the moment he was stopped in Sarajevo by a Muslim policeman. A few weeks before the outbreak of shooting around the city, Duško encouraged Vladimir to get a gun from the local SDS office, where weapons were being freely distributed to Serb residents who declared their readiness to fight. "Don't you know the Muslims want to kill us all?" Duško asked, incredulous when Vladimir said he didn't need to be armed. Duško left Sarajevo a few days later.

Vladimir and his wife, Dubravka, had a two-bedroom apartment in a nicely landscaped complex built in 1985 on the southwest side of Sarajevo. Many of their neighbors were career Yugoslav army officers who had been stationed with their families in Sarajevo for years. Near the end of March 1992, Vladimir noticed that the army families were all leaving. "It was weird," he said. "No one wanted to talk about it. Army trucks would suddenly pull up outside in the middle of the night, and people would start carrying down their furniture. One neighbor told us he was moving his family to Belgrade so he could care for his sick mother. One said he was being transferred. Others just left." No official announcements were made, but by the end of the month almost all the army families were gone, leaving half the apartments in Vladimir's neighborhood vacant.

Relations between the Yugoslav army and the Bosnian government were growing more strained by the day. At a press conference at the end of March, the Yugoslav army commander in Sarajevo, Col. Gen. Milutin Kukanjac, said the army would go where the "people" of Bosnia asked them to go, but the Bosnian Serb leadership would have to agree to any such move. Because the Serb party had already said it did not want the army to leave General Kukanjac was effectively saying the army would stay.

The *Oslobodjenje* reporter at that press conference was Djuro Kozar, who had covered the army for more than twenty years and maintained close relations with the top command. After the press conference ended, General Kukanjac called Kozar, a Serb, into his office. "Have you decided what to do?" he asked him.

"About what?" Kozar said.

Kukanjac looked at him for a long moment. "Whether you want us to take you and your family out," he said finally. When Kozar answered that he didn't see why his family should leave Sarajevo, Kukanjac cursed. "Didn't anyone talk to you?" he asked.

"No."

"Those damn SDS people," Kukanjac said. "They want us to do everything for them." He told Kozar that the Serb party was preparing for war and that all Serbs should leave Sarajevo as soon as possible with their families. Kozar said he would stay in the city anyway. Kukanjac walked over to his office safe, turned the lock, and opened the door. Taking out a pistol, he offered it to Kozar. "At least I can give this to you," he said. "You might need it." Kozar refused the gun, saying he had no use for it, and left soon after. He reported on the Kukanjac press conference in the next day's paper but kept his conversation with the general to himself.

Zvornik

Serb propagandists would claim the 1992 war in Bosnia was a popular revolt by the local Serb population, of the same character and tradition as the anti-Turkish uprisings of the Serb peasantry in the nineteenth century. But it began when a Belgrade gangster who called himself Arkan led his private militia in the pillaging of the town of Bijeljina in the far northeast tip of Bosnia, seven miles west of the Serbian border. An *Oslobodjenje* reporter was among Arkan's first victims. It was often called a civil war, but Arkan had close ties to Serbian President Slobodan Milošević, and the Belgrade-based Yugoslav army provided the Bosnian Serb forces with logistical support, troops, and weaponry. Key operations were launched and directed from Serbia proper. The war caught Bosnia and Sarajevo unprepared, and the hastily organized Bosnian government army was nearly routed at the start.

A Belgrade sweet shop owner, Arkan was wanted in Sweden for

armed robbery. His real name was Željko Ražnjatović. Belgrade journalists had identified him as an agent of the Serbian Interior Ministry's secret police, and Interpol suspected him of having worked as a hit man for the former Communist regime. Arkan and his militia, composed in part of hooligan fans of Belgrade's Red Star soccer team, first made their mark during the 1991 Serb-Croat war, when they led a campaign of mass murder, village burning, and looting in eastern Croatia, enriching themselves in the process. He hung the Serbian government flag everywhere his paramilitaries seized territory.

Bijeljina was a mostly Muslim town in a municipality where the rural villages were mostly Serb. Arkan and his men, known as Tigers, had the assignment of subduing the urban Muslim population. Dressed in combat fatigues and black stocking caps, carrying automatic rifles, machine guns, and grenade launchers, the Tigers overwhelmed the poorly armed Bijeljina police force within a day of their arrival on April 1, 1992, then went on a looting rampage through the center of town. Several leaders of the Bijeljina branch of the Muslim SDA party were rounded up and executed in front of the main mosque. The Tigers hoisted the Serbian flag above the police station and city hall, and within hours hundreds of Bijeljina Muslims were fleeing toward central Bosnia. They took with them only what they could carry on their backs.

From Bijeljina, Arkan and his men moved thirty miles south to the town of Zvornik, on the west bank of the Drina River, just across from Serbia. The Serb war campaign initially had two main objectives: to secure an east-west road corridor from Serbia across the top of northern Bosnia and to seize control of the entire Drina River valley, which bordered Serbia and had to be secured as a staging area for Serbian operations in Bosnia. Both missions required the seizure and "ethnic cleansing" of large amounts of territory. Zvornik, for example, was 61 percent Muslim, but under the war plan it was to be "liberated" and made into a wholly Serb city.

The longtime *Oslobodjenje* correspondent in Zvornik, Kjašif Smajlović (no relation to Ljiljana), phoned in three stories on Wednesday, April 8, 1992, the day the Arkan militia arrived on the outskirts of town. In one story describing the capture of four of Arkan's men by Zvornik police, Smajlović quoted one of the Tigers as saying they had come to defend the Serb population in Zvornik from armed Muslim extremists. A second story related Arkan's ultimatum that all Muslim residents of Zvornik either surrender their weapons or prepare to see their city become "another Bijeljina." Smajlović, himself a Muslim, evidently hoped that, if he reported the news straightforwardly and without editorial comment, Arkan's men would leave him alone.

Still, he worried. Before filing his stories Smajlović scrambled to get his wife and two children on a bus to Tuzla, forty miles to the northwest. It was not easy. Thousands of anxious Muslim residents had gathered at the Zvornik bus station and were fighting one another to get tickets out of town. Smajlović remained behind, although in a telephone conversation with an *Oslobodjenje* editor he admitted he was terrified and at one point broke into tears. On Wednesday night the outgunned Muslim defenders battled at their flimsy street barricades on the edge of town against local Serb militants backed by Arkan's militia. Early the next morning Smajlović phoned the *Oslobodjenje* office in Tuzla with the latest news. "This will be my last report," he told his colleagues, saying he planned to go into hiding. Within hours Arkan's Tigers and other Serb militia units had captured the Zvornik police station and moved through the town, killing as they went. Thousands of Muslim residents fled in panic, most seeking refuge in an old Turkish fortress on a nearby hilltop. Smajlović was not among them. Two Serb militiamen found him at the *Oslobodjenje* office and shot him dead on the spot. A woman selling cigarettes at a kiosk in front of the office building saw the men drag Smajlović's body out the front door by the feet and toss it in the back of a truck.

I visited Zvornik eleven months later, in March 1993. Since it had been conquered quickly, it had largely been spared serious war damage. Cafés and stores were open, and the streets were full of people, almost all Serbs. "The demographic picture is completely different now from what it was before the war," the "mayor" of Zvornik told me, portraying the murder or expulsion of 8,000 Zvornik Muslims as a simple population shift. Before the war, Branko Grujić had been president of the local SDS chapter. In the 1990 elections his party won just a quarter of the seats in the local legislative council, but by the time I visited, the Serb deputies had the city hall entirely to themselves. "We were very successful in this war," Grujić told me, sitting in the spacious wood-paneled office he had claimed when the elected mayor, a Muslim, fled for his life a year earlier. "We took this city in twenty-four hours. We had to, because the Islamic fundamentalists wouldn't leave us alone."

What had they done, for example? I asked. He thought for a few moments, toying with one of the brandy glasses his secretary had set on the table, then looked up. "They didn't like it when we wore our traditional Serbian clothes," he said. "They would yell at us in the streets. And when we realized they would fight us if we didn't live in their way, we had to organize our people and make this war. We had no other choice." Grujić didn't think the Zvornik Muslims would ever be allowed back. "They have a bad character," he explained. "They used to be Serbs, but they converted. They'll do anything for money. It's in their blood."

"There Will Be No War"

In Sarajevo people later claimed that the outbreak of war in the capital city caught them by surprise, even though five days passed between Arkan's first attack on Bijeljina and the Holiday Inn shooting on April 6. *Oslobodjenje* reporter Džeilana Pećanin later recalled that she was in a video rental shop when a news bulletin about the Bijeljina assault flashed on the store television. Customers, she said, stopped to watch the report, shaking their heads in concern, but then went back to picking out videotapes for their evening's entertainment, as if the news were from another country. Sarajevans, from President Alija Izetbegović on down, refused to believe that their city could be next.

Denial and disbelief worked entirely to the advantage of the rebel Serb forces, and Serb leaders did all they could to nurture such attitudes. Yugoslav army commanders played an important role in this regard, encouraging Sarajevans and Bosnian government officials to believe that the army troops were neutral and would serve as a buffer force around their city. General Kukanjac said he felt "sadness" at the developing troubles in Bosnia. "The Yugoslav army is doing its best to stop this tragedy," he told Sarajevo television. "It's urgent that we control the commanders on both sides."

On the basis of such declarations, Alija Izetbegović cooperated with the Yugoslav army right up to the outbreak of war in Sarajevo. The leaders of volunteer militias, such as a Muslim unit called the Green Berets, were so fearful Izetbegović might order them disarmed that they met in secret. On April 2, a day after the attack on Bijeljina, the Green Berets stopped a Sarajevo-bound convoy of Yugoslav army trucks and found a load of small rockets and grenade launchers hidden in a shipment of bananas. Not wanting to antagonize the army, Izetbegović ordered the militia to let the convoy continue to the army barracks with its load undisturbed.

The Serb leader best at deceiving Sarajevans was Radovan Karadžić. Shortly after the trouble began in Bijeljina, *Oslobodjenje* sports reporter Ahmet Pašalić went to see Karadžić in his SDS suite at the Holiday Inn. Pašalić had covered the Sarajevo soccer club for years and was friendly with Karadžić from the days when he was the team psychiatrist. A Muslim, Pašalić lived with his wife and fifteen-year-old daughter at the far end of the suburb of Dobrinja, near a Yugoslav army base where many heavy weapons were stored. The rumors of war had him worried, and he went to Karadžić for advice on what to do.

"I have one thing to ask you," Pašalić said. "I'm worried for my daughter. I will do anything on this earth to protect her. I want you to tell me: Is there going to be a war here?"

"As you know, Pasha, I have children myself," Karadžić said, "and on them I swear to you. There will be no war." It was exactly what Pašalić wanted to hear, and he went straight home to tell his wife.

On Saturday, April 4, Alija Izetbegović finally ordered a full mobilization of police reservists. He also requested the Yugoslav army to return the arms and military equipment they had collected months earlier from the Territorial Defense units under Bosnian government control. Radovan Karadžić was quick to condemn the order. "The people here are armed anyway, and tension is high enough," he said. "Putting more weapons in the hands of the people will only accelerate civil war." An EC mediator couldn't have put it better. Karadžić's worries had been noticeably absent when local SDS leaders were collecting guns from the federal army arsenal and distributing them to any Serb willing to fight. Although his bushy brows wrinkled in concern at the thought of the police mobilization, Karadžić had turned his own party into a paramilitary force armed with everything from hand grenades to T-55 tanks.

In any case, Izetbegović had few weapons to distribute, and the police mobilization was coming far too late to be of much military significance. The first mortar shell fell on Sarajevo's Muslim quarter one night later. More came each night thereafter, producing quick flashes of light against the black sky, followed by bone-jarring blasts that roared across the city and rattled windows in every direction.

Although Yugoslav army artillery units were providing the guns and the shells, *Oslobodjenje* attributed the attacks on the city to "SDS extremists." As had Izetbegović and much of Sarajevo, the *Oslobodjenje* editors had been clinging to the hope that the Yugoslav army would stay out of the fighting, and they were reluctant to report that army units were firing on the city or at least providing the weaponry. By attributing the attacks on the city to Serb "extremists," the paper was not even blaming the SDS party leadership. On the eve of the war, *Oslobodjenje* was still publishing SDS party communiqués and occasionally asking Serb party leaders for their analysis of what was going on. The day after Radovan Karadžić's apartment in Sarajevo was demolished by volunteer militia forces, *Oslobodjenje* carried a story from Tanjug, the Belgrade-based Yugoslav state wire service, quoting a Serb party official in Sarajevo as saying that "Muslim paramilitary formations committed a criminal act" on the Karadžić property.

The newspaper's final attempt at evenhanded reporting came on April 16. Gordana Knežević and Vlado Mrkić went to a Karadžić press conference held at his party's "crisis headquarters" in the Serb-occupied western Sarajevo suburb of Ilidža. No Muslim reporter dared go. Serb militiamen had set up barricades by then on all roads into and out of the city, separating territory under their control from the areas defended by forces loyal to the Bosnian government. After the press conference, Karadžić sat down for an interview with Knežević, Mrkić, and two other journalists.

Mrkić asked Karadžić who was shelling civilian targets in the Old Town. "I don't know," he said. "We know only that there are some boys who shot at the headquarters of the Green Berets and missed. This [bombardment of civilians] is a pity, but it is explained by the fact that there are boys up there who don't know how to shoot." Knežević asked if he knew that the wife of his medical clinic partner had been barred from her job in a Serb-controlled hospital simply because she was Muslim. "I am glad just to hear she is alive and healthy," Karadžić said. "If they cannot guarantee her safety, it's better that she does not go to work."

Did he know that 6,000 Serbs in Sarajevo had signed a petition saying he and his party did not represent their interests? "I forgive them all," Karadžić said. "Let them sign whatever they have to sign. May they just be safe." It was a glib and clever answer, but Gordana wouldn't settle for it. Did he really believe he and his party represented all Bosnian Serbs? she asked. Pressed, Karadžić acknowledged that "perhaps 8 percent of the Serbs in Bosnia are not for us."

On their return to the *Oslobodjenje* building, Gordana found Kemal sitting in the newsroom. She laid her tape recorder down triumphantly in front of him, saying, "You'll have a great Karadžić story in tomorrow's paper." She and Vlado typed up the interview in a straight question-and-answer format, and it ran the next day without accompanying comment.

The trip to Ilidža was the last time Gordana or Vlado was able to get past the SDS barricades around Sarajevo without a U.N. escort. It was the last time anyone from *Oslobodjenje* bothered to ask Karadžić to explain the shelling of Sarajevo. There would be no more SDS party communiqués in the paper. By the end of April virtually all the SDS sympathizers on the *Oslobodjenje* staff had stopped coming to work. In one last brazen act, Ljubo Grković, the reporter who had moved to Pale, came by the office to pick up his March paycheck. The building was by then under daily sniper fire from nearby Nedjarići, and Serb gunners under the command of Grković's boss in Pale were shelling the city every day. But Grković believed he was entitled to his wages. When a veteran pressman saw Grković in the newsroom, paycheck in hand, he came charging up to him with fists raised. "You goddamn Chetnik traitor!" he screamed. "How dare you come here?"

"Shut up, old man," Grković growled. The fifty-five-year-old pressman took a wild swing at him, but Grković punched him back hard in the face, sending the man sprawling across the floor. "I wanted them to see I wasn't afraid of them," Grković told me later in Belgrade when I asked about the incident. "I wanted to show that *Oslobodjenje* was my home as well as theirs."

That same day, April 25, Kjašif Smajlović's brother phoned *Oslobodjenje* offices to say he had learned from Zvornik refugees that Kjašif had indeed been killed. Two weeks had passed since anyone had heard from him, but his family and colleagues were hoping Kjašif had been detained or was in hiding. Kjašif had been with the paper for twenty years, and Kemal Kurspahić called the staff together to give them the news. Vladimir Štaka's eyes flooded with tears as Kemal spoke. He had met Kjašif ten years earlier while doing military duty as a young army recruit. As Kemal spoke of his death, Vladimir was remembering how Kjašif had gone out of his way to find some medicine for a Serbian family with whom Vladimir was staying. "Thinking about the killing of Kjašif that day was the first time I faced the reality of this war," Vladimir told me.

In an unsigned front-page column the next day, an *Oslobodjenje* editor wrote:

To [the SDS leaders] who have attacked Sarajevo media for reporting the terrors of war along the Serbia-Bosnia border only through

Muslim correspondents, we have this to report: There is one fewer. With the death of Kjašif Smajlović, *Oslobodjenje* has lost one of its precious people. . . . May this be marked against the honor of all those who would kill innocent people, people whose only fault is their different name, nationality, or religion.

For a Greater Serbia

On April 27, 1992, three weeks after Bosnia-Herzegovina won international recognition as a sovereign state, the governments of Serbia and Montenegro declared they were the sole heirs to the old Yugoslav federation. They claimed all rights to the name Yugoslavia, its United Nations membership, its assets, and its army. The Bosnian presidency demanded that in this case the Yugoslav army should either withdraw from its territory altogether or reconstitute itself as the republican army of Bosnia-Herzegovina. The proclamation of the new Yugoslavia, the presidency argued, constituted a formal break between Belgrade and Sarajevo and made the Yugoslav army a foreign presence on sovereign Bosnian territory. The federal army defied the presidential order. Senior army officers informed Alija Izetbegović that regardless of the change in Bosnia's international status, the army intended to remain in the republic until asked to leave by representatives of all three national communities. Because only the Muslims and Croats wanted them to go, the officers suggested, army units should withdraw just from those municipalities where Muslims and Croats were dominant. Bosnian government officials said the proposal only showed that the army considered itself the special protector of the Serb people.

In Sarajevo conditions were slowly worsening. At first the shelling occurred only at night. By day life went on more or less normally, with a few trolley cars running along the streets and pedestrians crowding downtown sidewalks. A burst of sniper fire at an exposed intersection might send everyone scattering, but then it would stop, and people would emerge from the doorways and continue on their way. So it went until dark, when the buses stopped, the streets emptied, and the shelling began again.

Before long, however, the shells were coming in the afternoons as well, and the sniper fire was getting so heavy that it was dangerous simply to move around. In the first seven days of the war, twenty-nine people died in Sarajevo from gunshots and shrapnel; the following week twice as many were killed.

Gordana and Ivo Knežević were increasingly concerned for the safety of their three children. The *Oslobodjenje* management had arranged bus and air transportation to Zagreb and Belgrade in mid-April for employees who wanted to send family members out of town, but Gordana and Ivo had been reluctant then to break up their family. They had moved back from Cairo just eight months earlier and wanted to remain in Sarajevo. For Gordana, leaving *Oslobodjenje* was unthinkable. As a Bosnian Serb she felt it was her duty to stand openly against Radovan Karadžić and the other Serb party leaders who were attacking Sarajevo and Bosnia in the name of her people.

But her high profile position at *Oslobodjenje* made Gordana vulnerable. As soon as she began writing anti-SDS articles, she started getting harassing phone calls, and with the approach of war they became more frequent and more frightening. The callers, never identifying themselves, would alternate between friendly warnings to stop writing "against Serbs" and open threats of harm if she ignored the advice. The worst were those calls in which someone threatened to

Ivo Knežević often stayed home with his son Boris, while his wife, Gordana, went to work at the newspaper.

(TOM GJELTEN)

kidnap six-year-old Olga. Gordana and Ivo stopped letting their daughter go anywhere without an escort. "She was my weak link," Gordana said. "If Olga had been taken, I would have done anything they wanted."

The calls stopped only when a fire temporarily knocked out the telephone system in Sarajevo, but by then the shelling was getting bad, and Gordana and Ivo feared the Serb forces might target their apartment building deliberately. They lived on the north side of the city, in a new residential neighborhood overlooking Sarajevo's Olympic Stadium, less than a mile from Serb-controlled territory. The area was shelled heavily in the first weeks of the war, and on the days when neither she nor Ivo could stay home, Gordana worried constantly. The *Oslobodjenje* offices in Nedjarići were on the far western side of Sarajevo, about six miles away, but every time Gordana heard on her office radio that her neighborhood had been shelled, she would ask someone at the newspaper to drive her home to check on her children. "It was unbearable," she told me. "I felt I had to do both things, care for my family and do my job. I thought both responsibilities were terribly important. Once you are a journalist, you cannot give it up just because there's a war going on. But you can't stop being a mother, either."

Apart from the security concerns, Gordana and Ivo had to worry about feeding their family. With all commercial traffic into Sarajevo blocked, the stores were soon emptied. Ivo, who did the family cooking, had to rummage each day to find something to prepare. With the situation deteriorating, Gordana and Ivo concluded they had no choice but to send Olga out of the city, with fifteen-year-old Igor accompanying her. For lack of a better idea, they decided to send them back to Cairo, where they still had friends who could care for them. Boris would stay behind. On Saturday, May 2, Gordana and Ivo walked Olga and Igor to the Sarajevo bus station and bought them tickets for an 11:00 A.M. bus to Belgrade. A foreign journalist agreed to accompany them and vouch for their identity at the Serb checkpoints. Gordana had made arrangements for another journalist friend in Belgrade to send them along to Cairo. They all sat for a few minutes in the station coffee shop before boarding began. Igor and Olga were told they would probably be gone for no more than a month or two, but their parents knew it could well be longer. Ivo, who was especially close to Olga, could not hold back the tears when he said good-bye to her.

Theirs was the last public bus to leave Sarajevo. Within minutes after its departure a fierce battle broke out in the center of the city, and Sarajevo was sealed off. For the next two years it would not be possible to enter or leave the city safely, except with the United Nations.

The Yugoslav army, having refused the government's order to leave Bosnian territory, came into the war directly on May 2, openly joining the Serb nationalists in their fight against the Bosnian government. The battle began after Bosnian police and volunteers surrounded the Officers' Club on the edge of the Muslim quarter and ordered the federal army troops inside to surrender their weapons. When the soldiers refused, the Bosnian fighters began firing grenades at the building. The Bosnian government later said the federal army soldiers inside the club had been shooting at civilians passing outside.

Federal army commanders immediately ordered an all-out artillery and bombing assault on the city in an effort to relieve the siege of troops who were stuck inside the club and at an army barracks nearby. Large-caliber field artillery guns positioned on the hilltops around the city—to defend Sarajevo, army commanders had said—started firing and did not let up for the rest of the day. Every five or ten seconds, deafening blasts thundered through the city, throwing up black clouds of smoke and debris, setting buildings ablaze, and showering the downtown streets and sidewalks with shards of glass, broken bricks, and shrapnel. The central post office, a splendid building from the city's Austro-Hungarian era, went up in flames. Igor and Olga Knežević heard the news of the Sarajevo shelling on the bus radio as they rode toward Belgrade. Gordana and Ivo, sitting by the radio in their kitchen, heard nothing about the bus being turned back and concluded that it was safely on its way.

Around midday federal army commanders ordered tanks from barracks in the suburbs to move on Sarajevo, evidently with the idea of cutting the city in half. One column prepared to enter the city from the west; other tanks, backed by Serb paramilitary forces, attempted to cross a bridge from the Serb-held south bank of the Miljacka River to government-held territory on the other side, a scant 200 yards from the headquarters of the Bosnian presidency. Neither effort succeeded. The tanks on the Miljacka bridge were halted by Green Beret volunteer fighters dressed in sneakers and blue jeans and equipped with rifles, gasoline bombs, and a single homemade cannon built from a drain pipe by one of their commanders, a sixty-year-old demolition expert who called himself Dedo. The federal army troops found themselves at a disadvantage in the close fighting. Four tanks attempting to enter the city were trapped and destroyed, and the others turned back. *Oslobodjenje* headlined its coverage the next day "Brutal Attack on Sarajevo." May 2, 1992, the Sunday paper reported, was "the most difficult day in the history of Sarajevo."

With no government army yet organized in Bosnia, the defense of Sarajevo and other cities was in the hands of local police forces, reorganized Territorial Defense units, and volunteer militia groups. Ex–Yugoslav army soldiers and officers who went over to the Bosnian side organized themselves as the Patriotic League. Another Sarajevo militia group named Bosnia 84 operated under the command of Jusuf "Juka" Prazina, a Sarajevo underworld figure whose "detective agency" specialized in strong-arm debt collecting. When the SDS paramilitaries were organized, the news of what they were secretly planning spread initially through the Sarajevo criminal world. Prazina and other businessmen with criminal connections were among the first fighters to volunteer their services in the defense of the city and were among the few who had their own weapons and were ready to use them.

Once it became clear that the federal army was siding with the Serb forces in Bosnia, hard-liners in the Bosnian government who had long favored a more confrontational stance began gaining the upper hand. The May 2 encirclement of the federal army barracks and Officers' Club was ordered while Alija Izetbegović was out of the country, participating in EC-sponsored negotiations in Lisbon. When he arrived at the Sarajevo airport that evening, the federal army promptly took Izetbegović hostage in a barracks nearby, declaring they would hold him until Sarajevo militia groups halted their attacks on the federal army installations in the city. He was exchanged the next day for General Kukanjac and about a hundred of his staff, who were to be escorted from their installations in Sarajevo to Serb-held territory outside the city under the direction of U.N. forces commanded by Brig. Gen. Lewis MacKenzie of Canada.

The evacuation was temporarily interrupted, however, when several Bosnian militiamen fired on the federal army convoy and demanded that officers turn over weapons and maps they were taking with them. At least six Yugoslav army soldiers or officers were killed in the attack. Izetbegović himself was furious that a safe-conduct agreement he had personally guaranteed had been violated by his own men, allegedly at the order of the hard-line Bosnian vice president, Ejup Ganić. Seeing Ganić later at the presidency building, Izet-

begović snapped, "Were you ready to sacrifice my life for forty rifles?"

One day later the Yugoslav presidency in Belgrade announced
that the federal army would withdraw fully from Bosnia by May 19.
But a condition was added to the order that gave it precisely the opposite meaning: Any soldiers or officers who were from Bosnia were
free to remain behind, along with their equipment. Because about 80
percent of the 60,000 to 80,000 Yugoslav army troops in Bosnia were
classified as natives of the republic, and because almost all of them
were Serbs, the effect of the May 4 order was that the bulk of the
army troops in Bosnia would from one day to the next become soldiers of the "Serb Republic." Any doubt that this transformation was
precisely what Belgrade intended vanished on May 8, when Gen.
Milutin Kukanjac was replaced as federal army commander in
Bosnia by Gen. Ratko Mladić, a Bosnia-born Serb nationalist who had
declared his intent to lead the Serb rebel drive in his native republic.
Yugoslav army officers were quoted in the Belgrade media as saying
Slobodan Milošević himself had insisted on the Mladić appointment.

Just four days after he was designated federal army chief in
Bosnia, Mladić announced he was leaving Yugoslav duty to take
charge of the Serb army. It was only a change of hats. Mladić would
stay in the same barracks, commanding the same soldiers (with new
Serb insignia sewn on their old Yugoslav army uniforms) and retaining most of the army arsenal in Bosnia: 14 fighter jets, 43 other fixed-
wing aircraft, 21 helicopters, about 300 tanks, and at least 600 pieces of
heavy field artillery. The Bosnian Serbs also inherited from the Yugoslav army hundreds of mortars and antiaircraft guns, thousands of
assault rifles and machine guns, millions of rounds of ammunition
and artillery shells, fleets of trucks and armored vehicles, and large
reserves of gasoline, diesel oil, and other fuels. The Bosnian government forces, in contrast, had at that point one airplane, which couldn't
be flown for lack of a protected airport, four helicopters, and a handful
of large-caliber artillery weapons. The defenders of Sarajevo had a
single tank, and they were surrounded on all sides. By mid-May the
Bosnian Serb army had taken control of about 65 percent of Bosnian
territory. The front lines would not change significantly over the next
two years.

On May 26, 1992, four Bosnian Serbs loyal to Radovan Karadžić
broke into *Oslobodjenje*'s office in Belgrade when no one was there. A
cleaning woman called the bureau chief, Branislav Boškov, at home

to tell him what had happened. By the time he reached the office, two of the men were changing the locks on the office door. They told Boškov the office had been "liberated" and asked him to leave. When he refused, one of the men pulled a gun and threatened to kill him. The "liberators" took possession of the office, the computers and other equipment located there, a Volkswagen Golf registered to *Oslobodjenje*, and another car belonging to Radio Sarajevo, with whom *Oslobodjenje* shared the space. Boškov called the Belgrade police, but they did nothing. He went to court in Belgrade to get the property returned, but the case went nowhere. City authorities told the Bosnian Serbs they could keep the *Oslobodjenje* office and all that they found there.

4

Humiliation

During the Sarajevo shelling of May 2, 1992, Senka Kurtović and several of her suburban Dobrinja neighbors squeezed into an apartment on the ground floor of their building, where the danger of being blasted was a little less. They huddled together on the edge of a bed, singing Bosnian folk songs at the tops of their lungs to ward off panic and drown out the sound of mortar and tank rounds exploding outside the walls. Listening to Radio Sarajevo at full volume that evening, they heard of the assault on the city by Yugoslav army artillery units and of the army's detention of President Izetbegović at its Lukavica base, which was just a few hundred yards east of where they were sitting.

Six years earlier Senka's father had purchased a tiny efficiency apartment for her in Dobrinja, a small but densely settled Sarajevo suburb built as an Olympic village for the 1984 Winter Games. Although it was removed from the city center, Dobrinja was located ideally for Senka's work at *Oslobodjenje*. The newspaper's high-rise office towers in Nedjarići were only a fifteen-minute walk away or a five-minute bus ride from the airport, which flanked Dobrinja to the west. But in May 1992, Senka and her Dobrinja neighbors found themselves on the front line of the Sarajevo war, and it was terrifying.

The battle zones around the city had been established in the first weeks of fighting and coincided roughly with ethnic lines of settlement. Most of the rural and semisuburban areas outside Sarajevo had a high proportion of Serb residents, and the Serb nationalist forces quickly gained control of roads into and out of the capital. The Serb nationalist party was also well organized in one downtown neighborhood with a large Serb population, Grbavica, as well as in the suburbs at the far western edge of the city, near Dobrinja. With 50,000 residents of mixed ethnic composition, Dobrinja itself was fiercely contested. The population was generally young and well educated, with little sympathy for nationalist thinking, and the suburb was well defended by volunteer militiamen (about 20 percent of whom were themselves Serbs) and ex-soldiers who had left the Yugoslav army. The Serb nationalist forces were desperate to gain control of Dobrinja because of its strategic location. Serb military leaders at that point were still hoping to occupy Sarajevo and force a partition of the city along ethnic lines.

After about a month of surprisingly strong resistance in all front-line neighborhoods, the Serb forces abandoned efforts to fight their way directly into Sarajevo. There would be no more incursions by tanks and infantry soldiers, such as was attempted on May 2. But the bombardment continued. The Serb leaders were not giving up on taking Sarajevo, only revising their strategy. The new plan was to undermine the residents' morale through shelling, sniper fire, and siege until their leaders would agree to a division of the city into separate Serb and Muslim areas. That goal would also be served by an orchestrated campaign to sow ethnic conflict in the city, in order to hasten its eventual division. Sarajevo would be made to suffer.

Life Under Fire

Senka usually walked to the *Oslobodjenje* offices through Nedjarići, an older neighborhood of small wood-frame houses and backyards choked with vegetable gardens, broken-down cars, chicken coops, and crowing roosters. Although residents of all national backgrounds lived there, a large number were Serbs—among them the family of Ljubo Grković, the *Oslobodjenje* reporter who went to work for the Serb party leader, Radovan Karadžić. When the war started in the spring of 1992, armed Serb militants under the command of Ljubo's brother Radvoje claimed Nedjarići for themselves. Although the front lines extended deep into government-controlled areas of Sarajevo, Nedjarići was connected on its west side to the Serb-held suburb of Ilidža, and it remained under Serb control throughout the Sarajevo war.

Senka continued to go to work through Nedjarići for much of the month of April, even after city buses had stopped running. "I think everyone in Sarajevo knew what Nedjarići represented except for me," she said later. "That was about the craziest thing I ever did." When she encountered a new barricade one day between Nedjarići and Dobrinja, Senka told the Serb gunmen positioned there that she worked at a nearby chocolate factory, knowing that the Serb nationalists disliked her newspaper.

On April 28 Senka finally decided that it was no longer safe to go out. Dobrinja by then was almost entirely cut off from the rest of Sarajevo. Yugoslav army troops occupied the airport to the west and were dug in all around their Lukavica base and on surrounding hilltops, evidently in support of the Serb nationalists. Army commanders were still claiming that their troops were neutral, but armed Serb civilians could be seen moving freely among the uniformed soldiers at all the army positions.

Radovan Karadžić and other Serb party leaders at the time were proposing a north-south division of Sarajevo, with all territory to the west designated Serb Sarajevo. The Serb side would include most of the New Sarajevo and New Town municipal districts, the radio and television broadcasting facilities, the *Oslobodjenje* offices, and the airport. Muslim Sarajevo would be limited largely to the Old Town and its environs. The pattern of Serb attacks on Sarajevo in the early weeks of the war was consistent with this territorial proposal. Twice Serb forces tried to fight their way into the city from the north and the south sides, aiming to link up at the Yugoslav army's Marshal Tito barracks in the center of Sarajevo. Had they reached the barracks and joined the Yugoslav army troops still based there, the Serb forces would have cut Sarajevo roughly into the eastern and western halves the Serb leaders had demanded.

Dobrinja was on the Serb side. Once they had it surrounded, Serb military leaders gave the people of the suburb an ultimatum: Surrender or be shelled. On May 2, when Serb and army forces launched their joint artillery attack on Sarajevo, Dobrinja took the heaviest hits.

The Yugoslav army tanks that had been parked on the airport runway for weeks with barrels pointed at Dobrinja finally began firing, as did tanks at the Lukavica base and more army tanks that were sitting on top of a grassy hill just to the north. Dobrinja shook under the barrage. The suburb was barely a half mile square, with high- and low-rise apartment houses clustered tightly together and no clumps of trees to shield the buildings from the pummeling gun and tank fire.

When she was not cowering with her neighbors, Senka wrote stories for *Oslobodjenje* about what was happening in her neighborhood and dictated them over the phone. She reported that food stocks were running low and that many of the shops were looted. From local civil defense officials, she got a count of people killed and injured by shelling and gunfire and phoned *Oslobodjenje* daily with the latest casualty toll. "We look more like animals each day, wild or domestic, depending on the day," Senka wrote in a May 5 dispatch. "We live as in cages, pacing from wall to wall, captured and helpless."

One day an incoming shell hit a building where Senka's uncle lived, and he and his daughter were seriously injured. Dobrinja had no hospital of its own, and the sick and wounded could not be evacuated because of the Serb checkpoints. Senka phoned the Serb party offices in Ilidža and asked for her former boyfriend, Dragan Alorić, thinking he could use his party connections to get a roadblock lifted. She located him at the Serb-controlled radio station in Pale, but he wouldn't intervene. "There's nothing I can do," he told her. "Call me when you have a real problem, like if you or someone in your family is arrested or taken away." Senka's uncle and his daughter had to be attended at a makeshift hospital set up in the basement of an apartment building by doctors who happened to reside in Dobrinja and were stuck there like everyone else. Dobrinja in the coming months was to become a model of communal effort and resourcefulness. Despite great odds, it never fell to the Serb army.

On the morning of May 9, Senka managed to escape from Dobrinja, making her way to the slightly safer neighborhood of Mojmilo, where her parents lived. It was a Serbian Orthodox holiday, and Senka and her neighbors could hear the Serb fighters on the hill behind their building singing Chetnik songs. "We should try it today," a neighbor said. "They might be in a good mood." He and another man volunteered to go up the hill to the Serb positions and try to talk to them. "If we get through, we'll wave for two more to come," he said. The men made it, and Senka and a friend went next.

Spotting the Serb militiamen at the hilltop, Senka called out in the friendliest voice she could manage: "Hello! We'd like to go to Mojmilo!" The Serb fighters waved the women up and took them to their unit commander, who warned them it was a free-fire zone but approved them to pass. With a bag of clothes slung over her shoulder, Senka dashed with her friend across another stretch of no-man's-land toward Mojmilo. The next day she reported for work at *Oslobodjenje*, running from one building to another until she reached the office towers. A café-hopping single woman barely a month earlier, Senka was on her way to becoming one of the newspaper's wartime stalwarts, a tireless worker who proved her courage over and over.

Sitting on the north side of Nedjarići, the *Oslobodjenje* building was even closer to the front line than Senka's apartment building had been. Serb gunmen occupied a school for blind children about a hundred yards to the south of the office towers, and the area between the two buildings was an open stretch of grass and gravel. From the day in early April when the office of editor Kemal Kurspahić was first hit, the Serb gunmen had been firing at the *Oslobodjenje* building regularly. Anyone entering or leaving the offices was at risk. By the first of May, most of the *Oslobodjenje* employees who lived in the city center had stopped coming to the Nedjarići building. The trolley buses that ran up and down Proleterske Brigade, the main east-west boulevard, were no longer operating, and even riding in cars was dangerous. The boulevard ran past the Tito barracks, and gunfire was so heavy along the way that the street was dubbed Sniper Alley by foreign journalists and U.N. soldiers.

Much of the *Oslobodjenje* news operation was transferred to a downtown office set up by Gordana Knežević in a building belonging to the Yugoslav railway company (the ZTO), across the street from the Bosnian presidency headquarters. Reporters would gather there each day, collect news, and write their stories. Someone would then get the unenviable job of driving the copy down Sniper Alley to the Nedjarići building, where the newspaper was put together and printed. Those writers, editors, proofreaders, and production staff whose responsibilities required them to be at the Nedjarići facility located some cots and blankets and began sleeping there overnight so as to avoid the danger that came with entering and leaving. Oddly, though, the building was not shelled. The speculation around *Oslobodjenje* in the first weeks of the war was that the Serb forces hoped to make the newspaper building the headquarters for their new

"Serb Republic" government and therefore deliberately spared it serious damage.

The shelling intensified on May 11, when an army artillery barrage left twenty-eight dead. The report that Gen. Ratko Mladić had taken command of a "Bosnian Serb army" prompted rumors that an all-out Serb attack on the city was imminent, and on May 12 European Community governments withdrew their eleven-member monitoring mission. They had been based in Ilidža, just west of Sarajevo, and feared being caught in the fighting. United Nations officials announced they were ordering the withdrawal of most of their peacekeeping troops as well, out of fears for their safety. The U.N. contingent, commanded by Brig. Gen. Lewis MacKenzie, had been posted in Sarajevo without a clear mandate; their mission was actually tied to the conflict in Croatia. In Sarajevo, MacKenzie had lately been occupied with the negotiation of an agreement between the Bosnian government and the Yugoslav army that would enable the army officers to leave the city safely. When army officers unilaterally backed out of the agreement, U.N. observers and Western diplomats suspected that it meant the troops had been ordered to stay at the Tito barracks in order to assist the Bosnian Serb forces in a second attempt to seize control of Sarajevo.

Early on the morning of May 13, fierce fighting broke out around Ilidža, and it grew more intense as the day went on. By nightfall the staff at the *Oslobodjenje* building in nearby Nedjarići were so nervous they could barely work. If the Serb militiamen positioned behind the building decided to launch an assault on it, there would be no one to stop them but a few security guards. The newspaper staff initially figured that the Serbs would not consider the *Oslobodjenje* building a military target. But that changed the next morning, when a dozen fighters armed with sniper rifles arrived at the front door and took up shooting positions on the eighth and ninth floors, overlooking the Serb positions in Nedjarići.

News desk editor Zlatko Dizdarević, who directed editorial operations in the building, noticed the soldiers coming in and asked the security guards if they had permission to be there. "They're Bosnian army," a guard said. Almost immediately a gun battle erupted between the Bosnian fighters on the eighth floor and the Serb militiamen in the school for the blind, while the newspaper staff hid in the basement. The Serb forces shot grenades at the building for the first time that day, and offices on the eighth floor were heavily damaged.

Around 10:00 A.M. the Bosnian soldiers left *Oslobodjenje*, but the

Serb forces continued shooting at the building all day. The departure of the Bosnian soldiers threw the *Oslobodjenje* security guards into a panic, and they announced they were abandoning the building as well. "We don't have a chance of surviving," one of them told Dizdarević. The *Oslobodjenje* workers did not finish producing that day's edition until 4:00 P.M., ten hours past their normal time. It was too late to bring the newspapers to the city, but a Sarajevo television announcer read the front-page stories on his evening news program. It would be one of only two days during the war when the newspaper was not distributed in Sarajevo.

For the next three days *Oslobodjenje* had no armed security staff at all. The newspaper workers decided that, in case of an assault from the Serb positions behind the building, everyone would escape through a hidden entrance on the front side. Among them they had eight pistols, each with eight bullets. Fahro Memić, the second editor on the news desk, stuck one of the guns in his belt and warned *Oslobodjenje* workers, only half jokingly, that he would shoot anyone who abandoned his workstation prematurely. With his thick black beard and stern visage, Memić could be menacing when he wanted to, and he was determined that the paper would continue to publish. He organized some minimal protection for the building against a Serb infantry attack, sneaking out to the parking lot and driving the paper's big delivery trucks one by one into positions blocking the building entrances.

Memić and his co-workers then gathered big bundles of old paper, stuffed them under the trucks and around the entrance doors, and soaked them with water to increase their density. Finally, they laid dozens of bottles on the floor behind the entrance doors, so that anyone coming in would stumble on them, make noise, and alert the staff to run for their lives. Dizdarević was meanwhile trying to persuade Bosnian authorities to send policemen to replace the security guards who had fled, but the government did not respond. In the end, one of the *Oslobodjenje* workers was able to convince four men from his neighborhood to come with their own rifles and stand guard at the paper.

But no assault on *Oslobodjenje* ever came. Once again the Serb attack on Sarajevo was an effort to break through to the Tito barracks, where the soldiers had abandoned any pretense of neutrality. Reporters visiting the barracks found the soldiers had taken the Yugoslav badges off their uniforms. "We are the Serb army of Bosnia," one said. In view of such statements, the pro-government forces saw the

Editor Fahro Memić supervised the copy desk and fought fires at the *Oslobodjenje* shelter in Nedjariči.   (© 1993 TEUN VOETEN/IMPACT VISUALS)

Tito barracks as an enemy outpost in the middle of their city and kept it surrounded. The Serb forces did not try again to reach it. But neither were the Bosnian fighters able to storm the barracks. Sarajevo was surrounded in turn by the Serb army, which threatened to level the city if the Tito barracks blockade was not lifted. On June 5 the federal army troops finally vacated the barracks under an agreement with the Bosnian government.

In the two years that followed, the Serb nationalists' hold on Sarajevo was unyielding. The forces encircling the city routinely blocked food, fuel, and medical supplies from entering, but the Sarajevo defenders were helpless. Every effort to break the siege of the city prompted a devastating artillery barrage from the Serb guns on the surrounding hilltops. Serb snipers positioned themselves in apartment building windows over downtown Sarajevo and picked off pedestrians, for no apparent reason other than to sow terror. The entire population was held hostage.

On May 27 two mortar rounds were fired into a crowd of about

150 people waiting for bread on Vasa Miskin Street, a pedestrian walkway in the city center. Twenty-two people were killed, and dozens were injured. A Sarajevo television crew arrived on the scene moments after the attack and filmed the carnage. A woman held her severed leg in her arms; a man sat in a puddle of his own blood, one hand reaching up to the camera in a plea for help.

The man's name was Hilmo Korjenić. He had just bought some ice cream for his ten-year-old daughter, Enisa, and was waiting for bread when the mortars landed. "I was the last in line," he told *Oslobodjenje* reporter Vlado Mrkić, who tracked him down weeks later in the hospital.

> As soon as I stepped up, it flashed. Nothing else. I looked around, but saw no one. Where are the people? Then I saw them—all flattened, wailing, screaming, howling. . . . I didn't immediately see that both my legs were gone. They were straight in front of me, and it looked to me as if they were complete. My shoes were still on, everything. . . . When I saw those people, I said to myself, "I'm going to die too." So I lay down and closed my eyes.
>
> And then my little daughter Enisa appeared. I leaned up to see what she was doing there, but when I opened my eyes, she was nowhere. That's what saved me. I called for help then. And all the way to the hospital, I was telling myself, "I don't want to die, I don't want to die." Enisa kept me alive. If she had not appeared, I would have bled to death, because all those people who did not call for help just lay down and bled and died.

The Vasa Miskin massacre stunned even the hardiest Sarajevans. "There are no words big enough either to console or to condemn," Mrkić said in an *Oslobodjenje* commentary. "Life will go on, because it has to. Time will wipe away the memories, because it is stronger than anything. But the shadow of the crime we have witnessed will remain for all days to come." Such graceful prose was a bit of a comfort to the people of Sarajevo in those awful times. If *Oslobodjenje* did nothing else, it dignified the city by taking note of its suffering.

The newspaper provided as well an example of how to carry on under horrible circumstances, day after day. The downtown *Oslobodjenje* work space in the ZTO Building consisted of one room, with six desks pushed together and a single telephone that worked only intermittently. Gordana Knežević was in charge, having replaced Miroslav Janković as deputy editor in early May, when Janković went to

Belgrade. She was assisted by Rasim Ćerimagić, who took her place as politics editor. Two dozen reporters and editors worked in the room, along with an *Oslobodjenje* secretary, and the place was always packed with people and thick with cigarette smoke. There were only seven or eight chairs and a handful of old manual typewriters. Tempers flared often and easily.

Reporter Vladimir Štaka, who had refused his friend Duško's offer of a gun in March, reported to work at the ZTO Building at the end of May. Two months earlier he and his wife, Dubravka, had moved into her parents' apartment behind the Holiday Inn, overlooking the Tito barracks and the hottest war zone in the city. Vladimir stayed home for a few weeks but then realized the war was likely to last awhile and decided to go back to work. He was motivated in part by a fear of being drafted into the newly formed Bosnian army. "When I saw we were entering war," Vladimir told me, "I knew people would be divided into two groups: those who could kill, and those who couldn't. I was one of those who couldn't."

Reaching the *Oslobodjenje* workroom downtown was a daily challenge. Vladimir clung to the sides of buildings, dashed across intersections, hid behind trees, and skipped all the main streets. At least a dozen times he saw people shot in front of his eyes. On one occasion Vladimir was running across a street when a man six feet away had his arm blown off by heavy machine-gun fire. "He didn't scream or anything," Vladimir recalled, "but his arm was completely gone. Blood was squirting from the socket." Vladimir kept running until he reached safety, then turned and yelled for help. Sarajevo radio regularly broadcast warnings to people not to stop in an exposed area to help a sniper victim, because of the great danger of being shot themselves. After reaching the ZTO Building, Vladimir was often stuck there. Serb gunners routinely shelled the presidency headquarters across the street so heavily that no one could leave the *Oslobodjenje* workroom for hours at a time.

Nedjarići

The challenge of keeping the paper publishing was most evident at the headquarters building in Nedjarići, where most of the editing and all of the production work was done. Editor Kemal Kurspahić organized the Nedjarići staff into three teams working in seven-day shifts, with the teams rotating in and out each Monday. In addition to editing the copy brought out from the downtown office, the journalists at the Nedjarići building took in news from *Oslobodjenje* correspondents outside Sarajevo; the reports were filed to the paper's office in Zagreb, Croatia, then dictated to Sarajevo over ham radio. The Nedjarići staff monitored the radio and television news programs and rewrote the main stories for the next day's paper. Later they would get a wire-service connection through Agence France-Presse, which provided them with international news. For their own safety they worked and slept in the building's bomb shelter, a vaultlike room two floors below ground level with thick steel doors. Until then no one at the paper had figured out a use for the shelter, which had been installed when the building was constructed in the early 1980s, in accordance with Yugoslav law. It turned out to be a godsend.

From the beginning of June 1992, the office towers came under daily shelling. Unable to get the building for themselves, the Serb forces had apparently decided to level it. One day the journalists noticed that a tank with the name Arkan (the Serb warlord who attacked Bijeljina and Zvornik in the first days of the war) painted on its side had pulled up behind the newspaper offices, about a hundred yards away. It fired several shells at *Oslobodjenje,* causing the building to shiver with each impact. In the following days the Serb forces started shooting incendiary grenades at the building, and at 5:00 P.M. on Saturday, June 20, the twin blue *Oslobodjenje* towers went up in flames.

"A strong explosion threw us out of our chairs," wrote an *Oslobodjenje* journalist in an account of the fire the next day. "It was followed by the sound of a large surface of glass crashing, and soon the street outside was bathed in the orange light of flame." The incendiary grenades had started a fire on the third floor of one tower and the fourth floor of the other. As smoke filled the building, writers and editors joined the security guards, maintenance workers, and printing staff using preinstalled fire hoses to fight the blaze. The fire spread upward, but water services had been knocked out that day in much of western Sarajevo, and the *Oslobodjenje* workers found they had no water pressure above the third floor.

Firefighters from three Sarajevo stations arrived on the scene and attached their hoses end to end in order to reach the upper floors of the building, but they had little success. The Serb forces continued to bombard the towers and the surrounding area to hinder the firefighting effort. The constant shelling and heavy machine-gun fire made it impossible for the firemen to fight the blaze from outside the building, and Serb snipers were shooting at anyone they could see through the windows. One firefighter was killed by sniper fire that night, and two others were wounded by shrapnel.

The *Oslobodjenje* workers fought the blaze alongside the firefighters. Fahro Memić, the editor who had organized the defense of the building against a ground attack a month earlier, was not assigned to work that week but heard the news of the fire over the radio. He jumped in his car and drove to Nedjarići to join in the firefighting effort. Hearing a firefighter ask two *Oslobodjenje* journalists to help with a task, Memić shouted, "Don't take those guys, they need to make the newspaper!" Turning to the journalists, he said, "You two go to the shelter and work! I'll go instead of you!" The firefighting continued all Saturday night, but in the underground shelter a small team was preparing the next morning's paper.

By early Sunday morning, twelve hours after it began, the fire had mostly burned itself out, and printing workers had put down their fire hoses and returned to the pressroom. At 6:00 A.M. the shift editor, Feto Ramović, called Kemal Kurspahić at home and told him the fire had been extinguished. Five minutes later he called back and said, "The presses are running." The two blue towers had been reduced overnight to hollow, charred frames, but *Oslobodjenje* had still been published. Memić, soaked to the skin and covered with ashes, loaded his car with newspapers and drove them to the distribution points in the city center, as was his daily duty.

The following day's edition was filled with shots of the burning building, a story about the firefighting, and a column by Kurspahić. "The ugly creatures obsessed with [ethnic] division shell *Oslobodjenje* every day and night," he wrote, "not understanding that the truth only spreads in fire. Two nights ago, they burned themselves up. . . . This newspaper of yours, dear reader, is reborn. The more difficult it is, the more passionate we are."

The Serb forces who destroyed the *Oslobodjenje* building gave me their side of the story when I visited the Serb-held part of Nedjarići in October 1993. Radvoje Grković, whose brother Ljubo had worked at the paper, was in charge of the assault. Ljubo did not participate, he told me, "for sentimental reasons." A local Serb commander named Jovo Šeovać said that he and his men were fighting for their own survival and that the *Oslobodjenje* building had been a threat to them.

"It's a miracle we're still here," he said. "We are like players on a soccer field, with the Muslims in the bleachers looking down on us from all sides." The Bosnian army controlled high-rise buildings to the north, east, and south of Nedjarići, and Šeovać and other Serb commanders claimed they had lost "hundreds" of their fighters to Bosnian snipers hiding in upper floors of the buildings. The *Oslobodjenje* towers, they said, had been especially troublesome. "That metallic facade and blue glass made it impossible for us to see the snipers through the windows," Šeovać said, "so they could shoot at us as they pleased. That's why we had to destroy the towers."

Šeovać took me to a house from which some of the fire against the *Oslobodjenje* building had been directed. The house had been under construction when the war began, so the outer brick walls were complete but the rooms inside had not yet been partitioned, leaving space for big guns. A grenade-launching weapon was set up on the ground floor, and on the second floor a 12.7-mm heavy machine gun was mounted on a tripod. Spent shell casings lay in a heap on the floor beside the gun, the barrel of which pointed through a tiny hole in the bricks toward the *Oslobodjenje* offices, about a hundred yards away. "Sometimes we can see them moving around in there," Šeovać said.

I shuddered as I remembered the times I had been in the *Oslobodjenje* building, peering out cautiously at this house and other structures, wondering where exactly the shooting came from. Viewed from the Serb side, what remained of the newspaper building was a broken, blasted mess. Looking across at the *Oslobodjenje* ruin that October day, I had the same thought I recalled having had on the Sarajevo side: how short the distance was between the two lines and yet how far away the other's world seemed. The sense of separation I felt was all the greater because I had traveled to Nedjarići that day from Belgrade and would return there without entering "Muslim" Sarajevo. I stood at the outer edge of Greater Serbia, looking across a stretch of no-man's-land to what the Serb nationalists considered enemy territory. The words "Fuck Off Moslems" were painted in English on the sides of a nearby house.

Back at the former army barracks, the local Serb commanders were eating a Sunday lunch. A group of women had prepared roast lamb and *pita*, a rolled pastry with cheese filling. Several loaves of fresh baked bread were in a basket, and the officers were passing a bottle of plum brandy around the table. Serb-controlled Sarajevo was not under siege, and there was no shortage of food. Barely 200 yards away, the *Oslobodjenje* management could only feed their workers a thin bean soup each day. As we ate the Serb commanders offered their analysis of the war. "Sarajevo," Šeovać said, "has always been a Serb city. It changed only in the last thirty years. Ilidža and Nedjarići were more than 90 percent Serb, for example. Just fifteen years ago, when it was farmland, Dobrinja was 100 percent Serb. And then they started moving Muslims in. They want to control everything. That's why we had to organize ourselves, to defend our homes and families."

U.N. Intervention

If the Serb nationalists seriously intended to starve Sarajevo into submission, they were frustrated in that endeavor by the United Nations. The international community decided it could not allow the city to be totally cut off from the rest of the world and negotiated an agreement with the Serb forces under which the Sarajevo airport would be turned over to U.N. control and a humanitarian airlift established. Over the next two years, more than 10,000 planeloads of food, medicine, and other humanitarian aid would be flown into the city, in addition to supplies trucked in overland. Until the airport was reopened, some city residents were actually gathering dandelions and nettles for food. Conditions eased only with the beginning of the U.N. humanitarian aid operation. Sarajevans would be fed.

But they would not be defended. United Nations commanders were not allowed to use military force in carrying out their relief work around Sarajevo and were therefore unable to do anything that went against the wishes of the Serb nationalists. Officials of the United Nations did not increase the number of relief flights without getting Serb consent, nor would they evacuate Sarajevo citizens without prior Serb approval. Sarajevo authorities were outraged by the U.N. attitude, but they were in no position to challenge it, because the U.N. Protection Force (UNPROFOR) troops kept the city alive.

Under the circumstances, people in Sarajevo came to view the UNPROFOR troops with a resentment born of dependence and disappointment. When they arrived in March 1992, the "blue helmets" were seen as a force representing international law and order in Bosnia, and they were received with fanfare. Four months later, after Sarajevans had realized the troops would take no action to protect the city from the besieging Serb forces, U.N. officials driving through Sarajevo were greeted with obscene gestures from people on the street. When U.N. Secretary-General Boutros Boutros-Ghali visited Sarajevo on December 31, 1992, he was surrounded wherever he went by protesters screaming, "Fascist!" and "Get out of Sarajevo!" But those same Sarajevans would stand in line a few days later for their one-kilogram cans of Edible Fat from Norway, their five-kilo bags of flour emblazoned with the twelve gold stars of the European Community, and their brown bars of smelly U.N. soap.

As a Sarajevo institution, *Oslobodjenje* had the same two-edged relationship with the UNPROFOR mission that the rest of the city had. *Oslobodjenje* journalists routinely criticized U.N. commanders for refusing to stand up to the Serb forces around Sarajevo. But when reporter Memnun Idžaković wrote in a commentary that UNPRO-FOR troops were "the same shit" as the Serb army, he very nearly lost his job. Were it not for sympathetic U.N. officials who quietly classified newsprint as humanitarian aid and authorized clandestine deliveries of diesel fuel to the printing plant, *Oslobodjenje* could not have continued publishing.

The man most widely blamed in Sarajevo for the development of bad feelings between the local population and the UNPROFOR troops was the first U.N. commander in Bosnia, Gen. Lewis MacKenzie. MacKenzie, who raced sports cars in his leisure time, was a veteran of more than thirty years' service in the Canadian Armed Forces, but his combat experience had come entirely through participation in seven U.N. peacekeeping missions, from Gaza to El Salvador. That experience instilled in him a belief that U.N. soldiering generally came down to the simple task of keeping two belligerent parties separated.

Five weeks after arriving in Sarajevo, MacKenzie wrote friends and family back in Canada about his new assignment. "Well, it's springtime in the Balkans," the letter began, "and history is repeating itself as the various ethnic groups seek to exterminate each other." This was as far as MacKenzie ever went in analyzing the conflict in which he found himself. His determination to position himself in the middle and cast blame equally in all directions enraged Sarajevans, who considered themselves victims of external aggression.

MacKenzie took Serb army commanders at their word when they said that they were not responsible for the bombing of the breadline on Vasa Miskin Street in May. He accepted their claim that the Bosnian army had laid a ground mine at the site and staged the massacre in order to win international sympathy. No U.N. investigation of the massacre was ever carried out, nor did U.N. officers interview any of the survivors of the blast. The "evidence" that it was a Muslim-laid mine came entirely from Serb military sources, and all of it eventually proved bogus. But MacKenzie told journalists and diplomats in Bosnia, in Europe, in the United States, and in Canada that he believed the breadline bombing to have been a Muslim "ploy." A senior U.N. official in former Yugoslavia told me that MacKenzie's bad relations with the Bosnian government stemmed from the May 2 convoy ambush, when he felt he had been tricked by Bosnian Vice President Ejup Ganić. "He was traumatized by the event, and he never forgave the [Bosnian] presidency for it," the official said.

Oslobodjenje's first formal contact with MacKenzie was on June 19, when he gave an interview to deputy editor Gordana Knežević at the UNPROFOR headquarters in the Post and Telephone (PTT) Building at the west end of Sarajevo. Gordana learned in the afternoon that MacKenzie would see her at 6:00 P.M. The shelling customarily began late in the afternoon, and a trip to the PTT Building down Sniper Alley at that hour would be hazardous. To complicate matters further, the single *Oslobodjenje* car available that afternoon had only enough gas in the tank to reach the UNPROFOR headquarters. Gordana and reporter Elvedin Kantardžić decided to go for the interview anyway, hoping U.N. officers might lend them enough gas for the return trip.

The PTT Building had in the preceding days taken several direct mortar hits, but it was of sturdy concrete construction, and the UN-PROFOR forces had sandbagged its perimeters, taped the windows to keep them from shattering, and made the building as fortresslike as they could. MacKenzie received Gordana and Elvedin in his third-floor corner office, which was decorated with framed pictures of the general standing by his beloved race cars.

Gordana was courteous but not deferential. She had a list of questions about "misunderstandings" between UNPROFOR and the people of Sarajevo. What, she wanted to know, was delaying the reopening of Sarajevo's airport? "Violations of the ceasefire," MacKenzie said. "Even if we succeeded in solving the technical problems and got the airport open and an air corridor established," he explained, "there is no pilot who would fly to Sarajevo as long as the fighting is continuing." The answer put much of the responsibility for improving conditions in Sarajevo onto the Bosnian government, because MacKenzie had said in previous public statements that he blamed the Bosnian side for many if not most of the ceasefire violations.

Gordana also wondered about the provision of U.N. transportation to the family of a prominent Serb nationalist, an incident that led some local people to label UNPROFOR "the Chetnik taxi service." She asked MacKenzie to respond to Sarajevans whose "sense of justice" was offended when he declared both sides "equally responsible" for the war in their city. She avoided, however, getting into an argument with the U.N. general, and she concluded the interview by offering MacKenzie an opportunity "to convey something to the citizens of Sarajevo." While some commentators and politicians in Sarajevo were already referring to the U.N. force in Sarajevo as "SERB-PROFOR" for its alleged partiality to the Serb nationalists, *Oslobodjenje* journalists let U.N. officers speak freely and often reminded their readers that Sarajevo depended on UNPROFOR assistance.

So did *Oslobodjenje*. Editor Kemal Kurspahić had instructed Gordana to inform MacKenzie that the newspaper was in danger of running out of newsprint and would need U.N. help in getting a new shipment brought across the Serb lines. After she finished the interview and turned off her tape recorder, she asked MacKenzie whether the UNPROFOR forces could help her newspaper. But he turned her down coldly, suggesting instead that *Oslobodjenje* do its part to support negotiations to end the war with the Serbs. "Once you make peace," MacKenzie said, "you'll have plenty of paper."

"Our newspaper didn't start this war," Gordana replied.

"Oh, all the media here have contributed to it," MacKenzie responded. Gordana was angered by MacKenzie's hostility, but she couldn't show it, because there remained the problem of the *Oslobodjenje* car and its empty fuel tank. On her way out of his office, Gordana explained the predicament to MacKenzie and asked whether he could authorize his soldiers to give her and Elvedin a little gas for the trip back downtown. MacKenzie refused again, saying he needed to keep UNPROFOR fuel exclusively for UNPROFOR use.

"Just two liters," Gordana pleaded. "We only need enough to get to the city. We can't make it otherwise."

"Sorry," MacKenzie said. "If we gave you gas, someone could say we were aiding one side in this conflict."

"But you've got *both* sides here," Gordana said. "I'm Serb, and he's Muslim," pointing to Kantardžić. MacKenzie still would not yield, and the two reporters were forced to head downtown on an empty tank. They had gone just under a mile when they ran out of gas near the headquarters of Radio-Television Sarajevo, one of the most frequently targeted buildings in the city. The shelling that evening was especially heavy, and the journalists were forced to spend the night on cots at the television building.

The MacKenzie interview was published as an *Oslobodjenje* "exclusive" on June 21. Gordana introduced it with a few biting words about U.N. neutrality in the Sarajevo war: "It is not easy to find someone in the UNPROFOR headquarters willing to admit that the building has been hit by any shells," she wrote. "And if the damage could be established, it would probably be said 'it is not known' which side is responsible." She noted that some people in Sarajevo "no longer believed in UNPROFOR," but apart from those comments the interview stood on its own, running in an unedited question-and-answer format along with a picture of MacKenzie in his office. Gordana did not mention the gas.

As the war dragged on, the newspaper's dependence on UN-PROFOR increased. The UNPROFOR troops sometimes seemed like an occupying army in Sarajevo, with absolute control over what could enter the city. Newsprint stocks were limited, and *Oslobodjenje*'s fate lay entirely in U.N. hands. If it ran out of paper, *Oslobodjenje* would have to stop publishing. The French organization Reporters sans frontières (Reporters without Borders) donated newsprint stocks to *Oslobodjenje*, but there remained the problem of how to get the paper past the Serb blockade around Sarajevo. When General MacKenzie said he would not approve a U.N. escort for trucks carrying *Oslobodjenje* newsprint, the editors and managers decided to cut back the daily press run and later the size of the paper, first shrinking it to sixteen pages and then switching from a broadsheet to a tabloid format.

After MacKenzie left Sarajevo, *Oslobodjenje* asked other U.N. officers if they could ship the newsprint stocks overland. MacKenzie's replacement, Gen. Philippe Morillon of France, initially approved the plan, but it was vetoed by Jeremy Brade, the Sarajevo representative of the U.N. High Commissioner for Refugees (UNHCR), which administered the humanitarian aid program for Sarajevo. A U.N. official in Sarajevo who worked with *Oslobodjenje* on the aid request said Brade came by U.N. offices at the PTT Building one day and ordered "this paper thing" stopped. "We don't want to be accused by the Serbs of supporting a propaganda machine here," he said.

Other U.N. officials saw a daily newspaper as serving a social function in wartime Sarajevo, regardless of its political line, and argued that *Oslobodjenje* should be supported in the same manner as other public institutions, such as schools. Friendly UNPROFOR officers said the newsprint could be brought past Serb checkpoints without problem as long as its intended use and final destination were not made public. The U.N. educational organization UNESCO, for example, approved a shipment of paper for "textbook publishing." It was actually meant for *Oslobodjenje,* and the supply kept the newspaper in operation for two months.

Once fighting in central Bosnia brought severe restrictions of overland convoys, however, a problem developed: The new head of UNHCR operations in Sarajevo, Tony Land, argued that priority in shipments should be given to items for which he felt the need was greater. "We need supplies for winterization, like plywood," he said, "and we need sleeping bags and hospital equipment. Newsprint for *Oslobodjenje* fits in there somewhere, but I'm not sure just where." Land formally barred *Oslobodjenje* paper from being included in the Sarajevo airlift, which operated under his authority. "I need 1,642 tons each week of food alone," he told me in early 1993. "Right now, about 1,200 is coming on the airlift. There's no room for newsprint."

Such disputes made *Oslobodjenje* editors and other Sarajevo citizens feel they were living under a colonial administration that arbitrarily decided what they needed and what they did not. On one occasion the newspaper managers conspired with the director of Koševo Hospital and an Italian humanitarian aid organization to sneak newsprint into the city. The Italian organization was ready to help *Oslobodjenje* but was kept from doing so by Land's regulations. The Sarajevo hospital director asked the Italians to send him "packing material" along with a regular shipment of medicine and other hospital supplies. Land was at the Sarajevo airport when the shipment arrived and noticed that some boxes for the hospital seemed especially heavy. He opened them and found the paper inside. The flat sheets were of the same dimension as a tabloid newspaper folded open. "Somebody get me a copy of *Oslobodjenje,*" he said. Sure enough, it fit.

Land didn't return the paper, but he was angry about the illicit shipment and reprimanded Gordana when he ran into her at the airport a few weeks later. Gordana didn't appreciate his scolding and snapped back, "And are you pleased with yourself for having uncovered such a crime? I am pleased we smuggled it," she continued. "Look at the papers in Belgrade. Shouldn't we be able to publish just the same?"

"Yes," Land said. "But you shouldn't smuggle."

Anxiety

The U.N. humanitarian aid operation provided Sarajevo with the minimum it needed to survive, but it was still a closed city. The Serb forces could make Sarajevans desperate without starving them. Senka Kurtović spent twenty consecutive days in the summer of 1992 in the cellar of her parents' apartment building in Mojmilo, living with them, her sister, and her nephew in a tiny storage room, with other residents camped out in cubicles on each side. Crowded together in the darkness, with gunfire and shelling outside, people slipped occasionally into hysteria. One hot July day, when the basement windows were all boarded up against the shelling and the air inside had become stifling, a woman ran into the shelter, screaming, "Here they come! They're coming! They're approaching the house!" With the Serb forces positioned so close, such an outburst could provoke panic among the whole group. That day Senka's mother calmed the woman and comforted the other residents by pouring buckets of precious water on the concrete floor to cool the room.

It was not the first time Andja Kurtović took a leadership role in her building, nor would it be the last. The daughter of a Jewish woman from Slovenia and a Croat Communist Partisan, she had been taught as a girl the importance of being courageous and having strong ideals, and she raised her two daughters the same way. "My mother always used to tell my sister and me she wanted us to be 'good citizens of the world,' " Senka said, "people who don't pay attention to race, nation, or religion, and who can live with all others, as long as they're basically good."

Senka was determined to get away for a break as soon as she could. Sitting on a hill between Dobrinja and Sarajevo proper, Mojmilo was almost as dangerous as Dobrinja had been and almost as isolated. The only open route to the rest of Sarajevo was across a short grassy field, in full view of Serb snipers, but by midsummer Senka had decided she wanted to go with the small group of people who sneaked in and out of Mojmilo each day. The grass was tall, and Senka and the others wriggled across on their stomachs to safe cover. Her father stood by the apartment building entrance, partly hidden, and watched, until he could see that Senka was safely on the other side.

"I was more worried about him standing there watching me than I was about myself," Senka told me, when I asked what went through her mind as she crawled in the grass. "I didn't feel afraid, because at a time like that you have no feelings at all," she said. "You're not outside of yourself. It's like when you're extremely happy; you don't have an awareness of how happy you are, you just experience it. It's the same with fear. You know he [the sniper] has his eye on you, you can feel his eye on you, you imagine him shooting, and you think only, 'My God, help me.' You think only about staying alive and making it through."

She made the trip several times over the summer. Once outside Senka moved in with Sarajevo friends for a few days or hitched a ride with an *Oslobodjenje* driver down Sniper Alley to the newspaper building in Nedjarići, where she would work with the staff, sleeping in the basement shelter for a week or so before heading back to her parents' apartment.

In the Koševsko Brdo (Hill) neighborhood on the north side of the city, thirteen-year-old Boris Knežević wanted to wander, but his mother wouldn't let him. As the shelling and shooting got worse, Gordana ordered Boris to stay close to the house if he went outside at all. The boundary she and Ivo set for him was the barricade that Sarajevo militiamen had erected on a street around the corner from their apartment building. Beyond that the street was open to sniper fire from Serb positions on a hill just to the north. Much of the time Boris hung out in the entryway of his building with neighborhood friends. They played Monopoly and Risk and listened to the radio or strummed a guitar that Boris had found when the Serb family who had been living upstairs left one day without notice.

In June and July shelling sent Boris, his parents, and the other building residents to the basement shelter as often as six times a day. Boris kept two duffel bags packed with the treasures he was determined to save in the event his home was hit. It was an odd assortment: Guns N' Roses cassettes, his writing journal, exams and papers from the private school Boris and his brother had attended in Cairo. As they had been for Gordana, the years in Cairo were a defining experience for Boris. He had loved that school, especially his English composition class and his American teacher. He carried his old Cairo papers down to the bomb shelter as if he were guarding the memory of that happy time against the terror of the present.

The transition from peace to war had been so sudden that it jarred everyone's sense of reality. Gordana was distressed to find she was losing her sense of time and season. "Ten times a day, I'm asking someone what day it is," she told me in June 1992, eleven weeks after the war began. "I can't remember anymore which month we're in; I don't know when the spring finished and the summer started."

I had just arrived in Sarajevo, and, while staying with the Knežević family, I was trying to reconstruct the order of wartime events. But Gordana was of little use. All the dates were blurred together for her, except for one: May 2, the day she and Ivo put their daughter, Olga, and their son Igor on a bus out of town. "That's my point of reference," Gordana said. "Everything happened either before that date or after."

The difficulty of that decision still hung on them. Ivo's thoughts were often on his daughter in Cairo. At age six she had a grown-up's worries. When the foreign journalist who accompanied her to Belgrade called her in Cairo to see how she was doing, the first question Olga asked was "Did you send some food to my mommy and daddy?" Ivo still thought of Olga as his little girl, but on the rare occasions when he and Gordana could speak to her on the phone, Olga sounded so wise and brave that it was hard for them to remember how young she was. She never cried on the telephone, although she told Gordana she did cry when she went to bed. "I just think about Daddy," she said. Igor and Olga seemed unsure of their welcome in the Cairo house where they were living and wondered how long they would be able to stay there.

"I can tell," Gordana told Ivo after one call. "They feel like homeless people."

Ivo took the pain of war more personally. When I asked in June 1992 what the worst aspect of the war was for him, he said simply, "The whole situation is humiliating." Ivo was an accomplished cook, but he had nothing in his cupboards but beans and macaroni. For a while he went to his office at the university, but once classes stopped meeting, there was no longer much point. "If you go to work," he said, "you're thinking all the time about how to get there and come back safely, and what will happen while you're away." So he stayed home, trying to read French philosophy but getting nowhere. I noticed a book by Foucault on the coffee table and asked Ivo about it. "I've been reading the last five pages for ten days now," he said.

Some Who Died

Two weeks after the *Oslobodjenje* fire, Kemal Kurspahić was seriously injured in a traffic accident. He was riding in a car driven by his general manager, Salko Hasanefendić, heading west down Sniper Alley toward the *Oslobodjenje* building. Hasanefendić's red Golf was going ninety miles per hour as it entered an especially dangerous intersection. A police car approaching from the right hit the Golf squarely on the passenger side. Kurspahić's right leg was crushed, and he screamed at Hasanefendić to help him get out of the car. The police-

man in the other car was slumped over his steering wheel, unconscious. In such cases snipers sometimes shot at the victims as they lay
helpless, but on this day several Bosnian soldiers were at a café
nearby, heard the collision, ran to the scene, and pulled everyone
from the cars and out of the line of fire within moments.

Such accidents were common in wartime Sarajevo. With stop-
lights not working and the traffic police engaged on the front lines,
drivers zoomed the wrong way down one-way streets and squealed
around corners at breakneck speed. In their eagerness not to be shot
or caught by a falling shell, Sarajevans were increasing their chances
of being killed or injured in a crash. There were many days in the
summer of 1992 when the casualty toll from car accidents exceeded
that from gunfire or shelling. The number of wrecked cars wrapped
around lamp poles, smashed against trees, or lying upside down on
the roadside indicated a city crazed by war.

Kurspahić was laid up for five months as a result of his injuries.
His right knee was completely destroyed, and the damage to his leg
from the childhood riding accident was aggravated. He was operated
on in Sarajevo and again in Zagreb, after U.N. authorities helped arrange his evacuation. In his absence Gordana Knežević took over
day-to-day editorial direction of *Oslobodjenje* and its staff.

In just ten months she had gone from living a peaceful life in
Cairo with her three children at her side to managing a wartime
paper with two of her children a continent away. Stress and a poor
diet were taking a heavy toll. She was losing weight, appeared increasingly haggard, and smoked constantly.

She accepted the additional authority thrust on her by Kemal's
injury but did not welcome it. She excelled at handling the dozens of
little daily crises that arose at the paper and in the lives of the staff,
but she was not wholly comfortable in a leadership role. The task
Gordana found most difficult was giving daily assignments, knowing they were potentially matters of life or death. Some staff members did what they were told without complaining. Others hesitated.
Columnist Gojko Berić flatly refused to leave his apartment, demanding that the paper send someone to pick up his commentary. The
paper's fifty-five-year-old senior photographer, Salko Hondo, was
also fearful. "Please don't send me to the front lines," he told Gordana. She complied, assigning him to take pictures at official functions or to accompany reporters doing interviews.

One day Gordana learned of a Sarajevo man who had dug a well
in his front yard and was bringing up water for his neighbors. It was

in a relatively safe section of the city, and she asked Hondo if he would stop and take a picture the next time he passed. Hondo told his wife about the assignment the next morning over breakfast. "I just have one little thing to do today, and then I'll come back, and we'll have another coffee," he said. She had the coffee waiting when she got the news that her husband had been killed by a mortar at the water line. Gordana was broken by his death. She phoned Kemal to say she could no longer send anyone anywhere. For two days she stayed home, unable to function.

Gordana made up for any shame she may felt as a Serb in a Serb-besieged city by becoming even more fervent in her support for the Bosnian state and more uncompromising in her opposition to the Serb nationalists. She was reluctant to settle for any outcome short of the total military defeat of the Serb army.

Vlado Mrkić also felt solidarity with Bosnia and Sarajevo, although he was unwilling to write in polemic terms about the conflict. Instead, he risked his life over and over, volunteering for tasks that others considered far too dangerous. Along with Fahro Memić, Mrkić often went to the *Oslobodjenje* building early each day to pick up papers and bring them downtown, where they and other *Oslobodjenje* reporters would sell the newspapers on street corners or leave them to be sold by others. In the afternoon Mrkić often volunteered to drive back to Nedjarići with that day's load of news copy from the downtown office.

After the 1991 Serb-Croat conflict, Mrkić was familiar with war conditions, but nothing he had experienced in Croatia compared with wartime Sarajevo. Dozens of times Mrkić was shot at by Serb snipers. A bullet grazed his forehead once, and another time a bullet passed through the sleeve of his jacket. "Vlado is among the bravest people at *Oslobodjenje*," Kemal Kurspahić said later. "He is one of those who did the most to save the paper."

To his Sarajevo readers, Mrkić was known mostly for his story-telling:

> Just as I stopped in front of the old parade ground, there was a ter-rifying explosion behind me. Ten meters back, I could see a cloud of smoke and dust. . . . A man carrying a young girl in his arms ran up. He was distraught and kept crying, "My child is wounded, my child. . . ." The girl was unconscious. Behind the man was a trail of blood. We sat them down on the front seat. I moved a hundred cop-

ies of *Oslobodjenje* out of the car and saw them blow away down the street.

. . . Everything that happened during the journey [to the hospital] passed as if in a dream. The girl, wounded in the back of the head, was unconscious. I didn't dare look at her. I could see a little arm swinging and hair sticky with blood clinging to a forehead. The man who was holding her never stopped speaking: "Faster, faster, friend! My child is still alive!" A little while afterwards, again: "She's warm, she's still warm, friend!" Then, "My God, she's getting cold, my child is getting cold!"

. . . In the [hospital] corridor, the man who had carried the girl took off his shirt, which was soaked with blood. Together we went into the toilets to wash our hands. He told me the girl was called Sanela. "Her father will lose his mind when he hears," he said.

"She's not your daughter?" I asked.

"No. But she was my favorite child on the block. Aren't all these children ours?"

. . . We went back to the old parade ground. There was blood everywhere: under our feet, on the doors of the car. At the place where we had helped the wounded, there were still large pools of blood on the ground. I gathered up the newspapers and took them downtown to a vendor. The next day, he said, "I didn't sell any of them. No one wanted to buy newspapers stained with blood."

Among the readers moved by the story was President Alija Izetbegović. "I read it and couldn't sleep," he said at an *Oslobodjenje* reception more than a year later. "I kept thinking of my own granddaughters."

In the late summer of 1992, Sarajevo was bleeding every day. On August 27 Serb gunners let loose another fierce artillery barrage, and the shelling continued all the next day, with hundreds of tank and howitzer rounds crashing in. Nineteen more Sarajevans died, and 145 were wounded. Radovan Karadžić, attending peace talks in London, claimed that the Bosnian government army had provoked the onslaught and that the Serb forces around the city were only defending themselves against Muslim zealots. "We can't stop it [the shelling], because we are endangered," he told the BBC in London. But the Serb shelling and gunfire were directed almost entirely against Sarajevo civilians, as they had been since the start of the war.

Death could come in an instant, to anyone. In the first minutes of the August 27 barrage, Željka Memić, the wife of *Oslobodjenje*'s firefighting editor Fahro Memić, was killed in front of their apartment building. Memić had just picked up a copy of *Oslobodjenje* from the man selling the newspapers on the corner and handed it and a loaf of bread to Željka, who was standing on the doorstep. He turned and headed back down the street toward the *Oslobodjenje* building. He had walked about a block when a shell landed with a tremendous roar and crash behind him. Memić ran back, but by the time he reached Željka she was already dead. Shrapnel from the exploding shell broke the kitchen windows of the Memić apartment on the fifth floor. One piece bounced off the kitchen wall and pierced the back of the sofa bed in the living room, where Željka's parents were sleeping. Fahro and Željka's fifteen-year-old son, Damir, was standing by the door to his bedroom, came out onto the apartment balcony to see what had happened, and saw his mother lying dead in the street below. The man selling newspapers was also killed, as was one other person nearby.

Five days after Željka Memić died, the Serb snipers in Nedjarići fired on a van full of *Oslobodjenje* workers as it was pulling away from the building, headed downtown. Amira Šehić, a thirty-year-old layout artist, was shot in the left shoulder and chest and lost the use of her left arm. Although she worked at one of the most dangerous places in Sarajevo, Šehić had displayed a casual attitude toward risk, but being shot changed her completely. Afterward she could not sleep if she heard shelling in the city, and sniper fire threw her into a panic.

The week of September 13–20 brought the highest casualty toll since the beginning of the war: 925 civilians in the city were hit by sniper or artillery fire, and 129 of them were killed. Reporters standing at the entrance to Sarajevo's Koševo Hospital watched as bullet-punctured ambulances and private cars brought load after load of wounded civilians to the emergency ward for treatment. The intensified shelling destroyed the last lines bringing electric power to the city, and doctors and nurses at the hospital were left to tend their injured patients without water or electricity. At the west end of Sarajevo, the Serb forces were moving steadily closer, having nearly routed the Bosnian army in fighting around the suburb of Stup.

One of the few places Bosnian government forces had made military gains was in Mojmilo, where Senka Kurtović lived with her parents. The Serb forces had been pushed off a nearby hill, and Senka and other Mojmilo and Dobrinja residents were able at last to come and go relatively freely. Senka had begun working regularly at the

Oslobodjenje room in the ZTO Building, catching a ride downtown each morning from Fahro Memić, Vlado Mrkić, or one of the other *Oslobodjenje* drivers. But Mojmilo residents still had to be vigilant because the neighborhood was regularly exposed to artillery and sniper fire. The local civil defense organization organized people to stand guard by their buildings, to make sure no snipers or saboteurs had a chance to enter. Men stood guard at night, women by day.

On October 15 Senka arrived home from work around 3:00 P.M. Her guard shift was due to begin an hour later. "You should rest," suggested her mother, Andja, "Angel" in Serbo-Croat. "Why don't I take your turn? You can take mine at six." Her mother was standing in front of her building chatting with neighbors shortly after four o'clock when a shell landed in the street. Andja Kurtović died five hours later.

"All my life, I'll ask myself why I let her take my shift," Senka said, her eyes flooding with tears. "She had just washed her hair, and it was still wet when I came home. I said, 'Why take my turn? It's cold, and your hair is wet.' But she insisted. I think she wanted to take my death."

I was often struck in Sarajevo by what seemed to me to be foolish behavior during periods of shelling, such as people standing in line for hours to get a pack or two of cigarettes when they should logically have been terrified to be out of doors. On the other hand, it was not Vlado Mrkić who was killed on the job, but his close friend Salko Hondo, the man who shied away from danger. Fahro Memić was twice hit and wounded by sniper fire as he drove wildly to and from the *Oslobodjenje* building, but it was his wife who died, and she was standing on her own doorstep. Senka Kurtović took many more risks than her mother did, but she survived the war and her mother did not. "If the shell or bullet has your name on it," a vendor in an open-air market once told me, "it will get you even if you're home in bed with the covers pulled over your head." If one were to remain active in Sarajevo, one became a fatalist.

5

Hatred

The consular officer at the Yugoslav Embassy in London took one last look at my passport before handing it back. *"Gjelten,"* he said, with some difficulty. "Is that some kind of Scandinavian name?" Norwegian, I said. The diplomat, a gray-haired Serb, slowly shook his head. "You'll never understand the Balkans," he said. "We're not like you. We all hate each other, and all the time we fight. It won't make sense to you."

I had heard this on almost every trip to Belgrade or through Serb-controlled territory in Bosnia over the previous two years. It was a standard Serb view: Interethnic hatred is natural and inevitable. Significantly, foreign journalists were told precisely the opposite in Sarajevo: that Bosnians had European values and that Sarajevo's record of multicultural harmony stood as a model for the world. The contradiction in outlooks was fundamental. The Bosnian Muslims, as a small nation stuck between powerful neighbors, had always feared conflict, knowing they would emerge as losers. An independent Bosnia could exist within its old borders only if it were a state in which Serbs, Croats, and Muslims lived peaceably. The Bosnian's best hope was that the "international community" would defend Bosnia as a country exemplifying Western ideals of tolerance and civil rights. The growth of ethnic hatred undermined their national interests and hurt their image.

But "Greater Serbia" nationalism benefited from interethnic conflict, so Serb leaders encouraged it at home and touted their bad neighborly relations before the world. In the Serbian national tradition, hatred separates the Serb people from their enemies and mobilizes them for battle. The Serbian state was originally defined by its struggle against the Ottoman Turks, and anti-Muslim sentiment has invigorated the Serbian national identity ever since. The revival of Serb nationalism in the 1980s and 1990s depended on a resurgence of bigotry against Muslims, and the more venomous it was, the more it energized the Serb war effort in Bosnia. While the Bosnian state depended on people staying together, the establishment of a "Serb Republic" on Bosnian territory required that people be set apart.

This could be accomplished by loading people onto trucks or railway cars and moving them—and this was done—but, because Muslims and Serbs were mixed in Bosnia like cornmeal and flour in the same bowl, dividing them would be easier if they were made to hate each other. Moreover, just as it served the Bosnian cause that the war be seen as a struggle in which the civilized world had a stake, it was to the Serbs' advantage that it be viewed as a conflict driven by ancient enmities. Outside military powers would in that case be reluctant to intervene. Ideologically the war in Bosnia was a conflict between those who had an interest in suppressing hatred and those who wanted to promote it.

On the Serb side, the war was fought so as to deepen distrust among the "nations" in Bosnia and to make living together impossible. Cities such as Sarajevo where Serbs, Muslims, and Croats coexisted were attacked in such a way as to drive their residents apart along national lines, while enterprises that exemplified a multiethnic model of life and work such as *Oslobodjenje* became targets of scorn.

The importance that Serb nationalist leaders gave to the goal of fostering animosity was evident in the priority they attached to propaganda. Television provided the opportunity to distill the message of divisiveness to its essence and pound it home. It was particularly effective because most Serbs in Bosnia lived in rural areas, where there was little exposure to other cultural influences and where education levels were relatively low; they were susceptible to simplified appeals based on traditional themes. When the Serb nationalist party took its place in the post-Communist Bosnian Parliament in early 1991, one of the first political battles it fought was for the establishment of separate media outlets for the "Serb" side. Even more significant, it was over the control of television that the struggle first turned violent: Serb police and armed militiamen seized a transmission center in northwest Bosnia on August 1, 1991, eight months before the war began across the republic. Serb nationalists immediately blocked Sarajevo television programming in the local area, replacing it with a Belgrade channel. As soon as the Serb nationalists organized their Serb Republic in Bosnia, they set up their own television station.

Serb-controlled Channel S programming revealed the ideological agenda of the Serb nationalist side, reduced to its fundamentals. First, anti-Islamic sentiments were induced. Against pictures of mosques, announcers warned that the Bosnian Muslims wanted to establish a fundamentalist Islamic state and intended to make Serb women cover themselves with veils. Having reminded Serbs of their ancient prejudices, the propagandists exploited their fears by labeling "Muslim" anything that stood in the way of the Serb cause. The Bosnian government and all its supporting institutions were *Muslim* entities, and *Oslobodjenje* became a Muslim newspaper. Channel S newscasters quoted "Muslim radio" in Sarajevo and reported attacks by the "Muslim" army. Even after the establishment of a federated Muslim-Croat government in 1994, Serb leader Radovan Karadžić stubbornly referred to his adversary as "the Muslim side."

After forty years of being told by the Communists that "brotherhood" was good, the Serb people heard the opposite from their leaders in the 1990s. Bigotry was now rational, not objectionable. Serb announcers spoke pejoratively of Muslims as *balije*—the equivalent of a white television anchor in the United States referring matter-of-factly to blacks as niggers.

In this regard a notable aspect of Serb propaganda was the portrayal of the Serb-Muslim clash as a conflict between the strong and the weak rather than simply a contest between good and evil. The Serbs were destined to come out on top in Bosnia not necessarily because justice was on their side but because they were brave and good fighters. The Muslims, by contrast, were depicted in the Serb media as pathetic losers, to be regarded only with contempt.

Serb newscasters, for example, made little effort to conceal that Muslim homes had been destroyed and Muslim residents displaced as a result of a Serb military conquest of some Muslim town. Such scenes were presented as evidence of Serb prowess and Muslim weakness. About pictures of Muslim civilian refugees walking along a road with bags in hand, a Channel S newscaster said, "Here we see lines and lines of *mujahideen* [Muslim fighters] and *bula* [Muslim religious women] running away from old Serbian ground." As tape rolled of bombed Muslim houses, he noted, "They tried to steal Serbian land, but they were simply beaten." The Serbs of Bosnia were told that they were a people bred for war and that military conquest was to be admired for its own sake.

A Primitive War

Given its enormous advantage in weaponry and logistical support, the Serb nationalist army was assured of a military victory in the Bosnian conflict from the beginning. But because the Serb war aim was not just to grab land but to change the way Bosnians identified themselves and to turn neighbors into enemies, the war had to be fought in an especially brutal way, and it had to be total. It was not enough that the non-Serb side be defeated: All traces of non-Serb existence had to be forever removed from "Serbian" soil. The Serbs' ambitious goals transformed what would probably have otherwise been dismissed as a minor regional conflict into a war with genocidal aspects.

I first encountered the Bosnian Serb army in June 1992 while following an UNPROFOR convoy across Serb-held territory in northeast Bosnia. Just outside the government-held town of Tuzla, we met a company of heavily armed Serb soldiers in the road. The convoy had stopped to wait for clearance from both sides to cross the combat line, and several soldiers came over to talk. One Serb fighter, long haired and with a bushy black beard, was clearly drunk. Pulling a flask from a pocket, he offered a drink of his *rakija,* a potent homemade brandy. Like the other fighters, he carried a Kalashnikov automatic rifle, but hanging from his belt he also had a long knife and, next to it, a butcher's cleaver. I asked what they were for.

"*Muslimani,*" he said, with a wide, gap-toothed grin. He pulled the knife from its sheath and slid it softly across his throat to show how he used it. And the meat cleaver? He held out his left hand and with the other hand made a chopping motion over the outstretched fingers.

Whether that Serb fighter actually slit Muslims' throats and cut off their fingers, I could not say. It occurred to me that he carried the knife and the cleaver mainly to intimidate. But abundant evidence soon indicated that the Serb offensive against the Bosnian Muslims would be the most brutal in Europe since World War II, and that much of the violence and criminality was officially approved as war policy at the highest levels of the Belgrade government. In 1942 Draža Mihailović declared that his Chetnik movement's aim was to create "a great Serbia which is to be ethnically clean . . . of all national minorities and nonnational elements." Fifty years later the Serb army in Bosnia was putting the Mihailović program into practice. The bloodier their conquest, the more Muslims or Croats were likely to flee.

Those who did not escape were given reason to regret it. Muslim men in Serb-conquered towns and villages were regularly rounded up and sent to internment camps, where many perished. Muslim women caught in the same situation faced the prospect of being raped by Serb soldiers. Croat and Muslim fighters also raped Serb women, though less systematically. Serb forces had an extra motivation: They wanted to drive the non-Serb population out of the territory they occupied, and an official policy of raping non-Serb women served that aim. A U.N. team of experts concluded that mass rapes in Bosnia-Herzegovina were carried out as "an instrument of 'ethnic cleansing.' " A European Community mission investigating Serb soldiers' rapes of Bosnian Muslim women reported that rape "cannot be seen as incidental to the main purpose of the aggression, but as serving a strategic purpose in itself."

Military victory represented only the first phase of the Serb nationalist war program. Nowhere was this better seen than in northwest Bosnia, where Serbs were in the majority and where, with the exception of the Bihać pocket, Serb nationalists took political and military control without firing a single shot. Muslims constituted only about a quarter of the prewar population in the region, but Serbs were determined to push them all out. In the municipality of Čelinac, local Serb authorities formally assigned the non-Serb population (1,440 Muslims and 79 Croats of 18,666 total residents) a "special status." They were not allowed to leave their homes after 4:00 P.M., to gather in public places, to swim in the local river or hunt in the forest, or to travel out of town without authorization. The message to Muslims was clear. Within a few months all but a handful had left.

The decrees in Čelinac, eerily reminiscent of Nazi edicts against Jews, were publicly condemned by the local office of the U.N. High Commissioner for Refugees (UNHCR), and they were soon dropped.

Authorities in other Serb-controlled towns in the region sent the same message to their Muslim residents in a less overt manner, relying on violence and intimidation. Telephone threats would be followed by firebombs in the night and selective murders, until entire Muslim communities were displaced. In Banja Luka, home to 29,000 Muslims, all sixteen mosques were destroyed.

In each case Banja Luka authorities claimed the perpetrators were unknown, but the next morning bulldozers would arrive on the scene and clear away the rubble. The site of the sixteenth-century Ferhadija mosque (first damaged in February 1992 and blown to pieces a year later) was turned into a parking lot. "You must not just break the minarets," a local Serb police chief explained to a reporter. "You've got to shake up the foundations, because that means they cannot build another. Do that," he said, "and they'll want to go. They'll just leave by themselves."

For the Serb nationalist war against the Muslims to be sustained indefinitely, however, it had to be fueled. Serb leaders accomplished this in part by declaring it a religious war. The Serbian Orthodox church, the patron of the Serb national cause for six centuries, played a vital supporting role in the war. After the bombing of the Ferhadija and Arnaudija mosques in Banja Luka, the local Orthodox bishop noted coldly, "They were in the wrong place." Metropolitan Nikolaj, the head of the Serbian Orthodox church in the Bosnian ecclesiastical province, assured Bosnian Serb soldiers that "God will allow us to achieve the objective we fight for and to divide Bosnia-Herzegovina fairly and for the benefit of the Serbs."

Religious fervor alone, however, was not enough to motivate Serb fighters in Bosnia, because the evidence of a fundamentalist Islamic threat in Bosnia was hardly compelling. But there was another motivation, unrelated to religion but as deeply rooted in Bosnia as the Serb-Muslim conflict itself: greed. In Ottoman times the Turks and their Muslim Slav allies in Bosnia had been the moneyed and landowning class, and Serb peasant uprisings against the Muslim "traitors to the faith" could also be explained as revolts against the rich. The archetypal Serbian heroes in the age-old struggle against Muslim rule were the seventeenth-century *hajduk* bandits who led raids on Turkish travelers from their villages in the Dinaric mountain range along the Adriatic coast. The anti-Turkish Chetnik guerrilla soldiers of the 1800s were inspired by the hajduk tradition. After the Turks abandoned Bosnia, the hajduk-Chetnik movement was kept alive with the Serb raids on Muslim farms in the Drina River valley in the 1920s and afterward.

The key element of the hajduk-Chetnik tradition was its association of war with looting. "On the barren heights," wrote Yugoslav historian Vladimir Dedijer, "life cannot be maintained without a leap over the fence into the barns of neighboring tribes to obtain food for one's immediate family and even distant relations." Dedijer, Tito's chronicler of the World War II Partisans, wrote that rural-born Serb Partisans were sometimes a problem for the movement because they brought with them "the old Dinaric tradition that the warrior should enjoy the fruits of his wartime exploits."

Like the peasant Partisans, many Bosnian Serb militiamen who volunteered to fight their Muslim neighbors in 1992 were raised in the Dinaric tradition. Many had long beards and wore fur hats, in the style of the hajduks and Chetniks, pinned World War II Chetnik insignia on their army uniforms, and saw their war service as a way to enrich themselves. The Bosnian Muslims were no longer big landowners in 1992, but they were generally more prosperous than their Serb peasant neighbors, as a result of years spent as "guest workers" in Austria and Germany, their domination of the business world, and their higher education levels. As soon as Muslim residents were chased from their towns in a "cleansing" campaign, Serb army fighters would move in and clear out their homes. Traveling in eastern Bosnia in the wake of a spring 1993 Serb offensive, I saw dozens of Serb army trucks hauling away refrigerators, television sets, washing machines, and furniture. In northwest Bosnia, Serb army officers from humble backgrounds could often be seen driving Mercedeses and BMWs bearing license plates from the formerly Muslim town of Prijedor.

The war in Bosnia began against a backdrop of unemployment in both Bosnia and Serbia, and economic stagnation increased greatly under the draining effects of war production and trade sanctions against the Serbian government. The opportunities for enrichment presented by the Serb war operation in Bosnia became increasingly important, even eclipsing the original nationalist themes. Serbian nationalism had been revived in 1986 with the publication of the Academy of Arts and Sciences "Memorandum" in Belgrade, but the Serb nationalist cause degenerated during the war in Bosnia to such an extent that it embarrassed the intellectuals who had inspired it. Dobrica Ćosić, the Serbian novelist credited with the modern revival of the Greater Serbia idea, was compelled in 1993 to condemn the destruction of mosques across Bosnia and to disassociate himself from Radovan Karadžić and the Bosnian Serb military leadership. The founder and intellectual heavyweight of the Serb nationalist party in Bosnia, Milorad Ekmečić, was similarly distressed at the way the "Serb Republic" and its army evolved. "The movement has been taken over by Chetniks and village people," he told me in the fall of 1993, disapprovingly. Neither Ćosić nor Ekmečić, however, was ready to admit that what had happened in Bosnia was a logical flowering of their Greater Serbia seed.

The rural character of the Serb war effort in Bosnia was reflected in the fact that most of the *Oslobodjenje* Serbs who left the newspaper at the start of the war out of sympathy for the Serb national cause stayed in Belgrade and ultimately distanced themselves from the crude propagandists in Pale and Banja Luka. Only Ljubo Grković, who went to work for Radovan Karadžić, seemed comfortable in the company of the Chetnik nationalists. Although Grković had been born in Sarajevo, his parents came from a village near the town of Gacko in eastern Herzegovina, where they had farmed. During World War II many Gacko Serbs were rounded up and killed by Croat Ustashe forces, and Grković's father raised his sons on stories of heroic Serb resistance. The elder Grković told Ljubo and his brothers how their grandfather had traded a bag of flour for a rifle and led his neighbors in the successful defense of their village.

Ljubo was determined to follow in the family fighting tradition and began carrying a gun while still working as a reporter, before the war began. When Gordana Knežević docked his pay one month for failing to meet his story quota, Grković snarled that he was going to kill her as soon as the war started. "I had my biggest problems at *Oslobodjenje* with other Serbs," Grković told me later in Belgrade. So much for his claim that Sarajevo was riven by ethnic conflict. The Grković bravado failed to impress his co-workers. With his well-rounded belly, slicked-back hair, and gold earring, the thirty-two-year-old reporter with a pistol tucked in his pants looked to his *Oslobodjenje* colleagues like an overgrown playground bully.

When the war started, Grković spent time in Pale with Karadžić, although he often visited his brother Radvoje, the commander of Serb volunteers in Nedjarići. He had never served in the army, but he learned how to use a weapon and occasionally took his place in the trenches opposite the Sarajevo defenders' front lines, along with Radvoje. Another brother, Milorad, was killed by a Bosnian army sniper a few weeks after the shooting began. In September 1992

Grković left Karadžić's staff and moved to Nedjarići to fight with Radvoje full-time. He participated in several actions, including an assault on the east side of Ilidža, when the Serb forces pushed the Bosnian army front lines back toward Sarajevo by several hundred yards. "We killed them like flies," Grković boasted. He said he stopped fighting in order to accompany Bosnian Serb fighters as a journalist. "I wanted to write about what they experienced in their own flesh and blood," he explained.

In the summer of 1993, Grković was with the Serb forces when they overran Trnovo, a Muslim town south of Sarajevo, and he wrote a firsthand account of the offensive for the Belgrade magazine *Duga*. His unit called itself the New Sarajevo Chetnik Company and, judging by Grković's tale, was distinguished for its primitiveness. He described the first encounter with Muslim fighters, a day that began with shooting on both sides and ended with shouted conversations across the front lines:

> We were calling on them to surrender and come over to eat with us. We promised to forgive their sins and to convert them to the faith of their ancestors, to baptize them according to Orthodox custom, with wine and brandy and mutton. But they don't like it when we mention food and drink. They immediately get nervous and start shooting. They are more often hungry than not, so every reference to eating makes them crazy. They start shooting wildly and curse our mothers.

The next day, according to Grković, his unit attacked the "Muslim nest" they had been taunting the night before:

> We poured a lot of bombs on the bunker, then we entered and fought them face to face. There was a lot of screaming. The fire was really heavy. The air was humid with blood. Somebody started singing, "Get ready, Get ready, Chetniks!" [a World War II song]. Then our people were caught up in mad ecstasy, and the voices became one voice. . . . In such a moment, even the biggest coward or wretched pacifist or cosmopolitan usurer forgets his fear and wants to kill. No one can resist this call from the roots. . . .
>
> [Afterwards] . . . bandages were put on wounded arms. There was a feeling of sweet emptiness, like after the creation of a work of art. When the fighting is over, one feels that he misses something, this spirit that went out from the body.

Later in his account Grković wrote with pride of his unit entering a previously inaccessible Muslim village that was protected by cliffs and surrounded by thick forests:

> We found everything as if life had continued until one second before. There were still fires in the ovens, and milk was on the stoves; it was as if the village were still alive. But not for long. We burned it.
>
> The flames looked like hands linked in a circle, waving over the village to make it disappear. The fire moved from house to house, roof to roof. . . . It was a beautiful fire. Our army was cold and tired, and we just stood there and stared into this blazing village that warmed our souls.

Grković seemed untroubled by the spectacle of aggression and destruction. Traveling with the Serb army as it fought and burned its way toward Trnovo was his final war project in Bosnia, however. In the spring of 1993, his brother Radvoje had given up the command of the Serb forces in Nedjarići. Ljubo relocated to Belgrade, then moved to Australia, where he had already sent his wife and children.

An Assault on Coexistence

Sarajevo, the Olympic city, was the supreme challenge for the Serb nationalists in Bosnia. About 120,000 Serbs lived in Sarajevo before the war (of a total urban population of 430,000), and without it any Serb victory in Bosnia would be incomplete. "We will never leave," Radovan Karadžić told a *Washington Post* reporter in January 1994, when the Serbs were under international pressure to lift their siege of Sarajevo. "We will make it the capital of our new state."

In making their claims to the city, Serb leaders sometimes got carried away. In the *Post* interview, Karadžić said that Sarajevo "used to be completely a Serb city." This was also what the Serb officer in Nedjarići told me on my visit there in October 1993. Such outrageous claims suggested that the Serb nationalists were unsure what to say about Sarajevo. The mere fact of the city's existence undermined their argument that people of different national backgrounds had to be separated.

Sarajevo was worse than Muslim; it was *mixed*. Croatian and Italian merchants from Dubrovnik established themselves in Sarajevo, as did migrating Sephardic Jews. The city was the headquarters for all Muslim communities in Yugoslavia, but it was also the seat of the Serbian Orthodox metropolitan and a Roman Catholic archbishop. And the communites overlapped; there was no Croat quarter, no Jewish ghetto, and no separate Serb section. A third of the residents were products of interethnic marriages. Asked by reporters how he explained the history of ethnic mixing in Sarajevo, Karadžić claimed it was imposed on the people by "outside forces" that were working for a unified Yugoslavia. "We didn't have any choice," he said. "We have been squeezed together by declarations. We felt terrible, all of us."

It appeared to some Sarajevans that the Serb army's unending attacks on their city were simple expressions of frustration, as if the Serb nationalists hated the city for all that it symbolized and were determined to destroy it. But other Sarajevans concluded that there was a logic to the seemingly mindless assault: The Serb nationalists, they argued, wanted to alter human relations in Sarajevo, to destroy the communal bonds that linked Serbs and Muslims and Croats as *Sarajlije*—Sarajevans. The Serb nationalists who attacked the city may have been deliberately prompting the Muslims and Croats of Sarajevo to hate Serbs in return. Such was the conclusion when Serb military commanders, in a body exchange with Sarajevo authorities, delivered the remains of three Muslim soldiers who had been decapitated, apparently while still alive, and of a Muslim woman whose throat had been slit and whose body showed signs of sexual abuse. Such actions made Serb-Muslim coexistence all the more unimaginable.

It was to such an end, *Oslobodjenje* reporter Vlado Mrkić argued, that the Serb nationalists probably ordered the May 1992 breadline bombing on Vasa Miskin Street. In an *Oslobodjenje* commentary on the bombing, Mrkić recalled other "dirty" actions by Serb nationalist forces he had witnessed as a reporter during the Croatian war. Writing as a Serb journalist in a largely Muslim community, he concluded:

> The killing of civilians in that way obviously has no military aim. It serves a dark psychological war, spreading despair, fear, futility, and mistrust between Muslims and Serbs in Sarajevo. It is the worst kind of terrorism the world knows, and one could even say it is of a kind unknown in the world until now. Here, in our Sarajevo, the goal of yesterday's massacre, among other things, is to cut those last delicate threads that have connected us, to kill the last,

barely visible ray of hope for the possibility of life together, to show
that we have become enemies till the end of time, enemies who
share nothing but death.

Mrkić raised the issue of morale again in his account of the suffering of a well-known Sarajevo actor, Nermin Tulić, who lost both his
legs to a mortar blast. "I am still full of life," Mrkić quoted Tulić as
saying several months after his injury,

> but there is hatred in me now. Not because my legs were cut off.
> The amputation is a joke; I have gotten used to it. But watching
> how my kids live, how thousands of children live, how humiliated
> and insulted we all are, how we have reached the bottom. That is
> why I started hating. Before, I had felt hatred only as an actor, in
> the theater. It was alien to me. But now it has come to me.
>   Whom do I hate? All criminals, I think. I do not want to say all
> Serbs, but . . . I feel this in me when I suddenly hear a shell explode,
> when I hear a detonation.
>   It is probably here that they have defeated me, by causing me to
> have this hatred. As for them having cut my legs off, fuck the legs!
> To feel hatred in yourself is worse than suffering from cancer.

That reaction undoubtedly suited the Serb nationalists, determined
as they were to divide Sarajevo into "twin cities," one for the Muslims and one for the Serbs.

In May 1992, when the breadline bombing occurred, the "Serb
Republic" leaders officially proposed that Sarajevo be made an
"open city," by which they meant that "according to their free will
and decision the citizens of Sarajevo be allowed to move from one
suburb and settle in another without being hampered by any side."
No mention was made of the right of people to *remain* in the suburb
where they lived; the Serb nationalists were determined to shift
populations. And in the areas around Sarajevo under their control,
the Serb authorities implemented such a program through force and
intimidation. There was nothing voluntary about it.

This was seen in Ilidža, the suburb of 67,000 residents that lay at
the far west end of Sarajevo, just beyond the line of confrontation between Serb and Bosnian government forces. Serbs constituted only 37
percent of the population in Ilidža, while Muslims made up 43 percent, Croats 10 percent, and people of mixed ancestry the rest. But the
Serb SDS party was well organized in Ilidža, and SDS paramilitary

forces took control of the suburb in the opening days of the war. As soon as they had consolidated police and military control, the Serb authorities began expelling the local Muslim population. Ilidža, they announced, would be part of "Serb" Sarajevo. Muslim residents were told they should exchange homes with those Serbs who lived in "Muslim" Sarajevo and wanted to move out.

Nikola Golijanin, a Serb who lived in the apartment just above Gordana and Ivo Knežević, arranged just such a switch in May 1992 with a Muslim family from Ilidža. Gordana and Ivo knew Golijanin and his wife only well enough to greet them and their fifteen-year-old son as they came and went. Nikola was an engineer with an Ilidža-based construction company; his wife worked for General Kukanjac, the Yugoslav army commander in Sarajevo. Nikola was always cordial, and at the beginning of the war in Sarajevo he offered to take his turn standing guard in front of the building along with Ivo and others who lived there. There was considerable sniper fire in the neighborhood, and residents had to be careful to control who entered their buildings. One day Nikola didn't appear for his guard shift, however, and no one in the building saw him or his family after that.

The Golijanin apartment was left locked, and no one disturbed it until a Muslim couple from Ilidža, Nazif and Fata Merzić, and their eighteen-year-old son, Kemo, arrived three weeks later with a key. The Merzić apartment in Ilidža and the Golijanin apartment in Sarajevo were both owned by the company that employed the two men, and Nazif and Nikola had agreed to exchange residences. Although they were not friends, they had known each other for twenty-seven years and happened to come from the same small town in Herzegovina.

But the experiences of the two families in the first weeks of war could not have been more different. While his Sarajevo neighbors were trusting Nikola Golijanin with the security of their building, Serb authorities in Ilidža were imposing anti-Muslim and anti-Croat measures that mirrored those established throughout Serb-controlled territory in Bosnia. Signs saying, "No entrance to Muslims and Croats," were posted on the front doors of the city hall, the police station, the post office, and all other public buildings. When Nazif Merzić went to his company to collect his paycheck, he was told Muslims and Croats would no longer be paid. Serb neighbors who before the war had been "perfectly normal" toward Nazif and his wife suddenly began avoiding them, even looking the other way when they met on the streets and stairways. In the seventy-two-unit apartment building where the Merzić family lived, all Muslim and Croat residents were ordered to keep their doors unlocked and be prepared for searches at any hour. In fear, Muslim and Croat families tried to visit one another secretly at night to discuss what to do. One by one they fled.

Nazif Merzić and his wife were the last to go. They had sent Kemo to stay with friends in Sarajevo at the first sign of trouble but were reluctant to leave themselves. Twice Nazif was arrested by the SDS authorities, interrogated, and warned to leave town. Each morning bodies of murdered Muslims had been turning up under the town's old Roman bridge, with slit throats. The third time Nazif was told he would also be killed if he did not go, and he took the threat seriously.

Nikola had been urging Nazif to consider an apartment exchange, and they met over coffee one morning to make the arrangements. The next day Nazif and Fata Merzić left Ilidža, bringing with them just two plastic bags containing their most valued possessions. The Serb authorities in Ilidža insisted that Nazif and Fata leave their new Ford Escort parked in their garage, so they had to walk out of town. They arrived at the Knežević building during a period of heavy bombardment, but they were oblivious to it. "The shelling was nothing," Nazif told me later. "We were free. Compared to what we had been through in Ilidža, Sarajevo was paradise."

When Muslim authorities in Sarajevo did not expel Serbs the way Serb authorities pushed Muslims out of their territory, Radovan Karadžić and other Serb leaders could always respond that the Muslims permitted an ethnically mixed Sarajevo only because they knew they dominated it numerically and culturally. But this did not explain why more Serbs did not move on their own to one of the separate "Serb" suburbs. At least 40,000 Serbs remained in "Muslim" Sarajevo in defiance of the Serb call for ethnically partitioned "twin cities." Faced with this fact, the Serb nationalists had two explanations: Either such Serbs were being held in the city against their will by the "Muslim" government in Sarajevo or they were traitors to the Serb nation who for opportunistic reasons had decided to align themselves with the Muslim side.

There were indeed many Serbs who wanted to flee government-controlled sections of Sarajevo during the war and were blocked from doing so by the Bosnian army. But it was not clear how many of these were fleeing persecution and how many simply wanted to escape from a besieged city. Many Muslim and Croat residents also wanted to leave, and the same movement restrictions applied to them. Army commanders were worried that if Sarajevans were allowed to depart freely, the city would be left undefended. In any case, there were thousands of Serbs who chose to remain in Sarajevo because they wanted to live in a mixed society rather than one organized along ethnic lines. Some had leadership positions, such as the deputy commander of the Bosnian army, Col. Jovan Divjak, and the president of the Bosnian Parliament, Miro Lazović, as well as Gordana Knežević, Vlado Mrkić, and the other prominent *Oslobodjenje* journalists who happened to be Serbs.

Serb propagandists dealt with the example of these Serbs by labeling them "Alija's servants," suggesting they were loyal stooges to the Bosnian president. Gen. Milan Gvero, a deputy commander of the Bosnian Serb army, once instructed UNPROFOR officials to inform Colonel Divjak that the Serb side would have no contact with him until Divjak "acknowledged" that he was no longer a Serb and had become a Muslim instead. "That's no problem," Divjak responded. "Tell Gvero I'll happily say I'm a Muslim, when he agrees to climb down from his tree and stand erect like a human." Two weeks later the UNPROFOR officer wryly told Divjak he had seen Gvero at the Sarajevo airport "eating bananas."

As one of the most determinedly multiethnic institutions in Sarajevo, *Oslobodjenje* was regularly denounced by the Serb advocates of ethnic partition, and the Serb journalists who worked there were targeted for vituperative personal attack. In July 1993 a Channel S program focused at length on the newspaper. The host was Dragiša Ćosović, a journalist who had worked at the weekly Sarajevo magazine *AS,* which had been published by *Oslobodjenje* printers. Ćosović opened the segment holding a recent issue of the newspaper before the camera. "This is the newspaper that is winning prizes all over the world," he said. "It spits on everything that is Serb."

Ćosović called Kemal Kurspahić *Oslobodjenje's* "chief mujahideen" and said Gordana Knežević was the paper's *dajdžinica,* its Turkish aunt. Reporter Vlado Mrkić was identified by name as one of several "ex-Serbs" working at the paper; they had so betrayed their people that they could no longer honestly call themselves Serbs. "Have they asked where they're going to live after Bosnia is ethnically divided?" Ćosović asked. "They will not be able to live in the Serb part, and Alija will throw them out like old rags." He hinted that the Serb authorities knew the whereabouts of Vlado Mrkić's wife and two sons, who were living in Belgrade. "Does he remember," Ćosović said

Oslobodjenje was published every day throughout the siege of Sarajevo, and the newspaper became a symbol of the city's tenacity. (DAVID BRAUCHLI/SYGMA)

menacingly, "that Mother Serbia is generously feeding his wife and children?"

Ivo Andrić

With Western journalists and other foreigners, Serb nationalists spoke often of the depths of ethnic hatred in their land in order to discourage outside powers from becoming involved in the Bosnian war. The effectiveness of this strategy was plainly illustrated by the impact of pronouncements made by Canadian Gen. Lewis MacKenzie, the first UNPROFOR commander in Bosnia, who appeared on television talk shows and before committees of the U.S. Congress to explain why the United States and other governments should stay out of the Bosnian war. Shortly after leaving Sarajevo, he told a Canadian reporter that he had witnessed "an intensity of hatred" there such as he had never seen. "If you believe that someday everyone is going to shake hands and make up and everyone's going to live happily ever after . . . I stopped reading fairy tales when I was five years old," MacKenzie said. The only answer for Bosnia and Sarajevo, he argued, was for the ancient hatreds to be settled through "some constitutional resolution," such as a partition along ethnic lines. After hearing of such remarks, Alija Izetbegović called MacKenzie "an ignorant man," but the Serbian-American media organization SerbNet was so pleased by what MacKenzie said that it offered to sponsor two of his speeches.

The debate over the depth of ethnic hatred in Bosnia, with all the policy implications attached to it, focused renewed attention on Ivo Andrić, the Bosnian writer who won the Nobel Prize for literature in 1961 for *The Bridge on the Drina,* among other works. Set in the Bosnian town of Višegrad, the novel chronicles four centuries of life around a great stone bridge built by an Ottoman vizier. Andrić focused on the complex and often conflictive relations among the four religious communities represented in Višegrad: Orthodox, Muslim, Roman Catholic, and Jewish. He loved Bosnia, but he also feared it, and he wrote unswervingly of the potential for cruelty in the Bosnian heart.

The centenary of Andrić's birth was in October 1992, at the height of the Bosnian war. It was commemorated by admirers on both sides, but with more enthusiasm among his Serb readers. Although he was born of a Croat mother (and an undetermined, but allegedly Muslim, father), Andrić was celebrated as a national hero in Serbia, where the government headed by Slobodan Milošević put his image on banknotes of varying denominations. His popularity with Serbs stemmed from the fact that Andrić placed himself in a Serbian literary tradition and wrote in Serbian dialect.

During the Bosnian war Ivo Andrić became useful to Serb nationalists in another, even more important, regard: His emphasis on the potential for violent conflict between the religious communities in Bosnia made it easier for the Serbs to claim that the Bosnian war was inevitable and therefore excusable. When the Bosnian government argued that the Serb nationalists were trying to poison the spirit of interfaith harmony that had prevailed in Sarajevo and elsewhere in Bosnia, the Serbs could counter that Andrić had regarded such tolerance as superficial and that he had seen passionate hatred seething underneath.

An Andrić story typically singled out was "A Letter from 1920," which begins with a chance meeting in a train station between a Sarajevo-born doctor of Jewish origin named Max and an old friend with whom he had gone to high school years earlier in Sarajevo. Max tells his friend that after leaving the Bosnian army that summer and spending three months back in Sarajevo, it became clear to him that he could not go on living there. When his friend asks the reason, Max answers simply, "Hatred." The conversation ends abruptly, but three weeks later the friend receives a letter from Max, in which he elaborates on his statement in the train station:

> Perhaps in Bosnia men should be warned at every step in their every thought and their every feeling, even the most elevated, to beware of hatred—of innate, unconscious, endemic hatred. . . . The rifts between the different faiths are so deep that sometimes hatred alone can succeed in crossing them. . . . (In these past few months I think I have had a good view of the real relationships between people of different faiths and nationalities in Sarajevo!) On every occasion you will be told, and wherever you go you will read, "Love your brother, though his religion is other," "It's not the cross that marks the Slav," "Respect others' ways and take pride in your own," "Total national solidarity recognizes no religious or ethnic differences."
>
> But from time immemorial in Bosnian urban life there has been plenty of counterfeit courtesy, the wise deception of oneself and others by resounding words and empty ceremonies.

Such passages served to caution foreigners visiting Sarajevo not to be too impressed by the appearance of interethnic harmony there. Ex–*Oslobodjenje* editor Miroslav Janković, an avid Andrić fan, told me when I saw him in the fall of 1993 that I could not understand Sarajevo without reading "A Letter from 1920."

"Bosnia is a perverted place," Janković said over dinner in a Belgrade restaurant. "It's not part of the civilized world." He said the collision of empires in Bosnia had made it an incomparably exciting and seductive land, with a mix of colors and rhythms all its own, but that this frontier heritage had also produced a predisposition to murderous violence and passionate hatred, and that Andrić understood and explained this better than anyone. Janković had left Sarajevo as a fervent Serb nationalist.

Not surprisingly, Ivo Andrić was regarded with some ambivalence in Sarajevo. A planned commemorative reading in the city on the anniversary of his birth was canceled at the last minute. The *Oslobodjenje* reporter assigned to cover the event wrote that the organizers realized it might "hurt the feelings" of Muslim refugees from eastern Bosnia, thousands of whom had seen family members murdered or had been expelled from their homes in Višegrad and other cities in the Drina valley—the area about which Andrić had written, and not always tenderly. Several Sarajevo intellectuals, however, rose to Andrić's defense when he was attacked. They included Avdo Sidran, a Muslim poet and screenwriter who was scheduled to speak at the commemoration. "I know every line of Andrić," Sidran told me, "and I don't think there's anything that can be considered anti-Muslim."

Max was a fictional character expressing his personally pessimistic viewpoint at a particular time in Sarajevo history. After all, Andrić titled the story "A Letter *from 1920.*" To argue that the words Andrić put in Max's mouth demonstrated the "truth" about interethnic relations in Sarajevo more than seventy years later seemed slightly farfetched. Characters in other Andrić stories are more positive in their assessment of social relations between Bosnians of different national backgrounds.

Those Serb nationalists who were tempted to use Andrić's writing to justify their proposals for ethnic partition also failed to acknowledge his obsession with bridges, which appear throughout his stories and essays:

> Of all the things that man raises and builds in this life, nothing in my eyes is better or of greater worth than bridges. They are more important than houses; more sacred, because more universal, than temples. . . .
>
> Thus, all over the world, wherever my thoughts wander or pause, they come upon mute and faithful bridges, as upon the eternal and eternally unfulfilled human desire to tie, to reconcile and link everything that our spirits, our eyes or feet suddenly find themselves faced with—so that there shall be no separations, no contradictions or partings.

Finally, Andrić emphasized the *cyclical* nature of conflict and reconciliation in Bosnia. In *The Bridge on the Drina,* he was sometimes harsh in his description of the malice and animosity felt by the Orthodox, Muslim, Catholic, and Jewish residents of Višegrad toward one another as they passed their lives in the shadow of the great stone bridge. But the 400-year time span covered by the novel suggested something else: For all the bitterness in their feelings, they managed to go on living together, century after century.

Andrić wrote of organic social phenomena, enmities that existed between real people. But what was introduced in Bosnia in 1991 and 1992 was a hundred times more horrible: state hatred, expressed by official media, turned into government policy, and implemented by an army equipped with automatic weapons, tanks, and heavy artillery. When I traveled through eastern Bosnia in the spring of 1993, with *The Bridge on the Drina* and other Andrić works fresh in my mind, I had only one thought: The Muslims were all gone. They had been murdered or expelled, and their mosques were blown up. The Bosnia that Andrić had described no longer existed.

I heard many Serbs in Bosnia—peasants, factory workers, and professionals—say terrible things about Muslims, but what struck me most about their language was how standardized it was. Rather than expressing personal prejudices occurring to them spontaneously, they were mimicking what they heard from their leaders, such as Biljana Plavšić, the vice president of the nationalist Serbian Democratic Party and one of the leaders of the "Serb Republic" in Bosnia. "My dearest wish," Plavšić told a Serbian magazine in Belgrade, "is to see the Drina valley cleansed of Muslims. I do not wish them any good, though in order to have my peace, I will have to give them something so they do not disturb me."

In the spring of 1994, an Associated Press reporter visited the town of Hadžići, thirteen miles west of Sarajevo. Before the war Hadžići had been two-thirds Muslim, but the Serb army had since overrun it, and all the Muslims had been forced to leave. "We will never allow the Muslims to return to their homes," the mayor said. "We will all die resisting it."

A Serb army captain told the AP reporter that the world was "nuts" to think that Hadžići Serbs "would ever walk the same streets with those fundamentalists," referring to his former Muslim neighbors.

A twelve-year-old boy named Borislav Sarenac, schooled by his Serb elders, said, "I do not miss my Muslim classmates one bit. It has been explained to me that while we were playing together, they were actually plotting behind my back."

6

Fighting Together, Falling Apart

The siege of Sarajevo was not unlike those of Leningrad, Constantinople, or others throughout the history of war in that its simple aim was to force the city's surrender. But the Serb nationalists had a political as well as a military agenda: They wanted to reorganize the city, dividing it into ethnic zones. This aim required that the social character of the city be broken down, so that neighbors would turn against neighbors and split naturally into ethnic blocs. The longer the siege continued, the more likely this was to occur, and the partition of the city that would follow a mass surrender would be that much easier to carry out.

The Serb strategy made the defense of Sarajevo more complicated. First, frontline soldiers had to prevent the Serb army from entering the city. Second, Sarajevans needed to stay alive and keep up their morale, in order to resist the temptation to give up. Finally, they needed to maintain Sarajevo *society*. Residents of all ethnic backgrounds fought valiantly on this front, and *Oslobodjenje* had a lead role. As one of Sarajevo's most prominent multiethnic enterprises, it had a large stake in the outcome of the struggle. But, as the city's leading newspaper, it also had a responsibility to cover events honestly, even when being forthright could make things worse. The longer the siege continued, the more difficult the challenge became; war inevitably eroded social links among the people of Sarajevo and made the city a less civilized place.

Resistance

Mortar shells fired on Sarajevo in the last days of May 1992 hit the radio and television broadcasting center, two mosques, dozens of residential buildings, and the figure-skating arena where Katarina Witt and Scott Hamilton won gold medals in the 1984 Winter Olympics. As they had on many previous occasions, Serb army commanders denied they were responsible, saying "the Muslims" were just shelling themselves. But an independent Belgrade television station broadcast what it said was a tape of an intercepted radio communication between Serb army Gen. Ratko Mladić and his unit commanders, recorded during the assault. The voice of General Mladić is heard giving his artillery officers their shelling instructions. "Fire on Velušići," Mladić says at one point, referring to a Sarajevo residential neighborhood. "There aren't many Serbs living there."

It was important for Sarajevo residents to realize that General Mladić and his fellow nationalists were trying to drive a wedge between Serb and Muslim residents by giving them different artillery treatment. If Sarajevans were aware of such deliberate efforts, it might spur them to work all the harder to maintain their communal ties. But Sarajevo residents heard something else in the Mladić tape that many regarded as equally important. The neighborhood he ordered targeted was not "Velušići," [Vel-*OO*-shee-chee], as Mladić said, but "Velešići" [Vel-*EH*-shee-chee]. The destruction of Sarajevo was being directed by a man who mispronounced the names of its neighborhoods.

For many Sarajevans the Mladić tape offered evidence of what they had always argued: that the Serb nationalists out to destroy their city were outsiders, rather than genuine *Sarajlije* like themselves. People who promoted ethnic division were uncouth peasants. To oppose the war was to defend the very idea of a city and the features that defined it—culture, diversity, art, and cosmopolitan life—and the fight took concentrated effort.

I was impressed during my first visit to Sarajevo in June 1992 by the lengths to which people went to maintain at least the appearance of their prewar lives. Gordana and Ivo Knežević invited me to accompany them one Saturday afternoon to lunch at the home of Slavko and Divna Pervan and their daughter, Lada. Slavko, a Croat, was a ballet instructor and choreographer who had planned the opening ceremonies of the 1984 Olympic Games in Sarajevo. Divna, a Serb, was an arts reporter at *Oslobodjenje*. Lada was a theater designer and painter. They lived in Sarajevo's Old Town, in an airy, high-ceilinged apartment full of antiques, books, and fine art. Among the other guests that day were *Oslobodjenje* reporter Emir Habul and Mustafa Demir, the secretary of Sarajevo's tourist organization, both Muslims.

Their apartment was near the Miljacka River, and the front door was unapproachable because of constant sniper fire from Serb positions a few hundred yards away, but the Pervans were determined to throw a Sarajevo party just like those of peacetime. They set their dining room table with their finest china and silver, and Slavko waited for us by the back door. He had a quarter bottle of plum brandy, enough to give each of his guests a single shot before lunch. The Pervans also brought out a bottle of homemade wine they had been saving since the start of the war. A friend had given them a piece of meat, and they cut it into nine pieces, each about two inches square. There was one piece for each person, along with two bite-sized chunks of broccoli and a spoonful of pickled beets. The portions were so small and the presentation so deliberate that the meal seemed more like a communion rite than a real feast. The point was simply to go on as if there were no war; to gather, drink, and eat as Sarajevans always had, and thereby to scorn the forces who were determined to weaken and divide their city. "Macaroni à la Karadžić!" Divna Pervan announced, as she set down a bowl of pasta unadorned by cheese, sauce, or seasoning.

Gordana dubbed efforts to cling stubbornly to prewar ways of life and culture "the Sarajevo resistance." Sarajevans who struggled to carry on with their old lives were hoping to avoid the fate of the people of Vukovar, the Croatian city where the population went underground when Serb rebels and the Yugoslav army began bombarding it. When the people emerged from their cellars months later, they found their city flattened and dead, and they were marched away at gunpoint.

The heroes of Sarajevo were not only Juka Prazina and other militiamen who fought in the trenches at the city's edge but also Mirsada Burić, who trained to represent her country in the 1992 Barcelona Olympics by running defiantly up and down the shell-ravaged streets of downtown Sarajevo. And Vedran Smajlović, a cellist for the Sarajevo Opera orchestra who for twenty-two consecutive days sat in a chair at the site of the breadline bombing on Vasa Miskin Street and played Tomaso Albinoni's Adagio in commemoration of the twenty-two people who died there. Zdravko Grebo, a former law professor at Sarajevo University, during the war set up a private station called Radio *Zid*, or Wall, whose mix of modern music, news programs, and provocative talk shows was intended to keep Sarajevo's "urban style and civilized environment" intact.

It was in this sense also that *Oslobodjenje*'s appearance each morning became so important in Sarajevo, more so to the staff than to the population as a whole. With his promise in April 1992 to publish the paper "every single day" during the war, Kemal Kurspahić had given his reporters and editors an objective to define their work lives and focus their energies. The *Oslobodjenje* staff knew that if they allowed themselves to skip publication every once in a while—when the shelling was especially heavy, or when their diesel oil or newsprint supply was dangerously low—such days would start coming closer together, and before long they would have lost the will to keep working. The afternoon paper *Večernje Novine,* in fact, suspended publication for a time during the worst of the war, although *Oslobodjenje* editors made one of their own pages available for their competitors to fill as they wished.

The *Oslobodjenje* staff produced a paper the night in June when their office towers caught fire and the night four months later when the battered tower frames finally collapsed in a heap. In the early weeks of the war, when Sarajevo was in chaos and under constant deadly fire, reporters and editors themselves stood on exposed street corners and sold the papers to passersby. Week by week the paper got smaller and thinner, and the press run was reduced. The pressmen reached the end of their newsprint and printed on wrapping paper or textbook stock or whatever else they could find, but they always produced a paper. During the early months of the siege, the staff of *Oslobodjenje* often pointed out, there were days when the only items available on the streets of Sarajevo were bread and their newspaper.

Oslobodjenje's publication achievement brought it worldwide attention, but it was only one example of the spirit of tenacity evident throughout the city during wartime. The courage and perseverance Sarajevans demonstrated under conditions of siege raised the question of whether people in Des Moines or Zurich or Winnipeg or Helsinki would have reacted the same way, given such a challenge. Was this a story about the universal indomitability of the human spirit, or was it a story about one unique city?

Sarajevo was clearly a distinctive case in its bridging of Oriental and Occidental worlds, and it was undoubtedly strengthened by the experience. To the extent that Sarajevans developed a strong civic spirit, it may have been precisely because they lived with the prospect of uncivil behavior and violence so close. In addition, Sarajevo straddled another divide for forty-five years by having one foot in Communist authoritarianism and the other in the capitalist West. It was a short plane hop from Sarajevo to Rome or Vienna, and Yugoslavs were allowed to travel freely, so Sarajevans were familiar with Western European fashion and culture. Yet Bosnia was the Yugoslav republic where Communist rule had been most repressive, where free expression was most limited. The experience of moving from this world to the other may also have toughened Sarajevans. During the siege city residents repeatedly told visiting foreign journalists that their values were *European,* and they were not simply pleading to be rescued. Sarajevans took those values seriously, because they did not take them for granted. Their connection to the West had always been vulnerable, which made Sarajevans all the more determined to preserve it when it was threatened.

Interethnic Strains

No matter how hard Sarajevans worked to hold on to their cultured ways, the odds were against them. The rise of nationalism on all sides in Bosnia after the 1990 elections introduced tensions that had not previously been evident, and when Radovan Karadžić and the other Serb party leaders called on Serbs to leave Sarajevo, the sudden rupture of social relations was painful.

Džeilana Pećanin's closest friend, Tanja, abandoned her at the beginning of the war. The two had studied English at Sarajevo University, spent their holidays together, and forged what Džeilana thought was a lasting bond. They watched their favorite film, *The Deer Hunter,* together countless times, memorizing lines of dialogue and reciting them back and forth—none more often then the scene when Michael and Nick promise that neither will leave the other behind in Vietnam.

But Tanja's father was a Yugoslav army officer, and her mother admired Slobodan Milošević, and when the Serb cause came up in conversation, Tanja stiffened. As a Muslim, Džeilana tried to avoid such questions, but some of their friends were not so careful, and Tanja could be drawn into argument easily. In the spring of 1992, Džeilana noticed that Tanja was becoming more distant. When Arkan, the Serb warlord who owned a pastry shop in Belgrade, launched his anti-Muslim campaign of pillage and murder in northeast Bosnia, Tanja joked about it. "I guess we'll all be eating cakes pretty soon," she said.

"That's not funny," Džeilana responded. Shortly after that Tanja stopped calling. In April 1992 she left for Belgrade without saying good-bye.

Džeilana was devastated by Tanja's sudden departure. Six months later, her father was killed by a mortar shell as he stood in line to collect water. The absence of her friend Tanja made his loss all the harder to bear, and Džeilana never stopped thinking of her. "Next to my father being killed, Tanja's leaving was the worst thing that has happened to me in this war," she told me.

Similarly, Senka Kurtović could not get over the way her ex-boy-

Oslobodjenje reporter Senka Kurtović stands outside her Sarajevo apartment building, a few feet from the spot where her mother was killed by a mortar shell in October 1992.   (TOM GJELTEN)

friend, Dragan Alorić, had concealed from her his knowledge of Serb war plans. As she sat in the cellar of her parents' apartment building during the heavy shelling of June and July 1992, Senka's thoughts often drifted back to the time she had last seen Dragan, the morning of April 5, just before he left Sarajevo to join the Serb party in Ilidža. With him in mind, she wrote an *Oslobodjenje* story in July that took the form of an open letter:

> How do you feel this morning, without these dear persons here on this sunny side of mine? Do you think of us sometimes? Are you thinking of us while you shoot at my windows? While you destroy the playground in front of my building? You know that your side shelled the nursery. How did you stand it, you who like all children as if they were your own? How could you be with those people, when they threw the shells on Vasa Miskin Street?
>
> On this sunny side of mine, people are still the same. They love and suffer. On this side of mine, I have to let you know you are no longer allowed. It is too late now to change your mind, to transform you. Too much evil has been sown, too much bloodshed. I've dreamed of you, and now I've finished dreaming of you. I'll never write to you again.

Nothing Senka wrote for weeks after got as much reaction. "That's the story of mine that people remember the most," she said. Almost everyone in Sarajevo during those first months of war had been hurt by someone close—a neighbor, friend, or lover who went over to "the other side."

Such feelings of betrayal nourished a collective anger in Sarajevo in the early stages of the siege, particularly among Muslims, who had nowhere to go and felt vulnerable. Neither Dželiana nor Senka broke contact with Serb friends who stayed in Sarajevo, but interethnic relations in general were inevitably strained. Once people felt abandoned by the most intimate of their Serb friends, they found it more difficult to trust again.

There was an element of logic in such caution. Regardless of how many Croats and Serbs and Jews and "Yugoslavs" joined the Muslims in defending Sarajevo, one fact remained: The forces on the enemy side were exclusively *Serb*. The Serb nationalists were fighting an ethnic war, on behalf of their people alone. Muslims did not volunteer to fight with the Serb army around Sarajevo, so there was no logical reason to suspect Muslims of secretly aiding the enemy. The only Sarajevans who deserted to the other side during wartime were Serbs. For a reason: The party attacking Sarajevo had organized a republic exclusively for the Serb people. Serbs in Sarajevo therefore had to be considered potential security threats in a way that Muslims could never be.

Thousands of Sarajevo Serbs were wholeheartedly committed to the Bosnian cause, and many fought heroically against the Serb nationalist forces and died alongside their Muslim and Croat neighbors. But there were also cases of Serbs who, after spending months declaring their aversion to the nationalists, suddenly slipped across the lines to Pale or Belgrade, either to assist the Serb side or simply to escape. Some Serbs fighting in the Bosnian army deserted, as did a few Serbs who had relatively high positions in the Bosnian government. Each time it happened more doubts were cast on the loyalty of those Serbs who remained in Sarajevo.

When Alija Izetbegović met in July 1993 with a delegation of loyal Serbs who were upset about their increasingly marginalized status, he said he could understand their unhappiness. "Unlike us Muslims, you had a choice," he told them. "You could have gone, and you chose to stay. And I know it's tough for you, because you are under the same shelling as the rest of us. But," he said, "you have to understand the position of the Muslim soldier who looks at the Serb in the trench next to him and doesn't know for sure if he can trust the Serb not to turn on him."

With some Sarajevans feeling rejected by trusted Serb friends and others warning of potential Serb traitors, the social environment was conducive to the growth of generalized anti-Serb sentiment, such as had exploded in the city in 1914. The Muslim-dominated Bosnian government, which was pushing hard to maintain its claim to all Bosnian territory, could not afford to have its political case weakened by an ethnic division of its population, and it made efforts to keep tensions in check. Izetbegović used the Communist-declared Victory over Fascism holiday on May 9, 1993, to reaffirm his opposition to ethnic discrimination or division. "This is a state also of Serbs, and a city of Serbs," he said, "and they [the Serb nationalists] will not force us to behave as they do." Sarajevo television, controlled by Izetbegović's Muslim party, was not always prudent. Serb viewers were offended in August 1992 when the station aired an interview with Ramiz Delalić, who had confessed to being one of the gunmen who shot at the Serb wedding party in the Old Town on the day of the independence referendum. But the announcers were generally care-

ful not to arouse national passions, and, in contrast to their Pale counterparts, they avoided ethnic slurs or inflammatory language.
Sarajevo authorities knew that the Serb nationalists would be quick
to highlight discriminatory policies or pronouncements as evidence
that Serbs were unsafe in the "Muslim" city. The Pale propagandists
would even make such charges without evidence. Their State Docu-
mentation Center for Investigation of War Crimes soberly reported
that Muslim militiamen at the Sarajevo Zoo "threw live Serb children
into cages with wild beasts. Serb fighters in the surrounding areas
have heard horrifying cries from the zoo."

In its August 1992 report, the war crimes center also claimed, "In
many parts of Sarajevo there are concentration camps and other
places in which Muslims are torturing and killing citizens of Serb ethnic origin." One alleged concentration camp was the Olympic Stadium, where according to the Serb authorities "over 6,000" Serbs
were imprisoned. A Bosnian militia leader named Zoran Čegar indeed rounded up several hundred civilian Serbs from Sarajevo in
May 1992 and held them at the stadium. His intent was to exchange
the detained Serbs for fighters of his own who had been captured and
imprisoned by SDS paramilitary forces. But the Bosnian government
immediately denounced Čegar's action, and the Serb detainees were
released within hours. The International Committee of the Red Cross,
the United Nations, the international delegations, foreign diplomats,
and relief officials who visited Sarajevo during wartime all failed to
uncover evidence of concentration camps for Serb civilians in the
city. Serbs in Sarajevo were never subjected to blanket restrictions
such as Muslims and Croats experienced in Ilidža and other Serb-
controlled towns.

But Serbs did face problems in Sarajevo, some serious and some
less so. In the summer of 1992, the most brutal case was the murder of
six members of a Serb family while they were eating lunch in their
home. An unknown assailant climbed over a wall into their backyard
and opened up on them with a machine gun. Other killings of individual Serb civilians were also reported in the first six months of the
war, although the cases were isolated. In September 1992 an ex-SDS
parliamentarian who had chosen to remain in Sarajevo, Milutin Najdanović, was taken from his home and executed, allegedly by Muslim militiamen, after he was accused of being a Chetnik informer.
The Bosnian government swiftly disclaimed responsibility, although
it did little to investigate the killing.

The handful of other SDS members or party officials who remained in Sarajevo after the start of the war faced interrogation at a minimum, and some were arrested and physically abused. One such case was that of Milorad Ekmečić, ideologist for and one of the founders of the SDS party. But he was released and allowed to leave the city freely. At that time Muslim SDA members and party officials throughout Serb-controlled territory were being sent to internment camps and usually ended up dead. For those Sarajevans struggling to maintain an atmosphere of tolerance and harmony in their city, these incidents were troubling. More significant, however, was the petty harassment that Sarajevo Serbs faced in their everyday lives. Because many Serbs had left the city and were attacking it, those who remained felt pressure to show their loyalty. Nearly all Serbs had stories of barbed comments by their non-Serb neighbors and acquaintances, generally heard during times of fierce shelling or siege-induced hardship.

Abusive behavior in the early months of war was encouraged by the chaos and anarchy that prevailed in the city and by the government's inability to exercise control over its own security forces. The criminals and underworld figures who were given responsibility for Sarajevo's defense led untrained and ill-disciplined militia groups. Although they fought and died heroically for Sarajevo, many never entirely gave up their criminal activities. Much of the looting of stores and shops that occurred in the first weeks of the war was carried out by armed gangs who freely roamed downtown streets wearing the badges of Sarajevo's re-formed Territorial Defense force.

Under the circumstances, searching for weapons in apartments sometimes served as a pretext for robbery. Serbs suffered disproportionately, because they were more easily judged suspicious, but the pattern was not rigid. Muslim and Croat apartments were looted as well, while some Serb residents never had their apartments touched. Danica Ugrica, the mother of *Oslobodjenje* Brussels correspondent Ljiljana Smajlović, was convinced that her flat was searched only because she was a Serb, and she left Sarajevo shortly after. But the newspaper's Muslim editor, Kemal Kurspahić, also had his apartment searched, not once but several times, probably because he lived near the front line.

Militia forces under the control of the "detective" Juka Prazina broke into Vladimir and Dubravka Štaka's empty apartment while they were living with Dubravka's parents downtown. Other apartments in the neighborhood belonging to army officers had been abandoned, and the militiamen apparently thought the Štakas had also left Sarajevo. Vladimir and Dubravka discovered the damage when they returned to reoccupy the flat. Friends had warned them that apartments in the area were being looted and taken over by refugees, and the Štakas thought it best to come back before their flat was given to someone else.

Arriving early one morning in late June, they found a police seal on the door and a notice to report to the neighborhood police station. Inside they noticed that Vladimir's laptop computer, a telephone answering machine, an assortment of video- and audiocassettes, and some of Dubravka's jewelry had disappeared. While Dubravka cleaned up, Vladimir went to the police to inquire, bringing with him a list of the missing items. A woman at the station checked Vladimir's documents, took the list, and assured him that there was no problem with the apartment and that she would check on the stolen goods. "But we have to discuss some other business," she said.

"What business?" Vladimir asked.

"We found a photograph in your apartment," the woman said, "that showed you were a member of a Chetnik movement." The photo was of Vladimir and Dubravka and some friends dressed up for an "end of socialism" costume party in 1990. One friend was in a police uniform. Vladimir was wearing a fur cap. The right-wing Chetniks, the most extreme and violence prone of Serb nationalist groups, were customarily bearded and fur hatted, just like Vladimir. In the photograph Dubravka had on a black dress and a scarf wrapped tightly around her head and looked like a woman in traditional Serbian Orthodox mourning dress. She had stuck the party picture on the glass door of a china cabinet in their living room, where Juka's men found it. "You are against Bosnia," the policewoman said to Vladimir.

"No," he countered, "you should check things out a little better. I am an *Oslobodjenje* journalist, I have a pregnant wife, and I have suffered enough in this war already." He was getting angry, but he was also scared. Seeing one policeman who looked relatively more educated than the others, Vladimir said to him, "This is a big mistake, believe me." It was no use. He was arrested on the spot, handcuffed, and taken by car to Juka Prazina's headquarters for further interrogation. "I was scared to death sitting in that car," Vladimir recalled later. "I knew Juka's people were criminals."

At the militia headquarters Vladimir was made to sit on a wooden stool facing a wall. One of Juka's men guarded him, armed with a laser-equipped pistol that aimed a beam of red light on its target. The guard toyed with the device, pointing the gun so that the red light danced around his head, until Vladimir lost his cool completely. "Do you intend to kill me?" he said, jumping off his stool.

"Yes," the guard said. "I think I'll shoot your ear off first."

"Well, my patriotism is bigger than your gun!" Vladimir yelled, just as Juka himself came into the room, hobbling on a single aluminum crutch. The twenty-eight-year-old militia commander, whose courage on the front line was legendary, had been wounded three times in the brief war and had several bullet fragments and bits of shrapnel still embedded in his body. His right arm hung uselessly at his side, and an aluminum rod was pinned to his left thigh. Bone thin, with a hollow face and deep-set green eyes, Juka Prazina had grown more fearsome in appearance with each injury. He glared at Vladimir.

"We have a tough Chetnik here," the guard said. Vladimir, his terror rising by the moment, repeated his story to Juka—that he was an *Oslobodjenje* journalist and that the picture that had gotten him in trouble was taken at a costume party two years earlier. "What should we do with him?" the guard asked Juka.

"Let's exchange him," Juka suggested, thinking of his fighters who had been caught and imprisoned by the Serb paramilitaries.

"For God's sake!" Vladimir protested. "They'll kill me!"

"But we can get one of our guys back in return," Juka pointed out.

"I *am* one of your guys!" Vladimir said. A well-known Sarajevo actor who had volunteered to fight with Juka's men walked into the room at that point and recognized Vladimir.

"Hey, Vlado, what are you doing here?" he asked.

"They say I'm a Chetnik."

"Juka, are you crazy? This is Vlado Štaka from *Oslobodjenje*," the actor said. Juka showed him the picture, saying it was suspicious. "Let him go, Juka," the actor insisted, and Vladimir was freed.

Vladimir Štaka was not embittered by his encounter with Juka and his men, and he did not regard his arrest as evidence that Serbs could not be safe under a Muslim-dominated Bosnian government. "This had nothing to do with a campaign against Serbs," Vladimir told me later. "These guys were criminals. They wanted our apartment."

Juka Prazina eventually ran afoul of the Bosnian government, and an order was put out for his arrest. He escaped from Sarajevo, fought for a while with the Bosnian Croat militia, then fled to Belgium. In December 1993 he was found dead in a highway ditch, shot in the back of the head. His bodyguards were suspected of the murder.

Serbs Writing on the Serb Problem

What to say about interethnic relations in Sarajevo was a question that bedeviled *Oslobodjenje* editors throughout the war. With its high proportion of Serb journalists, the newspaper had a lot to lose if an atmosphere of intolerance took hold. *Oslobodjenje* had political clout in Sarajevo, and its reporters and editors were determined to use their influence to oppose nationalist designs, as they had when they blocked the Muslim-supported proposal to reorganize the Sarajevo news media along national lines in 1991. No one could accuse *Oslobodjenje* of not caring whether a genuinely multiethnic model of life and work were preserved in Sarajevo. The question was how the newspaper could work for that goal.

If it had been peacetime, *Oslobodjenje* would have led the way in exposing any attempt to spread Muslim nationalism in Sarajevo or to subject non-Muslims to persecution, just as it had done during the Communist period and shortly thereafter. But under war conditions the issue was not so clear-cut. The paper's editors felt that the greatest danger to multiethnicity came not from the Sarajevo authorities but from the Serb nationalists who were determined to impose partition on the city. Any articles about the mistreatment of Serbs in Sarajevo would undoubtedly get instant attention in Pale; focusing on the problem would only aggravate it. Moreover, Sarajevo's reputation as a city where ethnic harmony still prevailed was one of the few things working in Bosnia's favor in the outside world. If it were sullied, Western governments would be even less likely to come to Bosnia's assistance. What to report under the circumstances was not clear. As a newspaper committed to professionalism and independence, but also to Bosnia and Sarajevo, *Oslobodjenje* faced such dilemmas constantly.

Oslobodjenje reporters and editors disagreed among themselves on this question. Gordana Knežević was inclined to analyze the political consequences a story might have and decide on that basis whether publishing it was wise. As a Serb, she was also more willing than some of her colleagues to question Serb claims of persecution. "I hear Serbs all the time complaining that they're not getting their proper share of humanitarian aid and then saying it's because they're

Serbs," she said. "What they don't understand is that everyone feels they're not getting their share. It has nothing to do with being a Serb."

Kemal Kurspahić was anxious to demonstrate his newspaper's professionalism, even in wartime. He showed latitude with both his Muslim and Serb reporters, giving them freedom to report as they saw fit. When the ex-SDS Serb politician Milutin Najdanović was murdered, Kurspahić assigned reporter Rajko Živković, himself a Serb, to investigate. "The idea was Kemal's," Živković told me. "He said he wanted the case enlightened from every angle." Reporter Živković was also one of the leading members of the Serb Consultative Committee, an organization that represented the interests of the Serb community in Sarajevo during wartime, and therefore had a private commitment to uncover any evidence of mistreatment of Serbs. Živković interviewed Najdanović's wife about the events preceding her husband's killing. Sarajevo police officials told Živković they had no information. His story quoting Mrs. Najdanović at length was published in *Oslobodjenje* in its entirety.

Vlado Mrkić, *Oslobodjenje*'s senior Serb reporter, specialized in describing human pain on all sides, and among his Sarajevo wartime chronicles were several stories about Serbs who suffered. Mrkić wrote about the murder of the six members of a Serb family in the summer of 1992 and of the killing of an elderly Serb man who lived with his Muslim wife in Sarajevo's Old Town. Because he also wrote many stories about Muslims dying under Serb sniping and artillery fire, he was not accused of caring only for his fellow Serbs. One day, however, a young man approached him in the street and warned Mrkić that he intended to kill him one day. "You're nothing but a Chetnik," the man said. "You should go to Pale."

In the early months of the siege, Mrkić was able to say what he wanted in *Oslobodjenje*, largely because he showed great subtlety in making his points. He could gently call attention to the daily indignities faced by Serbs in wartime Sarajevo, for example, by sneaking a few tart lines into the middle of an otherwise fervent appeal to Serbs to stand up for their city:

It has to be clear to the Serbs in Sarajevo: This city will not and cannot be liberated by their brothers in their tanks parked in six rows on the hills around here. . . . [It can be liberated] . . . only by those Serbs who are defending the city together with Muslims, Croats, Gypsies, and Jews. . . . By those Serbs who never for a single moment stopped believing in the idea of living together. . . . *By those Serbs now sitting in basement shelters, being told that every favor they are given will have to be returned sooner or later. By those Serbs who can be stopped in the street by any brat with a gun cursing their Chetnik mothers.* . . . Sarajevo can be liberated only by those Serbs who are ready to come out of their cellars and fight. [emphasis added]

As the war around Sarajevo became more deadly and the stakes higher, writing about sensitive issues became more difficult. Gordana Knežević took over direction of the newspaper after Kemal was injured in his car accident in July 1992. She was considerably more cautious about what stories should be published, and in what alphabet. Gordana was the prime force behind an *Oslobodjenje* editorial board decision in August to halt the practice of printing alternate pages in the Cyrillic script. There was no announcement or explanation of the move in the paper. Questioned at the time by foreign journalists who noticed it, Gordana and other *Oslobodjenje* editors said the Cyrillic computer had been damaged by shell fire, but that story was a concoction. Printing in the Latin alphabet was more economical, but the decision was political.

"Cyrillic lettering was connected in the minds of many people in Sarajevo with the Chetniks," Gordana told me. "We had to remember the paper was being read by people sitting in their shelters while Sarajevo was being shelled, and we felt that seeing the Serb alphabet was just making them angry."

Vlado Mrkić opposed the alphabet change, arguing that *Oslobodjenje* should demonstrate its continued connection to the Serb community. Increasingly, he was finding himself in conflict with Gordana Knežević and other editors over their views of the Serb predicament in Sarajevo and what should be said about it. In September Mrkić wrote a story about a group of elderly Serb women who were stuck for several days in the Sarajevo train station, waiting for the Bosnian Red Cross to bus them to Belgrade. The buses came to pick them up, but the Bosnian government held up the convoy temporarily while it tried to negotiate the release of three Sarajevo bus drivers who had been detained by the Serb forces in Ilidža. Mrkić described how the women, exhausted by their wait, struggled to make themselves comfortable in the bus seats. It was one of his trademark stories, evocative but without analysis. But, coming as it did at a time of intense Serb shelling of Sarajevo, with a dozen or more people dying every day, Gordana objected to the story.

"Couldn't you put in a few lines pointing out how these ladies happened to find themselves in this situation?" she asked. When Vlado refused to make any changes, Gordana killed the story. "I thought the readers were too sensitive to swallow it," she says. "I thought they'd say, 'What are those stupid *Oslobodjenje* people doing?' " As in her decision to drop the Cyrillic script, Gordana was thinking about how people in Sarajevo would react. Kemal later told me he would probably have let the story be published. As a Muslim himself, he worried less about what other Muslims might think.

Gordana was no less concerned about the fate of Serbs in Sarajevo than her colleague Vlado Mrkić and was not opposed to serious reporting on the question. She was determined, however, to avoid any exaggeration of the problems Serbs faced in Sarajevo. And she was insistent that the stories make clear that such problems developed as a consequence of the Serb nationalists deliberately trying to undermine multiethnic life in Sarajevo.

There was a danger in going too far with a political analysis of interethnic tensions in Sarajevo, however. By repeatedly trying to prove to the world that the war in Bosnia was not really a conflict between Serbs and Muslims, the Bosnian government and its supporters aroused the very ethnic tensions they were seeking to deny. Understandably anxious to show that Serbs in Sarajevo were not mistreated, Bosnian patriots called upon the Serbs regularly to testify to that effect. But this meant approaching such people *as Serbs,* when many wanted to be seen and treated simply as citizens of Bosnia.

The phenomenon was evident at *Oslobodjenje,* because so many Serbs worked at the newspaper. Foreign journalists routinely showed up at the downtown offices asking for an interview with "some loyal Serbs." Gordana Knežević did not like it, although she was usually willing to comply. Vladimir Štaka, because he spoke English, was often pursued and did not appreciate it. While he felt no kinship with the nationalists in Pale, neither did he necessarily feel like speaking out "as a Serb" on behalf of the Bosnian government.

"Now I feel more Russian than Bosnian or Serb," Vladimir told me in the summer of 1993, recalling that his mother was of Russian ancestry. In the 1991 census, he had classified himself as Yugoslav, not wanting to identify in any way with the Serb nationalists; but, with Yugoslavia gone, that was no longer an option. To call himself Bosnian in the current context was to turn the issue of his nationality into a political statement, which he also resisted. "So I decided to be Russian," he said.

A thirty-year-old *Oslobodjenje* reporter of mixed Serb-Croat background, Tihomir Loza, argued in a March 1993 column that, while Muslims were the main victims in the Bosnian war, it was harder "in a psychological sense" to be a Serb in Sarajevo. Like all Sarajevans, Serbs in the city were "exposed to the barbarity of Serb fascists," but in addition they had to carry the burden of their nationality. "There is no indication, let alone evidence, that the government has ever done anything in an organized fashion against Serbs in Sarajevo," Loza wrote. "But hardly a week can go by without someone from the government, probably acting on his own, undertaking to remind these Serbs that they are, lo and behold, Serbs."

7

Winter

I returned to Sarajevo in January 1993 after a six-month absence and was astonished at how wretched a place it had become. The conditions in the darkened city evoked images of siege from centuries past, with daily life reduced to a routine of scrounging for firewood, hauling water, and waiting for handouts. Played out in the streets of a modern European city, the Sarajevo war produced scenes of jarring incongruity, with smartly attired middle-class professionals in the roles of beggars and scavengers.

One day I visited a soup kitchen set up by the Bosnian Red Cross in a courtyard of one of the city's old mosques. Among the people in line was Marijana Madacki, a Sarajevo-born Croat woman in her midthirties with rosy cheeks and sad blue eyes. She was dressed as if she were headed for a hike in the woods. Her blond hair was tucked neatly under a red scarf, and she wore a blue windbreaker over a wool sweater and a flannel shirt. Nine months earlier she had been the front desk manager at a hotel in the suburb of Ilidža. The day I met her, she stood holding a small stew pot, waiting patiently for her four ladlefuls of bean soup—the daily relief allotment for herself, her two daughters, and her husband, Josep, who before the war had been a graphic designer for a Sarajevo publishing firm.

Until the previous August they had lived on the top floor of an old villa that once served as the German consulate. The building sat prominently on a low rise near the Bosnian presidency headquarters, and it was hit twice by Serb gunfire. On the second occasion a tank shell crashed through the roof and exploded in the Madacki bathroom, blowing the bathtub to bits and leaving rubble and plaster a foot deep on the floor. After that the Madackis moved into an abandoned apartment nearby, using their old place for salvage. Josep converted a kerosene stove for wood burning, and he and Marijana ripped the wood flooring out of their former apartment to use as kindling.

The day after I met Marijana at the soup kitchen, I went to see her and Josep at their old house, where they were spending much of their time. I found Marijana in the backyard tending an open fire over which a large vat of water was simmering. It was the family laundry. Smoke hung in the air, and ashes settled on Marijana's head and shoulders as she slowly stirred the clothes in the rusty steel drum. The yard around her was littered with debris, and there were holes in the earth where tree stumps had been dug up. An old woman whom Marijana did not know was gathering twigs and branches and stuffing them into a bag.

Josep was in the house, chopping up a tree trunk he and some neighbors had dragged into the front hallway. He was clumsy with the ax, and many of the blows bounced off the trunk wildly. I noticed his left thumb was bandaged and asked him about it. "It was an accident," he explained, eyeing the ax warily. "I'd never had one of these in my hands before." The trunk was from a magnolia tree, one of several that had shaded his backyard. Josep had planted one of the young trees himself and did not want them touched, but strangers had shown up one day and begun cutting the trees, and Josep couldn't stop them. More people came the next day, and Josep and a friend decided they should take a tree down as well. "I was very sorry about it," Josep said, "but better I have one for myself. I needed wood also." He and his friend cut off the branches and with help got the trunk into the house, where it lay as a treasure at the foot of an ornately built wooden stairway. Each night Joseph locked the house to keep the magnolia log safe from those who might be tempted to steal it.

War did not deepen community solidarity in Sarajevo, as might have been expected, but weakened it. Not because of rising ethnic tensions; people simply withdrew into their own worlds and focused on their family survival needs. There was almost no electricity when I arrived in January; the power lines had been sabotaged or damaged by shelling. Temperatures had dropped into the freezing range in November, earlier than usual, and the Serb army around the city had cut the natural gas flow to a trickle. Only people with stoves and wood to burn could warm their homes at all, and probably just one room at that. The rest closed their doors, covered their broken windows with plastic, and shivered day and night. The boundaries of neighborly compassion were drawn ever more narrowly and in the worst of times barely extended beyond the threshold of one's own home.

The only part of Sarajevo where communality and the rule of law still prevailed in the winter months of 1993 was the distant suburb of Dobrinja, where *Oslobodjenje* reporter Senka Kurtović had lived until she escaped to her parents' apartment on May 9, 1992. A few days later the Serb army had cut Dobrinja entirely off from the rest of Sarajevo. Volunteer militia forces had entrenched themselves around the perimeter of the suburb and defended it successfully, but Dobrinja remained in total isolation for two months. In July, Bosnian government forces finally succeeded in dislodging the Serb army from an adjacent hilltop and broke through to the Dobrinja front lines. From May to July local authorities and community leaders had organized for survival, dividing Dobrinja into sectors and then subdividing it by street and building, designating someone at each level responsible for the residents in that unit. A community security force, a hospital, a dental clinic, a media center, and even a grave-digging squad had been organized. What little food stocks as could be found were distributed on an equitable basis.

The self-help approach was maintained even after Dobrinja was reconnected to Sarajevo. When I visited in February 1993, almost every resident had an assignment, based on skill and interest. One group of men had organized an emergency carpentry team. Whenever an apartment was damaged by shelling, the volunteers would go to the unit and make repairs. In another shop men produced primitive wood stoves from scrap sheet metal—road signs, locker doors, stove tops, or anything else they could find—and offered them to whoever was in greatest need. Across the street a crew was kept busy stuffing old rice and flour sacks with sand and sewing them shut, for use in the protection of storefronts and entryways exposed to shelling. Unlike Sarajevo, Dobrinja had no black market. Every box of food and item of humanitarian aid that came into the suburb went directly to a central warehouse. No one went unfed; no ill or injured person was left unattended. The suburb was regarded as a wartime wonder—the People's Republic of Dobrinja, as visiting journalists dubbed it.

In the manner of other socialist rulers, however, the Dobrinja authorities relied on police powers to maintain community discipline. Residents could come and go only with special permission. Those, like Senka Kurtović, who left the community and did not return risked having their homes seized. Senka's apartment was turned over to refugees, and she got it back only after the intervention of her brother-in-law, a Bosnian army officer. Local military commanders took their security concerns so seriously that at one point they cut telephone lines with Sarajevo proper, so as to be sure that Dobrinja was entirely under their control. Dobrinja leaders told me that their community worked so well that Sarajevo city people tried to sneak into the suburb, thinking they could live better there. "We survived against all odds," a Dobrinja man told me. "They could benefit in Sarajevo from our example, but the people there are too selfish."

Fear, Hardship, and Loneliness

The main Bosnia news story in early 1993 was the peace negotiation cochaired in Geneva by Cyrus Vance for the United Nations and Lord David Owen for the European Community. *Oslobodjenje* covered the talks closely and offered comment on the negotiations almost every day, but deputy editor Gordana Knežević fretted that her readers were paying little attention. "All they want to know," she said, "is which neighborhoods are being shelled, where the water is running, and what day is the humanitarian aid being distributed." It was a time of private struggle, when people had no idea what to expect and prepared for the worst.

After her father was killed in October 1992, Džeilana Pećanin and her mother had each packed a suitcase with spare clothes and toiletries, ready for some day when they and other Muslims in their neighborhood might have to flee a Serb army advance. Džeilana stuck her university diploma in her suitcase; her mother put family photographs and important documents in a spare handbag that she kept on a shelf of her bedroom closet. Having heard many stories of Serb soldiers seizing money and valuables from refugees, they wondered how they could hide their cash savings if they ever had to flee through Serb lines. Džeilana's long hair offered an answer: Her mother sewed ten German one-hundred-mark bills into a cloth hair clip, which Džeilana could wear without raising suspicion. Her mother's anxiety was excessive but understandable. Already widowed by the war, she feared she had also lost her only brother, who had been seized with his family at their home in northeast Bosnia and taken to a Serb concentration camp.

Gordana Knežević had recruited Džeilana to the *Oslobodjenje* reporting staff in November 1992, a month after an incoming mortar shell killed Džeilana's father while he was waiting to draw water behind his apartment building. Džeilana, thirty-one, was left alone to care for her mother. Gordana needed reporters with good English skills to cover the work of the United Nations and other international relief agencies in Sarajevo, as well as the visits of foreign dignitaries. With the reporting experience she had acquired while working as an interpreter for foreign journalists, Džeilana would be an important

Reporter Džeilana Pećanin covered the United Nations Protection Force (UNPROFOR) in Sarajevo.

(TOM GJELTEN)

addition to the *Oslobodjenje* staff, particularly on the UNPROFOR beat, which she shared with Vladimir Štaka.

Vladimir's wife, Dubravka, had given birth to a baby girl on October 19, 1992, a day when the city was under especially intense bombardment, and water, telephones, and electricity had all been cut. With the help of Dubravka's father, Vladimir installed a wood-burning cookstove in his living room. But the stove, a porcelain-encased unit three feet high and a foot wide, was not large enough to heat more than a single room, and the fire burned out quickly if left untended. When he or Dubravka got up in the night to change little Maja's diapers by candlelight, it was so cold they could see their breath. They bundled the baby as best they could; Maja learned on her own that she was warmest sleeping on her stomach.

Elementary baby care involved hours of work and great ingenuity. Dubravka figured out how to make diaper covers from the plastic wrapping of toilet paper packages. Vladimir was kept busy finding firewood and water. There was a public tap in the neighborhood, but he had to stand in line for a turn and then haul jug after jug up to their third-floor apartment. With a baby whose diapers always needed laundering, plus two adults who had to eat, drink, and keep clean, the water never lasted long. Always hungry, short of sleep, and working six or seven days a week at his *Oslobodjenje* job, Vladimir soon caught a winter cold that turned into pneumonia. By the end of the winter, he weighed only 130 pounds, down from 180 before the war. His cheeks were hollow, his arms were spindly, and his collarbone stood out sharply through his shirt.

In addition to the difficulties at home, Sarajevans constantly faced the risk of death or injury from shelling. Walking home from *Oslobodjenje* one day, Vladimir was caught in a mortar barrage. Hearing a shell fired off in the distant hills, he paid no heed; three seconds later the incoming round landed a mere block from him. When Vladimir heard another outgoing round a few minutes later, he immediately ducked for cover; this time the shell came even closer. He started running, only to hear a third detonation in the distance. "I felt like someone was watching me with a binoculars," he said. He dove behind a brick wall and covered his head with his hands. The mortar landed on the other side of the wall, knocking bricks loose and throwing up a cloud of dust and debris. Stunned by the blast and covered with grit, he lay without moving until rescuers came to pick him up, although he was uninjured.

There were few precautions that could be taken against shelling,

Oslobodjenje reporter Vladimir Štaka lost fifty pounds during the war, but reported to work at the newspaper faithfully each day. (TOM GJELTEN)

and almost everyone who moved about in Sarajevo had at least one such close call. Gordana Knežević was once knocked flat and temporarily deafened by a shell that landed about thirty yards from her as she walked near the downtown *Oslobodjenje* office. A man I met at the Red Cross soup kitchen told me he thought every day about being hit by a shell as he walked between his home and the kitchen. "I never know whether to hurry or slow down," he said, "because you could be heading toward it, or it could land behind you." Prepared for the worst, he went everywhere with a Yugoslav army–issued field bandage taped to his jacket.

I could see fear in the people I met walking along Marshal Tito Street in downtown Sarajevo. Although the sidewalks were crowded, I was often struck by how quiet it was: no horns honking, no clanging trolley cars, no hawkers shouting, no street-corner gabbing. Just the trample of feet on pavement and the squeak of carts loaded with water jugs. People hurried along, their faces clenched in scowls. Some held the arms of companions, but they did not talk. Everyone stared straight ahead. At the sound of an explosion in the distance, faces would flinch, but only for a moment and without a change of expression.

I learned there was a difference between surrendering oneself to destiny and being reckless. The first was frequently necessary in Sarajevo; the second never was. One winter afternoon I was sitting with Vladimir and some other *Oslobodjenje* reporters in their workroom in the ZTO Building when a mortar round exploded nearby with a tremendous boom. We could not see anything through the plastic-covered windows, but we soon heard the shouts of soldiers and policemen calling for help and, more dimly, the cries of people injured. I took my tape recorder and started off, thinking I should go to the scene, but Vladimir ran after me.

"Don't go!" he yelled, just as I headed out the front door. He had stopped at the top of the stairs behind me and clearly did not want to come farther, although he was also thinking he should accompany me if I insisted on going. The site of the shelling was just around the corner. I could see Vladimir was frightened, and he was asking me not to go as much for his own sake as for mine. I was violating a rule: You go out during shelling if you must, but you do not tempt your fate. I stayed back.

More than 250,000 shells had fallen on Sarajevo as of that date, according to Bosnian authorities. At least 8,000 people in the city were reported dead or missing, and more than 60,000 were said to have been injured from shelling or gunfire.

Among them was Amira Šehić, the *Oslobodjenje* layout artist wounded by a Serb sniper in September. Although she had recovered from her chest wound, the bullet damaged nerves in her shoulder, and her left arm dangled limp and motionless. Twice a week she went to the hospital for therapy, but her doctors said she would not improve without surgery. When I came in January, Amira had not yet told her parents of the injury. They lived in Stolac, a mixed Muslim and Croat town near the Herzegovina battlefront, and Amira feared upsetting them. Unable to get dressed or wash her hair without help, Amira was living in Sarajevo with her cousin. A few months later *Oslobodjenje* editors managed to get her evacuated on a U.N. aid flight. Reporters without Borders arranged surgery and medical treatment for her in Paris.

Amira was fortunate to work for one of the few Sarajevo companies still functioning. *Oslobodjenje* employees were paid a token salary and got benefits that set them apart from other workers in the city. As long as the Sarajevo bakery was operating, a batch of bread was delivered each day to the downtown *Oslobodjenje* office, and each journalist who showed up for work could take a loaf home. The envelope of Bosnian dinars *Oslobodjenje* workers got every two weeks was virtually worthless, but in addition they were given ten packs of cigarettes. The newspaper had owned 700 tobacco and newspaper kiosks in Bosnia, and the company had a huge cigarette inventory at the start of the war. The biweekly allotment served as a kind of currency wage, because cigarettes were tradable for anything in the market. A pack was worth a big bag of kindling; ten packs sold for about fifty dollars.

Although the war had been a great equalizer—an incoming mortar shell did not distinguish between government ministers, children, soldiers, and dogs—the division between haves and have-nots remained sharp. People with money could secure minimal comforts. One entrepreneur who prospered during the siege was Nurija Kizo, an Old Town metal shop keeper who before the war built air-conditioning equipment, heating ducts, and other metal appliance parts. Foreseeing a winter without gas or electricity, Kizo designed a square steel woodstove about two feet high, with two compartments, one above the other. Wood was to be burned below; the upper chamber was for baking. The top of the stove was flat and could be used for boiling water or cooking a pot of beans or rice. When the war began Kizo had a stockroom full of sheet metal, drawers of rivets, and all the hand tools he needed. By early fall he was hammering out a stove a day, each selling for 300 German marks (about $180). "It's not expensive in the least," he told customers who were upset by the price. "A stove like this will last you twenty years."

Sarajevans who didn't have 300 marks for a custom-made unit either endured the cold or built stoves of their own, using tin buckets, oil drums, or whatever material they could find. Installation also required improvisation. Most Sarajevo apartments built since World War II lacked accessible chimneys, so residents generally had to punch their stovepipes through exterior walls or push them through windows. By the end of the winter, the sides of the modern high-rise housing blocks on Sarajevo's west end were all splotched with black smoke marks, and hundreds of tiny stovepipe ends stuck out all over like whiskers on an unshaven face.

Finding firewood was an even bigger challenge. Because few Sarajevo families had used wood for heat before the war, there were virtually no reserves on hand when the city was sealed off by the

Serb siege. Most of the wood collected came from the trees that were cut down along city streets. The leafy city park where I had watched Olympic runner Mirsada Burić do wind sprints in June was by the following January an empty lot strangely crisscrossed by sidewalks. Men with chain saws and special government connections had cut all the trees down and chopped them up. Low-quality firewood sold for about $200 per cubic yard, a quantity that might last a month. Many Sarajevo families spent their life savings this way. Still green, the wood burned slowly and gave off more smoke than heat. The sooty air smudged people's faces, and without warm water or good light to wash by, some people stayed dirty for days.

For the Knežević family, the winter of 1992–93 was the hardest period they would face during wartime. Gordana and Ivo got a small woodstove like those made by Nurija Kizo from a friend for 50 German marks (about $30), but it was inadequate. Ivo put the stove in Boris's room, because it was the smallest in the apartment and the easiest to heat. He and Boris dismantled the bunk bed Boris had shared with Igor, and they stored the pieces in the basement. Boris moved his mattress into his parents' room. The boys' bedroom became the Knežević kitchen and living space. A small mattress was tucked in a corner as a makeshift couch, two stuffed chairs were brought in from the living room, and some kitchen shelves and a small worktable were set up against one wall.

The Kneževićs spent long winter evenings in the little room, often with a neighbor or two. It was dark by 4:00 P.M., but candles were a luxury, to be brought out only on special nights. A single candle sold for $6 in the Sarajevo market and would burn to a stub in one long evening. Ivo made a small lamp out of a marmalade jar filled with water and a little cooking oil, which floated on top of the water in a thin layer. The wick was a string stuck down into the oil through a hole in the jar lid. The lamp burned with a tiny flame that consumed the precious cooking oil slowly and provided a flicker of light in a dark room.

Ivo built a fire in the early evening, cooked a meager meal, and kept the fire going until the room was warm, at which point he let it die down to save wood. Only when it became uncomfortably cold did he build the fire up again. After an exceptionally frigid December, the wood supply he had originally budgeted to last all winter was nearly depleted.

When I arrived in January 1993, I found the Kneževićs disheartened. Gordana had lost twenty pounds since I had seen her last, and

Ivo looked older and wearier, with new lines around his eyes and a looser, thinner face. They were worried about their children Igor and Olga, who had been forced to leave Egypt after the family with whom they had been staying announced they could no longer accommodate them. Gordana scrambled to get Igor placed with a new family in Manchester, England, and she arranged for Olga to get to Zagreb, where she could stay with Croatian friends. The arrangements complete, she and Ivo worried how the children would manage away from each other.

They were also concerned about fourteen-year-old Boris, who was increasingly despondent. When Nazif, Fata, and Kemo Merzić had moved into the apartment vacated by the Serb family upstairs, Boris had been delighted. Kemo, it turned out, was also a heavy metal fan, and Boris had shared his Guns N' Roses and Metallica tapes with him, because Kemo had left his cassette collection back in Ilidža. Although they were five years apart in age, the boys had become good friends, spending hours together in the basement shelter during periods of shelling and in the building entryway during periods of calm. Kemo had brought down a guitar the Golijanin boy had left behind when he and his parents moved to Serb-held territory. Kemo wasn't interested in learning to play, so he had given the guitar to Boris, who was. Kemo told Boris all about life in Ilidža; Boris told Kemo about his time in Cairo.

But Kemo had joined the Bosnian army in September, volunteering to fight with the Dragons of Bosnia brigade on the front line west of the city, back near Ilidža. Boris saw him only every week or ten days, when Kemo came home to visit his parents. No one else near Boris's age lived in his building, and, when it got dark each afternoon, he was left alone.

Three-sided War

Gordana and Ivo and other Sarajevans who followed the news were discouraged by the negotiations in Geneva, where Cyrus Vance and Lord Owen had presented a peace proposal. The Vance-Owen Plan called for the reorganization of Bosnia into a federation of ten semiautonomous provinces, nine of which would be identified with a particular ethnic group: three provinces for the Serbs, three for the Muslims, and three for the Croats. The tenth province, Sarajevo, would be governed jointly. The provinces would have their own security forces and retain power over media, social, and education policies. Federal authority would be limited mainly to foreign affairs and monetary policy, and there would be no central army. To expedite the Geneva talks, the mediators separated the negotiation of the constitutional plan from the settlement of the provincial boundaries.

The Bosnian government disliked the Vance-Owen Plan because it legitimized ethnic partition. The organization of the peace talks was itself telling: Bosnia's elected president, Alija Izetbegović, was treated by the mediators simply as a representative of the Bosnian Muslims, just as Radovan Karadžić was considered the leader of the Bosnian Serb community and Mate Boban the Bosnian Croat representative. The Vance-Owen proposal, however, guaranteed the survival of a Bosnian state, and Izetbegović agreed in January 1993 to back the constitutional framework, as did Boban. Karadžić said his own approval of the draft legal outline would have to be ratified by his "parliament," which consisted of those Serb deputies from the former Bosnian Parliament who supported Karadžić's Serb nationalist party.

The Serb nationalist deputies met on January 20. Although Karadžić argued in favor of approving the agreement, his speech reflected the same bottom-line intransigence that he and other Serb leaders would display in later peace discussions. Karadžić declared that the Serb people in Bosnia should not yield in their determination to have an all-Serb state or give up any land they considered essential to their interests. "I advise you to accept this document in order to do what's possible now and to prepare for what will be possible in the future," Karadžić said. Because Vance and Owen had separated the constitutional and territorial aspects of their plan, Karadžić was able to tell his deputies that approving the draft legal outline would not commit them to the proposed division of Bosnian territory. "Forget the maps," he said. "You Serbs are the masters of your own land." The Serb nationalist deputies followed Karadžić's instruction and approved the constitutional design, although the vote was virtually meaningless without an agreement on a territorial split.

The Karadžić speech was broadcast by the Serb radio station in Pale, just outside Sarajevo. At home Gordana and Ivo Knežević heard it on their battery-powered pocket radio. Their next-door neighbor Kana Kadić was visiting that evening, and Gordana had lit one of her few remaining candles. Ivo listened to Karadžić with palpable contempt, stretched back in his chair and staring at the ceiling. He would never forgive the man on the radio for having started a war that smashed his life to pieces and separated him from his daughter.

Across the room Kana sadly shook her head as Karadžić spoke. She did not follow politics, but she knew that what he said was bad for Muslims and bad for her Bosnia. Her head scarf came unfastened, revealing strands of gray hair, but she didn't bother to tie it up again. Gordana and Ivo, a Bosnian Serb and a Bosnian Croat, were her friends.

Outside Sarajevo, however, tensions were growing between Muslims and their non-Muslim neighbors, and the adoption of the Vance-Owen peace formula aggravated them. The Geneva agreement not only failed to end the war in Bosnia but provoked a new one. Before the accord Croat nationalists in Herzegovina were nominally allied with the Bosnian government. The Bosnian Croat forces, while functioning as a separate militia, had fought alongside the Muslim-dominated Bosnian army against the Serb forces and in theory were grouped with the Bosnian army under a single high command. The war in Bosnia still had the character of a Serb nationalist revolt against a recognized legal government.

But by treating the Bosnian delegation simply as a Muslim entity alongside Serb and Croat parties, Vance and Owen undermined the Sarajevo government's legitimacy and redefined the Bosnian war as a three-sided conflict among ethnic factions. Not surprisingly, within weeks the fighting was conforming to that characterization. Bosnian Croat nationalists interpreted the Geneva plan as giving a green light to their old idea of having a Croat ministate comparable to what the Bosnian Serbs had set up for themselves. The three provinces Vance-Owen had designated as "Croat" incorporated territory adjacent to Croatia proper and gave the Croat nationalists everything they wanted for their statelet, making it a de facto extension of Croatia itself. Once the Vance-Owen map was formally introduced, the Bosnian Croat leaders saw no more reason to collaborate with the "Muslim" government in Sarajevo. The Vance-Owen map had not been adopted officially, but that minor point was disregarded.

Within days of the approval in Geneva of the constitutional portion of the Vance-Owen Plan, a special session of the Bosnian Croat "assembly" ordered that all Bosnian government army forces operating in the three "Croat" provinces submit immediately to the command of the Bosnian Croat army, known by its acronym in Croatian as the HVO. The Bosnian army units refused to yield, and fighting soon broke out among the rival armies, especially in central Bosnia. Over the violent objection of Bosnian army soldiers, HVO militiamen hoisted the Croatian flag over public buildings in towns they claimed to be theirs under the Vance-Owen Plan. "Now we know what H V O stands for," a Serb television newscaster noted: *"Hvala, Vance-Owen* (Thank you, Vance-Owen)." The Bosnian Serb leaders could not conceal their delight that one of their principal war aims, the rupturing of the Muslim-Croat alliance, was being facilitated by outsiders. Serb nationalists had portrayed the Bosnian war from the beginning as a three-way ethnic conflict, and it was finally fitting their description. If the Muslim-Croat fighting persisted, Sarajevo and other multiethnic communities would inevitably crack along ethnic lines, just as the nationalists had predicted.

The HVO forces were soon expelling Muslim residents from towns and villages under Croat control, as Serb nationalists had done during their occupation of Bosnian territory months earlier. Moderate Croats suggested that Croat hard-liners had realized that the Serb nationalists would not be punished for their "ethnic cleansing" campaigns in Bosnia and therefore decided to follow the Serb example. Before long Muslim-led Bosnian government forces, seeing no reward for holding the moral high ground, joined in the criminality and began chasing Croat villagers from areas under Muslim control. The Vance-Owen peace plan for Bosnia was ultimately dropped as a result of the Serb side's failure to accept the proposed territorial division, but the Muslim-Croat fighting it provoked continued throughout 1993 and cost thousands of lives on both sides.

Although he called it an act of betrayal, Bosnian President Alija Izetbegović could not have been entirely surprised by the Croat turnabout, given the history of Croatian claims on Bosnian territory and of Serb-Croat collusion against the Muslims. Croat nationalists had never shared the Bosnian commitment to a state where citizens had rights as individuals, independent of their religion or nationality. Instead, the Croats believed in ethnicity-based citizenship. This was the basis of the state in Croatia, where the government had declared the republic "the national state of the Croatian people." Non-Croats were classified as members of "other nations and minorities," and it was not long before they learned this phrase meant second-class status, even for residents born and raised on Croatian territory.

Croat authorities introduced a new citizenship certificate known as a *domovnica*; it was granted automatically only to people who could prove Croatian ancestry, and it thereby provided a mechanism for discrimination against non-Croats. When *Oslobodjenje* launched a Zagreb-based weekly edition in March 1993 for distribution in Europe, Croatian authorities said they would license the operation only if the director had a *domovnica*. More seriously, refugees from Bosnia received differential treatment on the basis of their nationality. Catholics from Bosnia who declared themselves ethnic Croats were automatically entitled to all refugee benefits, even if they had never set foot in Croatia, and their children were free to attend public school. Bosnian Muslims, by contrast, were routinely denied access to schools and other public institutions, because they were of the wrong religious and national heritage.

Oslobodjenje editor Kemal Kurspahić's eleven-year-old son, Mirza, whom Kemal had sent out of Sarajevo in the fall of 1992, was not allowed to enroll in school in Croatia because as a Muslim he couldn't get a *domovnica*. Gordana Knežević's daughter, Olga, was able to attend classes in Zagreb because the family with whom she was staying told the school authorities that Olga's father was a Croat. But when Gordana visited the school at the end of the year, the teacher told Gordana that she would not be able to certify Olga's attendance unless Gordana provided documents attesting to the girl's Croat ancestry. Gordana and Ivo refused, and Olga got no credit for the school year.

Obituaries

On February 17, 1993, Boris Knežević's eighteen-year-old upstairs neighbor and fellow Guns N' Roses fan, Kemo Merzić, died during fighting on the west side of Sarajevo. Shot in the chest, Kemo lay slumped in a frontline trench for two hours, awake and fully conscious. The gunfire around him was so heavy, however, that he could not be evacuated, and he slowly bled to death. Turning in his final moments to two young Bosnian soldiers at his side, Kemo said, "Which of you is going to be brave enough to go and tell my parents that their only son is dead?" One of the fighters visited Nazif and Fata Merzić the next day with the news.

For days Boris was unable to think of anything else. Sitting alone in his cold apartment, he pondered every hour of his friend's last day, as the visiting fighter had related it. Boris imagined himself in Kemo's place and wondered what had gone through his mind. He pictured the scene, heard the sounds of battle, and felt the pain of the injury. For months he had been keeping a journal of his daily life, in English, and he felt an urge to write about Kemo as well. But Boris couldn't describe his death the way he had other incidents; too many important elements of the story were unknown. When he finally put his thoughts on paper, it was in the form of a short story, with the details filled in as Boris fantasized them.

> As soon he had prepared the gun, he crouched in the trench, took out the sandwich his mother had so carefully wrapped in aluminum foil earlier that day, took a bite, and gave one to each of his comrades.
>
> "What is it, son?" his mother had asked.
>
> "Emergency. A Chetnik offensive in Azići. All have to be there, even those who are on leave, like me."
>
> She had packed him a few sandwiches with the homemade bread she had baked that morning, using their poor reserves of flour, as the bakery hadn't worked for days, and with some tinned meat from the food his father had managed to bring. She cried as they said good-bye, and he left all so suddenly, with tears in his bright blue eyes. She patted his short black hair, and it felt like the fur of a puppy under her hand. She simply said, "Take care of yourself."

Boris said in his story that Kemo had a rifle equipped with a grenade launcher, which was indeed the main antitank weapon used by Bosnian soldiers around Sarajevo. He wrote that Kemo and his fellow soldiers had been assigned to occupy a factory, lay mines around the building, and be prepared to blow it up if they were forced to retreat. He described Kemo as feeling "a swelling in his throat" as he prepared to make the dash to the factory, angry at "the goddamned leadership" for considering him "disposable." Boris told how Kemo broke down a steel door to enter the factory, how he got caught in a gun and grenade battle with Serb soldiers inside and was injured, how he struggled back with his comrades to the trenches where they had started, and how he lay in his trench realizing he was about to die.

In telling the story, Boris switched from third-person to first-person forms, as his own emotions took over. Boris imagined that Kemo (Kemal) thought in his dying moments of his girlfriend, a Serb, who had left Sarajevo for Belgrade at the start of the war.

> Couldn't she have stayed like so many other Serbs and Croats, like Slavko and Vedran and others who fought with him? Why did it have to be her, he thought, but then again if it was someone else's girlfriend, that other person would now be wondering the same

thing, and it had to be someone. Yours is the shortest straw, boy, so it's a stupid question. . . .

"Come on, don't talk crap, you'll be okay," one of the men said, but the man's words had no effect.

You idiot, Kemal thought. But it doesn't matter, I'm not scared at all. Just sad, very sad. There was so much I could have done and wished to do. But anyway it was my choice. I have an uncle in Hrasnica who is the commander of a battalion, and he could have put me anywhere I wanted, away from the front, but I refused when he asked me. All my life I wished to know how it feels to die, except I didn't want it so early.

In a short article he wrote later for *Children's Express*, a news service in the United States distributing stories and interviews by children, Boris described Kemo Merzić as "my best friend and neighbor" and said his death was "the worst thing that happened to me in this war." It stood out as an event that put everything else in perspective. I mentioned to Boris one day that a rocket attack on a building visited regularly by his father had destroyed the office next to the one Ivo used, and that he was lucky not to have been killed himself. "Didn't that make you nervous?" I asked him. I thought Boris was amazingly nonchalant about the incident.

"You don't understand," he said. "It doesn't matter as long as you're still alive."

On his weekly visits home, Kemo had told Boris many stories about close calls on the front line, but none counted in the end, only the story of the day he died. You either survive or you don't. In response to a *Children's Express* question about the "worst thing" about wartime in Sarajevo, Boris wrote with youthful clarity, "The worst thing in war would be death itself. We can live through cold, hunger, lack of electricity, water—but death, no."

Virtually everyone in Sarajevo had someone dear—a friend, a neighbor, a family member—who died during the war. "We live eyeball-to-eyeball with death," Gordana said. Several nights a week someone would knock on her apartment door and hand Gordana a death notice to be published in the newspaper: a piece of paper with a name, the date of death, and a brief prayer or message of farewell. At the *Oslobodjenje* office downtown, soldiers stopped by every day, often with a handful of notices. As a community service the newspaper published a single obituary free of charge for anyone whose death was war-related. Additional notices, signed by other friends or family members, cost the equivalent of about thirty cents each. Typically, two pages of the eight-page newspaper each day were taken up entirely with obituaries. And they were read, just like the news pages. With families and friends in Sarajevo cut off from one another, and with so many people dying, reading the *Oslobodjenje* obituary pages was often the only way to learn who among one's acquaintances had died.

Occasionally the obituaries themselves suggested a story, as in the case of a Sarajevo Serb who died fighting as a soldier in the Bosnian army. The man's wife, a Muslim, announced that her husband had died "defending Bosnia." The man's parents, less convinced of the rightness of the Bosnian army cause, announced in their own notice that their son died "as an innocent victim of this tragic civil war." More often, the *Oslobodjenje* obituaries were simply a sad accounting of family pain:

In painful memory of our beloved brother **FERID (son of MEHO) PILAV.** Dear brother, words cannot express the sadness and the pain that your parting has left in my heart, but as long as I live, your memory will be with me. Forgive me for not having been able to organize your burial as I would have liked, but you were so magnificent that any burial would have been too modest for you. With love, your sister Ferida.

22 December. A week has gone by since **SLOBODAN (son of PETAR BARISIĆ** gave his life while defending his city, at the dawn of his twenty-sixth year. Today, we will all be present at his graveside at the Lav cemetery at 11:00 A.M. Forever bereaved: father Petar, brother Željko, cousins Milan, Duško, Bosko, and Mitar, grandfather Zdravko, and other friends and numerous neighbors.

20 December. A week of intense suffering since the death of our dear **ISMET (son of IBRO) MULAOME-ROVIĆ).** Dear Ismet, It is difficult to accept your absence. Time can do nothing to ease the pain we have felt since your parting. You left behind in our hearts a feeling of emptiness, but we will never lose our cherished memories of your generosity, or of your beloved face, always smiling and radiant. We will love you always. Your family: your wife Senada and daughter Nejira.

We are profoundly sorry to inform family, friends, and neighbors of the death of our beloved son, brother, and husband **ADNAN (son of HAMDO) RUSTEMPASIĆ,** who entered into the kingdom of Heaven on 12 January 1993 in his 31st year as a martyr defending his city. The funeral will take place on 15 January in the Muslim cemetery. The bereaved family.

22 December. Seven days ago, our **ZAIM MUHIĆ** gave his life for Sarajevo and Bosnia. Your wife Emira, your father-in-law Avdo, your mother-in-law Selveta, and your brother-in-law Eno.

Our dear husband, father, and brother **LUBOMIR (son of MILAN) JOKIĆ** was slain by the fire of a murderous sniper on 13 January 1993, in his 46th year. His funeral will take place on 15 January at 11:45 A.M. in the Lav cemetery. His bereaved family: wife Azemina, son Vladimir, daughter Vedrana, mother Ljubica, sister and brothers Jadranka, Vitomir, Aleksandar, as well as countless other loved ones and friends.

To the newspaper's readers, the *Oslobodjenje* obituaries provided an ethnic breakdown of death in Sarajevo, apparent even to those who didn't know the deceased. Slobodan and Lubomir are Serb names; Ferid, Ismet, Adnan, and Zaim were Muslims.

The UNPROFOR Connection

Foreign visitors to besieged Sarajevo were naturally touched by the suffering they saw in the city, and when Sarajevans complained that the world had abandoned them, our uneasiness inevitably deepened. Those of us who came and went regularly did little favors for people, carrying letters in and out, contacting family members outside, or bringing them candles, vitamins, and batteries, to alleviate our own discomfort as much as theirs.

Officials serving with the United Nations Protection Force (UN-PROFOR) in Sarajevo were put in an especially difficult position. While journalists and others who worked alone could offer little more than token assistance, U.N. personnel had the resources, opportunities, and authority to make a big difference in the lives of many Sarajevans, if they were motivated to do so. The policies UNPROFOR officers had to follow in carrying out their humanitarian aid mission sometimes seemed indulgent of the Serb army and insensitive to the Sarajevo population; but, as individuals, the officers could bend the rules and make extra efforts to help people, and many did. As the major personal connection between Sarajevans and the outside world during the darkest months of siege, friendly UNPROFOR officers were warmly regarded. *Oslobodjenje* in particular benefited from special UNPROFOR assistance, as soldiers and officers supplied diesel fuel for the newspaper's generators and facilitated the shipment of newsprint. As a result of this division of roles into private and official capacities, a U.N. official might seem generous one day and cold-hearted the next.

Col. Patrice Sartre was a good example. As commander of the Sarajevo airport in late 1992 and early 1993, the French UNPROFOR officer ordered his troops to catch and turn back Sarajevans trying to cross the airport tarmac to government-held territory on the other side. In line with UNPROFOR policy, he sometimes authorized a share of Sarajevo's humanitarian aid to be diverted to the besieging Serb forces in return for their cooperation in permitting U.N. convoys to pass unhindered through Serb checkpoints around the city. But Colonel Sartre was also one of the UNPROFOR officers most willing to help Sarajevans in need. He became acquainted with *Oslobodjenje* reporters and editors and visited their ruined headquarters on the front line in Nedjarići. Realizing the danger they would be in if Serb forces ever decided to rush the building, Sartre offered to have an armored vehicle ready for their rescue. He helped arrange U.N. press accreditation for Gordana Knežević, enabling her to fly out of Sarajevo on a U.N. aid flight and make a quick trip to New York to pick up a journalism award. After Sartre heard how much *Oslobodjenje* reporter Emir Habul missed his four-year-old daughter, he stopped one day in the town of Fojnica, where the girl was living with her mother and grandparents, took a Polaroid picture of her, and brought the photo back to Habul in Sarajevo.

In November 1992 Sartre threw a party at a downtown Sarajevo restaurant he had rented for the occasion. Hooking up an UNPRO-FOR generator, he turned on all the restaurant lights and had tables set for more than a hundred guests. He donated cases of French wine from his airport stockroom and asked the cook to prepare dinner for everyone who came. "The restaurant was the only sparkling spot in Sarajevo that night," recalled Gordana, who was there with Emir Habul and other *Oslobodjenje* journalists. Sartre sent out a fleet of armored vehicles to collect his invitees, all but a few of whom were local people. Government ministers and Bosnian army officers came, as well as musicians, artists, and other notable citizens. No one accused Sartre of showing poor taste with his display of extravagance in such difficult times; he had reminded Sarajevans of their old lives, and they appreciated it.

Two months later, however, Sartre was a central figure in an incident that plunged UNPROFOR relations with the Bosnian government to one of the lowest points they would reach during the war. UNPROFOR soldiers were taking the deputy Bosnian prime minister, Hakija Turajlić, in a U.N. armored vehicle to meet with a delegation of Turkish aid officials at the airport. At a checkpoint on the way back to Sarajevo, Serb fighters backed by two Serb army tanks halted the vehicle, which was painted white and clearly marked with U.N. insignia. During a confrontation that followed, a Serb soldier shot Turajlić six times at close range, firing into the vehicle over the shoulder of Colonel Sartre, who had positioned himself in front of the open back door. Turajlić died within minutes.

Bosnian government officials were enraged that the U.N. troops had failed to protect Turajlić and even allowed the vehicle door to be opened, enabling the Serb soldiers to see him inside. They were angry at Sartre, who had sent UNPROFOR reinforcements away, thinking it would be better to negotiate with the Serbs than to stand up to them. And they heaped scorn on Gen. Philippe Morillon, a former French Legionnaire who had replaced Gen. Lewis MacKenzie as UNPROFOR commander in Bosnia and was Sartre's superior officer. The former chief of staff to Turajlić wrote a wrathful commentary, calling Morillon an "assassin" for having "handed over our Hakija Turajlić . . . so that he [Morillon] could breathe easier and listen to the Chetniks. . . . This is what kind of man Morillon is," the aide wrote, "[and this is] what his subordinates are like."

Oslobodjenje published the anti-UNPROFOR letter in its entirety, although the paper's writers were reserved in their own commentary on the incident and largely spared Sartre from criticism. They showed similar restraint in their writing about the UNPROFOR troops in Sarajevo throughout the war. Through the U.N. operation the newspaper was tied to the world outside Sarajevo. In the view of the *Oslobodjenje* editors, UNPROFOR was not the enemy. Nothing would be accomplished by attacking UNPROFOR officials, and much could be lost.

Gordana Knežević's ten-day trip to New York was a disorienting journey back in time to a place of peace; the contrast between that world and Sarajevo was so great as to be almost unbearable. On one of her first days outside, Gordana sat in a hotel atrium and stared entranced at the glass ceiling, as if she had never seen skylights or plate windows before. After eight months of shelling in Sarajevo, the sight of all that unbroken glass was beyond her comprehension.

Gordana worried on that trip that if she allowed herself to relish the comforts that surrounded her she might lose focus on her mission, which was to speak for her newspaper and her city abroad. She was afraid to relax, to open her eyes, even to taste the food, thinking it would make returning to Sarajevo too painful. She kept plastic-wrapped sandwiches in her handbag and avoided eating in fancy hotel restaurants. Still, she felt guilty, remembering Ivo and Boris back in their cold, dark flat. In every hotel room she scooped up the little shampoo bottles, matches, and ballpoint pens, and stuffed them in her bags, thinking that, by collecting supplies, she would be helping her family.

Returning turned out to be even worse than she had feared. Sarajevo had suffered a terrible cold snap while she was away, and Ivo and Boris had run completely out of wood. Going into the bathroom, Gordana noticed that the shelves were missing. Ivo had taken them down and burned them. Her cosmetics were piled in a corner on the floor.

8

War, *Oslobodjenje,* and Democracy

With the coming of spring 1993, Sarajevans dared for a few weeks to think that the worst was behind them and that the Geneva negotiations might even lead to peace. Under pressure from his Serbian and Greek allies, Radovan Karadžić finally approved the territorial reorganization of Bosnia proposed by Cyrus Vance and David Owen. The Bosnian government had accepted the plan weeks earlier, and Lord Owen announced that the Karadžić signing on May 2 represented the start of "an irreversible process."

Two weeks later, however, Bosnian Serb voters vetoed the Vance-Owen Plan in a referendum. In Washington the Clinton administration retracted earlier threats to intervene unilaterally in Bosnia, with Secretary of State Warren Christopher characterizing the country as a "morass" into which the U.S. government did not care to step. Vance resigned in frustration. With the external pressure on them removed, the Serb forces around Sarajevo tightened the siege, hoping to get the Bosnian government to accept the old terms of surrender.

The flow of water into the city was cut again, power lines that had been rebuilt were rebombed, and the shelling increased.

Their hopes raised and then dashed, Sarajevans went into the second summer of war more demoralized than ever. Instead of beginning the work of healing and reconstruction, the city slid back into a mean-spirited authoritarianism fueled by anger and despair. The legislative council of the Old Town municipal district decreed that professionals who had left the city during wartime could face criminal charges upon their return. The hoodlum gangs that had rallied to Sarajevo's defense at the beginning of the war turned their attention to profiteering and extortion, and city officials let them get away with it. Intolerance spread, and liberal reformers worried that the Bosnian government was on its way to becoming an undemocratic regime not so different from others in the former Yugoslavia and across Eastern Europe.

The changing political environment presented *Oslobodjenje* with a new challenge. There were disagreements in Sarajevo over what war policies the government should follow, when militancy should give way to negotiation, and how strenuously to fight crime and corruption. By publishing every day of the siege, *Oslobodjenje* had demonstrated its heroic spirit and won international acclaim, but now the newspaper needed to promote and inform a public debate and to defend democratic values, as it had in 1990 and 1991 during the transition from Communism to a multiparty system.

Against this goal, *Oslobodjenje*'s performance was less impressive. The newspaper was generally unquestioning in its coverage of the Bosnian government in the summer of 1993, and it contributed little independent reporting on the deteriorating social and political climate in Sarajevo. Some of the paper's longtime supporters began to question whether *Oslobodjenje* really deserved all the journalism awards it was receiving; within the newspaper disaffected staff members were quick to join in the sniping. Zlatko Dizdarević, the former news desk editor who had long rivaled Kemal Kurspahić and Gordana Knežević for leadership of the paper, confronted the editor in chief one day. "Let's be real, Kemal," he said. "We're not the best newspaper in the world. For the international community, we are a symbol of the situation in Sarajevo, that's all. We're a good movie story."

In fact, the editors never represented their newspaper as the best in the world, and much of the criticism directed against them was unfair. When *Oslobodjenje* had declared its political independence in 1990, Bosnia had been at peace. In the summer of 1993, the country was at war, Sarajevo was under daily assault, and journalists were no longer sure of the line between independence and disloyalty. It would not have been an easy determination for any newspaper to make, and *Oslobodjenje* had the added burden of having labored for nearly fifty years under Communist rule. The journalists had just begun to learn new professional habits and standards when the war began, and the conditions of life under siege had set them back. They were exhausted, afraid, bitter, and confused.

"I'm losing my ability to analyze," Gordana Knežević had told me when I visited Sarajevo in June 1992. "You need a cool head for that, and I don't have it anymore." Twelve months later war had dulled her thinking and that of her colleagues all the more.

Keeping *Oslobodjenje* going from one day to the next was chal-

Oslobodjenje's wartime editorial board stands outside the ruins of the newspaper's headquarters. From left: Midhat Plivčić, Feto Ramović, Muhammed Džemidzić, Zlatko Dizdarević, Rasim Ćerimagić, Gordana Knežević, Kemal Kurspahić, Emir Hrustanović, and Fahro Memić.   (*OSLOBODJENJE*)

lenge enough. August 30, 1993, would be the fiftieth anniversary of the newspaper's founding. The one commitment shared by everyone on the staff was to reach the anniversary with the paper's wartime publication record unbroken. Beyond that their priorities were to stay alive themselves and to keep their families together. For a vibrant and independent press to flourish in Sarajevo, the war would have to end.

Thugs at Large

One warm afternoon in July 1993, I watched as a shiny black Mercedes jerked to a stop next to the open-air market on Marshal Tito Street. The car was immediately surrounded by a half dozen young men. The driver, a dark-haired man in Ray-Ban sunglasses and a gray T-shirt, slowly got out of the Mercedes and walked around to open the trunk. Inside were three big burlap sacks, each filled with 500-gram (about one-pound) bags of coffee beans. The driver counted out several bags for each of the men gathered around him, took a stack of German marks in return, got back in his car, and drove off.

The coffee came from traders on the Serb-controlled side of Sarajevo. The man with the Mercedes had arranged for it to be smuggled across the front lines by paying off both Serb and Bosnian army commanders. He then sold the coffee at a huge profit to the young men on the sidewalk, who in turn resold it in the market—for about $33 a pound. With the exception of humanitarian aid items, virtually everything on sale in besieged Sarajevo arrived in this manner, under the eyes of Bosnian army soldiers all along the way. One consequence of the Serb encirclement of Sarajevo was that the city's frontline defenders enjoyed almost total control over its black market economy, and local military commanders became rich as war profiteers. Because several of them had been involved in illegal activities before the war, they brought expertise to their new careers. As the siege of Sarajevo dragged on, a powerful criminal class emerged in the city, largely supplanting the old business elite.

Juka Prazina, the former loan shark and repossession man who led his own militia force, controlled trade in the Stup area on the west end of Sarajevo until he ran afoul of other Bosnian army units and fled the city. With Prazina gone, much of Sarajevo's underground economy was left in the hands of Ramiz "Ćelo" (or "Baldy") Delalić and Mušan "Caco" Topalović, the commanders of the Ninth and

Tenth Mountain Brigades of the Bosnian army. Their units controlled front lines all along the south side of Sarajevo, a hilly area where clashes between Serb and Bosnian fighters were frequent and fierce but where there was also considerable smuggling.

Delalić and Topalović had both joined the Muslim Green Berets militia at the beginning of the war and, like Juka Prazina, had been given command of their own army brigades as reward for their strong leadership and their bravery in frontline fighting. As did Prazina, however, both men had connections to Sarajevo's prewar underworld, and both used their army positions to enrich themselves through smuggling and other illicit activities. Ćelo Delalić allegedly ran a prostitution ring. Caco Topalović's specialty was banditry. In the portion of Sarajevo they controlled, Caco's fighters routinely stopped U.N. officers, aid workers, and foreign journalists and robbed them at gunpoint of their flak jackets, fuel, cash, and cameras.

Because the Bosnian government depended on Ćelo's and Caco's contributions to the defense of Sarajevo, city authorities tolerated their operations even when their criminal behavior tainted Sarajevo's image as a city of goodwill and tolerance. Both commanders were associated with incidents of anti-Serb violence and abuse. Ćelo publicly boasted of having been one of the gunmen who shot at the Serb wedding parade in the Baščaršija neighborhood on referendum day. After the war began he was known for personally arresting and beating up any Sarajevo Serb he suspected of collaborating with the Serb nationalist army. Caco's men, meanwhile, were implicated in the murders of at least three Serb civilians in the Old Town district during wartime. In another instance of Caco's vigilante terrorism, his soldiers shot their way into the studios of Sarajevo's Radio M and blew up the sound equipment. The provocation: The station's disc jockeys had included some Serbian folk songs in the mix of music they played. "During the war I have endured all kinds of danger, including snipers and shelling, but I have never been so afraid as I was last night," said station director Emina Ibrić, a Muslim, the morning after the attack.

The actions of the Ninth and Tenth Mountain Brigades in the summer of 1993 contributed to a widespread sense of anarchy in Sarajevo that lasted until Interior Ministry troops arrested the renegade commanders in October. The government's inability or unwillingness to control Ćelo and Caco in the meantime angered law-abiding citizens. *Oslobodjenje*'s reluctance to highlight their criminal activity, though understandable, undermined the newspaper's reputation as an independent journal committed to the defense of democracy.

Especially scandalous was Caco's practice of rounding up men on the streets of downtown Sarajevo and trucking them off to dig trenches along the front lines, supposedly to keep Caco's soldiers free and fit for combat. Caco told a local journalist that he had ordered the operation after coming to Sarajevo one day with a wounded soldier and finding the cafés full of able-bodied young men who because of government connections (or bribes) had been exempted from soldiering. For several weeks in the summer of 1993, Caco's "Dig for Victory!" roundups were so frequent that many Sarajevo men were loath to set foot downtown for fear of being caught. Only those cafés whose owners paid protection money were safe from the raiders.

Caco's men were more likely to dragoon Serbs than Muslims, but any man could be taken to dig. Caco's favorite targets were Sarajevo artists and intellectuals, whom he regarded as soft and cowardly. A mediocre musician himself, Caco was apparently anxious to humiliate men whose talents were more notable than his own. One of the first men his soldiers sent to the hills was Vedran Smajlović, the Sarajevo Opera cellist who had honored the victims of the Vasa Miskin bombing by playing an adagio at the site of the massacre each afternoon for twenty-two consecutive days. The performance caught the attention of the world, but Caco Topalović decided that Smajlović, a Muslim, had not served his country adequately, and he forced him to dig trenches for seven weeks within shooting range of Serb snipers.

On Saturday, July 3, two *Oslobodjenje* journalists were grabbed. Vedo Spahović, a thirty-six-year-old general assignment reporter (and a Muslim), was walking to the newspaper's downtown office when he was stopped by a toothless man in a Bosnian army uniform. The man checked Spahović's press card and identity papers, then told him to join about a dozen other men in the back of a truck parked about twenty yards away. As Spahović was climbing into the truckbed, he noticed that the toothless soldier had gotten into an argument with another man in the street. When the man refused the soldier's order to get into the truck, the soldier lowered his rifle and shot the man in the foot, then hit him in the chin with the rifle butt, sending the man sprawling to the ground. The men who came after him were more obedient.

Tomo Počanić, a semiretired sportswriter who went to the *Oslobodjenje* office mainly to play chess with his old friend Vlado Mrkić, was nabbed at the same spot about a half hour after Spahović was taken. A young soldier approached the white-haired Počanić as he came walking down the street and asked his age. "Fifty-eight," Počanić answered.

"You'll do," the soldier said, "move over there." He motioned toward a group of men who were being held at gunpoint nearby.

"I knew immediately what was going to happen," Počanić, a Croat, recalled later. "If they had just come to my house and told me I had to make my digging contribution," he said, "I would have accepted it and gone without complaint. But as it was, I had no way to get word to my wife that I had been taken, and she worried easily." Počanić and the others in his group were driven to Caco's brigade headquarters, where he ran into Spahović. The men were marched straight up a hill to a frontline position, handed shovels, and ordered to dig.

The next day Spahović and Počanić managed to send a letter out with a soldier, notifying *Oslobodjenje* colleagues that they were on Trebević Mountain, southeast of Sarajevo. Witnesses to their abduction had by then already reported to the newspaper management. Telephones were not working in Sarajevo at the time, so Vlado Mrkić went to Počanić's apartment to tell his wife what had happened to him. *Oslobodjenje* reporter Dželiana Pećanin, who was a neighbor to Spahović and often rode to work with him, brought the news of his

Veteran reporters Vlado Mrkić (l.), a Serb, and Tomo Počanić (r.), a Croat, met at the *Oslobodjenje* office every day to play chess.   (TOM GJELTEN)

kidnapping to Spahović's nieces, who had been staying with him since their mother, his sister, was killed by a mortar shell.

The *Oslobodjenje* journalists were freed on July 8, after five days of frontline duty, a far shorter spell than most diggers had to endure. They walked back to the center of the city, exhausted and filthy, in the same clothes they had been wearing when they were picked up. Of the two Počanić was the less shaken by the experience. He had maintained his trademark sense of humor on the mountain, and his good-natured teasing had helped to lift Spahović's spirits through the most frightening moments. After he returned Počanić was philosophical about the experience. "It's like everything else in life," he said. "It happens, and then it's over." A Croat in a mostly Muslim city, Počanić did not let his faith in the Bosnian ideal of tolerance and civility be diminished by the rough treatment he had received from Bosnian army soldiers. "I support the participation of all Sarajevans [in the war effort]," he told me, "in any way they can. I cannot drive a tank or shoot," he said, "but I can dig, so that's what I should do."

Vedo Spahović felt less charitable. From the mountain he headed directly to the downtown *Oslobodjenje* office, where he sat in a daze for several hours, talking about his ordeal to anyone who would listen. "We were digging on the forward line, about fifty meters from the Chetnik [Serb] positions," he said. "Caco's soldiers were *behind* us." Spahović said he was terrified constantly and ate only twice during the entire period. At night his group of diggers slept on a hard floor in an unfinished house with no roof. Each man was given a blanket, but, because they had only light street clothes to wear, they shivered all night long.

The five days on the mountain were the most horrifying Spahović had experienced during the war. But, because his suffering came at the hands of Muslims like himself, its major effect was to confuse his previously sharp moral understanding of the conflict. He no longer saw the line that divided victims from aggressors as running neatly around the perimeter of his city; for him it now also existed inside Sarajevo. "Now," Spahović told me, "I would say the main victims in this war are simply the common people." Among those digging alongside him in the Trebević trenches was a sixteen-year-old boy whose parents had both been killed by shelling. The boy had been living with his grandmother and was grabbed by Caco's soldiers on his way to fetch water.

Unreported News

The realization that there were genuine villains on the Bosnian side
as well as among the Serb nationalist forces was one of the key developments in Sarajevo in the summer of 1993. But the story went
largely untold in the pages of *Oslobodjenje*. A brief mention of Caco's
June 7 attack on Radio M was buried inside the paper, and the perpetrators were not identified as Caco's soldiers. Ćelo's well-docu-
mented criminal activity—of concern to Sarajevo police commanders
and to officials at the Bosnian Interior Ministry—was not laid out for
Oslobodjenje readers to consider. And, for all they had to say about
their time on Trebević, neither Vedo Spahović nor Tomo Počanić
wrote one word about their experiences. Caco's roundups were not
chronicled in *Oslobodjenje*. The paper limited itself to quoting vaguely
worded government communiqués that shed little light on what was
really happening in the city.

The immediate reason for the silence was a concern that Caco and
Ćelo might order reprisals against *Oslobodjenje*, or anyone who col-
laborated with it. Kemal Kurspahić had not wanted the abduction of
Spahović and Počanić reported because he and other editors were
working through their Old Town connections to get the reporters released, an effort that ultimately paid off. With respect to other cases,
it was hard to find people willing to speak openly and knowledge-
ably about abusive or corrupt military commanders. When the cellist
Vedran Smajlović was freed on July 11, after forty-seven days in the
trenches, he spent more than an hour telling Gordana Knežević everything he knew about Caco's digging operation, but he insisted
that no article be written.

Similarly, an actor named Zoran Besić ran into *Oslobodjenje* reporter Djuro Kozar one day and told him about being dragged off a
theater stage and sent to dig. But when Kozar referred to the incident
in an article, Besić demanded that the newspaper publish a note saying the conversation with Kozar had never taken place. Not wanting
to get Besić in trouble, Kurspahić agreed to the retraction. "I'm not
surprised no one wants to be quoted," he said. "If the Bosnian army
high command and the Bosnian police can't control these guys, talking about them could put somebody's life in danger."

At a July editorial board meeting, Kurspahić proposed the prepa-
ration of a special two-page spread in *Oslobodjenje* on "crime and
public safety" in Sarajevo. Other editors weren't convinced the project was a good idea, however, and it was never carried out. Gordana

Knežević in particular was reluctant. The extent of her cautiousness became apparent one day when an American newspaper reporter had his car broken into and his flak jacket stolen outside the *Oslobodjenje* offices by uniformed men, presumably from Caco's brigade. Upset by the incident, Gordana sent Dželiana Pećanin to the local police station for a statement, thinking it could be the basis for a news story. The police refused to comment, however, and Gordana concluded that *Oslobodjenje* shouldn't say anything either.

"If we printed that robbery story and someone got annoyed with it," she explained, "they could come up to *Oslobodjenje* and finish the job. We would need armed guards to run a story like that." The attack on Radio M had shown what a media enterprise could expect if it made Caco Topalović angry. At one of the editorial board meetings where *Oslobodjenje*'s coverage of potentially controversial stories was discussed, Gordana suggested that "staying alive" should be the paper's guiding editorial policy. She readily conceded that her insecurity exceeded that of her boss. "There is a difference between Kemal and me on this," she told me. "Kemal is ready to be taken to dig. I'm not." As a Serb in Sarajevo, Knežević may have been especially sensitive to the threat of vindictive attacks from war-crazed fighters.

Oslobodjenje's hesitation to report on Caco and Ćelo's activities stemmed also from a fear of their political clout. In the Old Town district, where they were headquartered, the men had a near-cult following. Like good warlords they had spread the benefits of their acquired wealth around the neighborhood, where Muslims made up 80 percent of the population in 1991 and an even greater share during wartime. The residents admired Caco and Ćelo for the bravery they had shown in battle; Serb gunners regularly targeted the neighborhood because of its concentration of Muslim residents. "The defense lines of our district are the firmest in the city because of those two men," Old Town Municipal Council President Selim Hadžibajrić told me in August 1993.

The Old Town district was the heart and soul of Muslim Sarajevo and the stronghold of the Muslim SDA party, which controlled the Bosnian government. Hadžibajrić and other Old Town politicians were from the hard-line nationalist wing of the party and notably unsupportive of *Oslobodjenje* and other institutions associated with the model of a secular, multiethnic Bosnian state. But challenging the Old Town political establishment by reporting on Caco and Ćelo's misdeeds would have meant attacking part of the government's power base, and in the summer of 1993 *Oslobodjenje* was not ready to do that.

The Official Line

Since the Serb nationalists had launched their drive to partition Bosnia in early 1992, *Oslobodjenje* had been supportive of the Bosnian government, largely forgoing the role of an opposition newspaper. This was a turnabout from the days when Kemal Kurspahić had taken the lead among newspaper editors in Yugoslavia in the move to challenge state authority. In June 1990 *Oslobodjenje* had told its readers that it was assuming "a critical stand toward the [Communist] Party and power." A year later the newspaper took Bosnia's first non-Communist government to court in a bold move to preserve its political independence. In 1992 and 1993 Kurspahić and other editors characterized their paper's position simply as "pro-Bosnia," justifying their support for the Bosnian government with the argument that the Serb nationalist drive to divide the country meant that all who believed in a united Bosnia should join in its defense.

The paper generally accepted government analyses of the military conflict in Bosnia, even when the claims of victory were inflated and the denials of setback disingenuous. When fighting broke out in central Bosnia between the Muslim-dominated Bosnian army and the Croat militia forces, *Oslobodjenje* consistently characterized the army's actions as justified and Croat moves as aggressive, to the dismay of Croat leaders in Sarajevo, who had hoped the paper would take a more evenhanded approach. The newspaper was not subject to government censorship, but there was no need for it, because *Oslobodjenje* editors rarely printed war-related news that came from unofficial sources, even when they knew it to be accurate. "There is a military brain," Gordana Knežević said. "We don't know what could be damaging or dangerous, so under these war circumstances, we are very cautious about what we publish."

Oslobodjenje was not alone in its move from opposing the Bosnian government in peacetime to supporting it in wartime. The Social Democratic Party (the reformed Communists) had led the opposition in Bosnia to all ethnically oriented parties, including the Muslim SDA, but once the war began it swung solidly in line, even to the point of joining the SDA-dominated government.

Still, *Oslobodjenje*'s pro-government slant was controversial. Muhammed Filipović, a university philosophy professor who cofounded the Muslim party in 1990 only to denounce it a few months later as too nationalist, complained about the paper's unquestioning perspective even while contributing to its opinion page. I was in the *Oslobodjenje* offices one day when Professor Filipović, a tall, slender man in his seventies who went everywhere dressed in a suit and tie and wearing a straw hat, dropped off one of his commentaries. He customarily criticized his old colleagues in the Muslim party for their inattentiveness to the interests of non-Muslims in Sarajevo.

"Give this to Gordana," Filipović said, handing the typewritten article to the receptionist. "And tell her not to pass it through political control!" Gordana, who had admired Filipović since the days when she had studied philosophy under him at Sarajevo University, entered the room just in time to hear his comment and politely objected. "Oh, come on," Filipović snapped. "Everyone knows you are a government publication."

Oslobodjenje's detractors pointed, for example, to the numerous interviews with government ministers that ran unedited in the paper's wartime pages. One of the most unjustified on journalistic merits was with Rusmir Mahmutćehajić, the government's minister of energy; it was published in two parts on consecutive days, taking up an entire page each day. Among those who criticized such fawning treatment of government officials was Zdravko Grebo, the founder of Radio Zid, known in Sarajevo for its irreverence. Grebo had been close friends with Gordana and Ivo Knežević for years and spent many long evenings with them during wartime, but he still complained about *Oslobodjenje*. "They were better before the war," Grebo told me. "I regard them now as a loyal state newspaper."

Sarajevans who considered *Oslobodjenje* too cozy with the government had gotten fuel for their accusation in March 1993, when the Bosnian presidency named Ivo Knežević as minister of information, although the circumstances of his selection made the appointment less controversial than might have been expected. As a Social Democrat and an ethnic Croat, Ivo balanced the Muslim SDA members who dominated the cabinet, but for the same reason he had little power. Major political strategy decisions would be made without his input, even when they concerned media questions. When the government appointed a new general director at Radio-Television Sarajevo, Ivo heard about it on the evening news with everyone else.

The Burden of a Communist Past

A key difference between *Oslobodjenje* and such media enterprises as Zdravko Grebo's Radio Zid or *B-H Dani* (Bosnia-Herzegovina Days), a lively newsmagazine that made its debut in wartime, was that *Oslobodjenje* had for forty-seven of its fifty years been under the control of the Communist Party in Bosnia. While the newspaper staff had unanimously rejected Communist ideology and were genuinely committed to the establishment of democracy and a free press in Bosnia, some patterns of thinking from the era of Communist rule were inevitably carried over into the post-Communist period. When combined with feelings of patriotism and practical considerations of security and survival, these old habits made the demonstration of political independence a more complicated exercise for *Oslobodjenje* in wartime Sarajevo than it otherwise would have been.

During the Communist period *Oslobodjenje* had taken its cues from its Party bosses, who directed news coverage with the Party's political agenda firmly in mind. Independent, open-ended reporting was not encouraged, because of the danger that it might uncover information or attitudes that did not fit "the Party line." The *Oslobodjenje* staff rejected much of this disposition in the transition to democracy, but not all of it. Some editors continued to argue that the newspaper should have a single political line, as opposed to the more freewheeling approach characteristic of Western newspapers. The difference under democracy was that, rather than the Party, the senior editors, assembled as the editorial board, would determine the paper's political line. The occasions that called for such consensus were at first relatively infrequent, and the principle was on its way to being abandoned in the post-Communist period. But it reappeared under wartime conditions and became increasingly important. At *Oslobodjenje* improper analysis was considered more egregious than an error of fact.

Consistent with this idea was the emphasis put on commentary over straight news stories. Of the fifty-six editorial staff members in wartime, seven were full-time columnists. In a typical eight-page wartime issue, *Oslobodjenje* carried four or more commentaries. The "In Focus" column ran on the front page. All of page 2 was devoted to opinion pieces, with the left-hand column given over each day to one of the paper's staff commentators. Other opinion articles, by staff reporters, editors, or guest writers, took up the rest of page 2 and were sprinkled through the remaining pages. With two or three pages devoted to obituaries each day, the space available for straight news was severely restricted.

The value attached to opinion writing in Sarajevo was evident in awards the Bosnian journalists' association bestowed on the *Oslobodjenje* staff in 1993. Vlado Mrkić, one of the few veteran *Oslobodjenje* journalists who still went out and talked to people, wrote down what they said, described what he saw, and refrained from offering his opinions, was named "best writer," as though his work were noted primarily for its aesthetic merit. The 1993 award for "best journalist" went to Gojko Berić, a columnist who did no reporting at all. A fastidious and demanding man before the war, Berić couldn't handle the terror, chaos, and unpredictability of Sarajevo under siege. He closed himself in his apartment in April 1992 and did not come out again for more than a year. But he wrote lucid commentaries, and at *Oslobodjenje* that ranked higher than stories based on enterprising footwork.

As editor Kemal Kurspahić had taken an important step toward freer expression by promoting a diversified "author journalism" in place of the single (unsigned) Party viewpoint that the paper had presented during the Communist period. "In Focus" was written by someone different every day. But the adherence to a single line was still evident: One stricture set by the editorial board was that the conflict in Bosnia should never be characterized in commentary as a "civil war" for which all sides were to blame. On three occasions *Oslobodjenje* desk editors killed columns by staff commentator Slavko Šantić when he implied such a view.

The tradition of holding to an agreed editorial line partly explained the newspaper's cautiousness. The editors did not look to the ruling Muslim party for guidance, and they insisted that they had not surrendered their independence. But the newspaper was allied with the government in wartime, and the editors were reluctant to challenge it without a good reason. With Sarajevo under daily assault and Bosnian statehood in jeopardy, that reason was not often apparent.

Confronting state authority had been easier in 1990 and 1991. When *Oslobodjenje* broke its ties to the League of Communists, the need for democratic reform was already indisputable. A year later, when the newspaper stood up to the ethnic parties who controlled the government and wanted to take control of the media, the issue was similarly clear: *Oslobodjenje* was defending its professional integrity. The situation in Sarajevo in 1993 was far murkier; it was not always obvious where and when the newspaper should take a politically independent stand.

Reporting the Caco/Ćelo business forthrightly could have led the newspaper into the ongoing political battle in Sarajevo between the Muslim nationalists based in the Old Town and Center municipal districts (majority Muslim) and the secularists whose constituency was in the suburban New Town and New Sarajevo districts, where Serbs and Croats and residents of mixed ancestry made up more than half of the population. *Oslobodjenje* reporters and editors were clearly part of the latter group, but they were unsure that wading into the middle of this struggle was smart under the circumstances, and the editorial board decided against it.

The paper was similarly hesitant in its coverage of a debate in the summer of 1993 over the negotiating stance the government should take in Geneva, given the Serb nationalists' rejection of the Vance-Owen Plan. In June, Slobodan Milošević and Franjo Tudjman presented a new proposal for dividing Bosnia, with the Serbs and Croats each getting their own minirepublic and the Muslims and anational "Bosnians" squeezed into a tiny landlocked state in the middle. The proposal represented everything the Bosnian government had opposed from the start, but it was backed by international mediators David Owen and Thorvald Stoltenberg, a Norwegian diplomat who had replaced Cyrus Vance. Bosnian President Alija Izetbegović seemed unsure what to do. In Sarajevo the population was exhausted, and some people were clamoring for peace at any price. "Sign, Alija, even if it's only for your backyard!" was the graffiti written on a building wall near the presidency headquarters.

When Gordana Knežević visited her contacts at the presidency, she found them despairing of Izetbegović's leadership. "I don't know what Alija stands for," Vice President Ejup Ganić told her. "The boat is drifting on the sea," another Izetbegović adviser said, "and nobody is manning the tiller."

Gordana chose not to write about those conversations, however. She and other *Oslobodjenje* editors felt that calling attention to Izetbegović's indecisiveness would serve no obvious purpose except to undermine the government. For a news organization to provoke its government simply for the sake of being adversarial might have been considered normal in an American or Western European newspaper, but *Oslobodjenje* political editor Rasim Ćerimagić told me he considered such a tendency "yellow journalism." He viewed Radio Zid and *B-H Dani* disdainfully because they were politically unfocused.

"These media have independent journalists," Ćerimagić said, "but there's no editorial body that gives them direction. People here are getting confused between media freedom and media anarchy."

Oslobodjenje journalists were aware that their editorial philosophy bore traces of Communist-era thinking, and they freely acknowledged that their paper did not yet meet the professional standards of Western European or American newspapers. "Between journalism in Romania and journalism in France or Britain," Gordana told me, "we're about in the middle, which is where we've always been." In this regard the paper suffered simply from inexperience with Western journalistic style. The editors knew they should publish more news based on their own reporting, and they did when they could. In November 1993 reporter Emir Habul wrote honestly of the unprovoked murder of two Franciscan priests by Bosnian army soldiers near the central Bosnian town of Fojnica, where he was living at the time. UNPROFOR correspondents Vladimir Štaka and Džeilana Pećanin were similarly diligent. If a U.N. press officer announced that the Bosnian army had launched an offensive, violated a ceasefire, or attacked civilians, Štaka or Pećanin reported exactly what the spokesman said, without regard for whether the Bosnian army press center was presenting a conflicting version of the events.

One of the major obstacles in *Oslobodjenje*'s evolution as an independent newspaper, in fact, was a lack of understanding and support from the Bosnian government. Government officials clung even more stubbornly than *Oslobodjenje* editors to the idea that the paper should express only a "correct" interpretation of the news. At a media forum organized in June 1993 by Information Minister Ivo Knežević, a Sarajevo police commander criticized *Oslobodjenje* for quoting one cabinet minister making a derogatory comment about UNPROFOR and a second minister whose words were more diplomatic without explaining to the readers which of the two was speaking "for Bosnia."

"The problem of who represents Bosnia," Editor Kurspahić responded, "is not for the media to resolve. We are not going to censor public statements. If there are things that should not be said, that's for you to decide, not us." In the Communist period *Oslobodjenje* editors would have followed Party instructions and known whom to quote and whom to ignore. The police commander and other government officials who thought like him were nostalgic for the political orderliness of that time and expected *Oslobodjenje* to stick to a "Party line" model even in the absence of Party mentors.

Oslobodjenje's development as an open and independent newspaper in the Western tradition had been halted, and perhaps even reversed by the war. The staff's commitment to a Western journalistic ideal remained, but for the moment other aims had a higher priority.

Surviving

While its critics saw *Oslobodjenje* as overly deferential to the Bosnian government, most of the editors believed they operated near the maximum practical limits of their independence, given the circumstances. The staff regularly complained that government officials seemed hostile to them and distrustful of their intentions. Although the paper supported the government, it was not under the government's direct control as it had been in the Communist period, and as its counterparts *Vjesnik* and *Politika* in Zagreb and Belgrade still were. *Oslobodjenje* editors suspected that top government officials in Sarajevo resented their independence, modest though it was.

"They would like to call up and say, 'We'd like a column attacking Lord Owen tomorrow,' " Gordana explained. "And then they'd want to open the paper the next day and find it. That's the way it was with *Oslobodjenje* in the Communist days." Alija Izetbegović and other top Bosnian leaders were "cool" toward the newspaper, in Gordana's view, not bothering to keep them informed of presidency events or securing a place for them on official trips, as the government did for Sarajevo television reporters. Information Minister Ivo Knežević obviously had good relations with the paper, but he did not have enough power to make a difference.

In April 1993 the government took *Oslobodjenje* off its list of "priority" diesel users, meaning it would no longer get a share of the limited government fuel stocks. The move nearly killed the paper. For most of the summer, the flow of electricity was suspended in Sarajevo, and *Oslobodjenje* relied heavily on its own diesel-fueled generators to power printing presses, computers, work lights, televisions, and the ham radio. With its two automobiles, the paper needed 100–120 liters of diesel a day to continue minimum operation.

The UNPROFOR troops were one source. Gordana went to the headquarters of an Egyptian U.N. battalion in Sarajevo, hoping that the rudimentary Arabic she had picked up while working in Cairo would impress them enough to inspire their charity. The battalion commander gave her a hundred liters and told her to come back the next day for another fifty. Other UNPROFOR officers also chipped in with regular diesel deliveries. Still, there wasn't enough. The newspaper was able to continue publishing only because it had a cash reserve with which it could buy diesel on the Sarajevo black market at a price of $10 to $15 a liter. The money came from international awards the paper had won for its perseverance in publishing. During one four-week period that summer, the *Oslobodjenje* manager spent about $20,000 in prize money on black market diesel, with most of the money going into the pockets of Ukrainian U.N. soldiers, who were known in Sarajevo as the most reliable diesel suppliers.

The newspaper's concern about its diesel supply was a factor in the editors' decision to run the lengthy interview with Energy Minister Rusmir Mahmutčehajić in July 1993. The editors were willing to compromise their independence a bit and court government favor if doing so meant that they could continue publishing, day after day. Virtually no objective stood higher. This was another difference between *Oslobodjenje* and *B-H Dani* or Radio Zid: The latter two were more willing to take risks. Radio Zid was forced off the air on several occasions in the summer of 1993 when it lost its electricity supply, and *B-H Dani* published only irregularly. With just a few weeks to go until the fiftieth anniversary of its debut, *Oslobodjenje* was determined to avoid any such interruptions.

In the view of its editors, the newspaper stood on its history and had no need to prove itself. Put on the defensive by those who said *Oslobodjenje* wasn't very inspiring in its content, the staff could argue that it was good enough for Sarajevo readers to snap up the 3,000 or 4,000 copies distributed each day as soon as they hit the streets. Many who couldn't find a copy to buy would cluster tightly around a billboard on Filipa Kljajića Street, where a copy of *Oslobodjenje* was posted each day for passersby to read.

With its multiethnic staff, *Oslobodjenje* made a political statement in wartime Sarajevo simply by its continued existence. It defied nationalists on all sides, inside as well as outside Sarajevo. Although it published no exposés on Caco and Ćelo's criminal activities in the Old Town district, *Oslobodjenje* still made enemies among its Muslim politician-defenders. Selim Hadžibajrić, the district council president, criticized the newspaper for employing too many Serbs and Croats and "not defending Muslim interests." By continuing to publish every day, *Oslobodjenje* defied its detractors, regardless of the slant of its reporting and commentary, and the editors concluded it would be counterproductive to provoke the ruling party further.

Personal Stakes

On a masonry wall in the center of downtown Sarajevo, a graffitist
with a can of red paint tagged the city, in English, QUARTER OF
CONSTANT PAIN. Around the corner, in the same spray-painted
red lettering, was the kicker: OVDJE NIKO NIJE NORMALAN (Here
Nobody Is Normal).

Sarajevo under siege could not be understood in conventional
terms. A modern European city had been transformed into a great
prison, a place of torture and deprivation from which there was no
escape and where the future was a darkened haze. With each passing
month hope and sanity were harder to sustain. Collective work and
activity grew more perfunctory, as Sarajevans were caught up in
their private anxieties. *Oslobodjenje* became less a group operation
and more an enterprise of disconnected individuals. What may have
appeared to be professional or philosophical disagreement among
staff members was often the consequence instead of their varying experience of the war at a personal level.

For Vlado Mrkić, a turning point was the broadcast by Channel S,
the Serb nationalists' television station in Pale, in which the announcer denounced him by name as an "ex-Serb" and "Alija's servant" and questioned whether "Mother Serbia" should continue to
harbor his wife and sons. Mrkić was so upset by the threats that he
would barely speak to anyone at *Oslobodjenje* afterward. He was already irritated by the increasing demands from his editors that he
take a more explicit political stand in his writing, and after the Serb
nationalists attacked him, Mrkić felt alienated from everyone and
grumpier than ever.

He continued to show up at *Oslobodjenje*, but only to play chess.
He slipped quietly into the office, always wearing the same rumpled
black jacket, glanced around glumly, and sat down to arrange the
chessmen. "Where's that dirty Catholic?" he would mutter, referring
to his Croat friend Tomo Počanić. If Počanić were not available,
Mrkić played someone else, though reluctantly. Počanić, who had
covered chess tournaments in Yugoslavia as a sportswriter, was one
of the few men around the newspaper who could beat Mrkić regularly, and they played nearly every day, often drawing a little crowd.
After several games, played mostly in silence, Mrkić would get up
and leave, without saying good-bye to anyone but his chess partners.

When Mrkić quit writing for *Oslobodjenje,* the newspaper became
less interesting to read. Mrkić contributed real-life stories rather than

polemics, and he consequently saw human suffering everywhere he looked, without affixing good or evil labels to his characters. "In the reportage of Vlado Mrkić," a Sarajevo critic wrote, "one hears the voices of those people whose misfortune it was to have history play with them against their wishes."

Mrkić was not one to complain publicly about his troubles in Sarajevo, but he agreed to sit down with me and an interpreter one day after I helped him make contact with his wife in Belgrade via a satellite telephone. Mrkić told me he was only taking a "time out" from his *Oslobodjenje* writing. "I needed a break to solve some of my family problems," he said, although he did not know when he would return to work. "I'm exhausted," he explained. "I've written about everything in Sarajevo I can think to write about. After a while, all death looks the same. There's nothing more to say. The words are worn out."

A local journalist came over to greet Mrkić and offered him a cigarette. Mrkić didn't smoke, but he took two cigarettes from the pack and put them in his shirt pocket. With two daughters to support and virtually no income, Mrkić had become frugal. The frown on his pale, stubbled face was the mark of a troubled man. The summer was going badly, and he was feeling isolated. Having chosen to remain in Sarajevo, Mrkić worried that it could become a Muslim city in which he would have no place. "I know," he said, "that if a 'Muslim' state is made here—a state for which Muslims have died—I'll probably have to give up my apartment in Baščaršija. But I don't want to be ordered to leave," he said. "Where can I go? Now I can't go to the other side either. This is my personal drama."

Mrkić had been employed by *Oslobodjenje* for twenty-six years, but, with the hardening tone in the paper, he felt his contribution was not appreciated as it had been in the past. Although he was still popular among most readers, some Sarajevans accused Mrkić of obscuring the true nature of the Bosnian war by treating everyone as a victim, a charge he considered unfair. "I know who the aggressor is," he said, arguing that his selection of people to profile left no doubt as to who was suffering most. "But after telling their stories," Mrkić said, "I don't then say, 'So you see, this is how Serbs kill Muslims, or this is how Muslims kill Croats.' I write objectively, but for many people, that is not enough." Mrkić told me he was no longer encouraged to write stories about Serbs being attacked in Sarajevo, such as he had during the first year of the war. The realization depressed him, as did his own diminishing ability to be moved by the tragedies around him. "All of us," he said, "have begun to leave our principles behind. War has destroyed everything in us."

Gordana Knežević was similarly disheartened. She too foresaw that she and her husband could come under pressure to turn their apartment over to Muslims who had been displaced from their own homes by the Serb army, and the thought terrified her. But Gordana always focused on the larger political context: She felt that the Bosnian government, though controlled by the Muslim national party, was still the best hope for those who believed in a pluralist Bosnia. Gordana's great worry was that the international mediators and Western diplomats would persuade the Bosnian government to accept the Milošević-Tudjman partition proposal, which would have meant the establishment of a Muslim republic in Bosnia with Sarajevo as its capital. She advocated an uncompromising line in the Geneva talks. In an "In Focus" commentary in July 1993, Gordana scolded those war-weary Sarajevans who were ready to surrender to the Serb demands: "Our tiresome daily worries about survival," she wrote, "are bringing us to a collective memory loss. Sarajevans are forgetting who put us under siege and whom we are still fighting." Negotiations over partition, she argued, "have been tried already and did not lead to the peace we desire so much."

With her advocacy of the "combat option," as one of her *Oslobodjenje* colleagues described it, Gordana was publicly identified with one side of the debate over the Geneva peace process. Between her professional responsibility to remain neutral on a key government policy question and her duty as a patriotic Bosnian to argue for what she believed right, there was no contest: Patriotism came first.

Gordana's willingness to put her journalistic talents at the service of the Bosnian government was evident in the way she and her colleague Rasim Ćerimagić came to the assistance of Sarajevo authorities in their conflict with Fikret Abdić, the Muslim businessman who had built a small political and financial empire in the Bihać region of northwestern Bosnia. After the war broke out in 1992, Bihać was cut off from Sarajevo, and Abdić began acting independently of the central government. Instead of fighting with the Serbs and Croats whose forces surrounded his enclave, he did business with them, offering them a share of his black market profits in exchange for their guarantees of safe passage for his supply trucks. His willingness to deal with the enemies of the Bosnian government enraged Alija Izetbegović and other Bosnian leaders but impressed David Owen and Thorvald Stoltenberg, who were desperate for a peace agreement. When the rest of the Bosnian leadership decided to boycott the negotiations temporarily to protest the Milošević-Tudjman partition plan, Owen and Stoltenberg invited Abdić to Geneva in an obvious attempt to undercut the government.

On the way home from Vienna, where they had picked up two awards for *Oslobodjenje*, Gordana and Rasim ran into Abdić and Stoltenberg at the Zagreb airport and quickly figured out what was going on. They immediately reported the story in *Oslobodjenje*. Their aim, according to Rasim, was "to alert the government to what was going on."

About a month later Abdić wrote to the Bosnian collective presidency, of which he was a member, urging them to accept the Milošević-Tudjman partition plan. "It has to be explained to all Bosnia-Herzegovina citizens that there will be no military intervention," Abdić argued. "The only alternative left is negotiations." An *Oslobodjenje* reporter got a copy of the letter and suggested that it be published.

Gordana and Rasim, however, viewed the letter as an attempt by Abdić to undermine Alija Izetbegović in Sarajevo and urged that *Oslobodjenje* ignore it. Other members of the newspaper's editorial board disagreed, saying the letter expressed a viewpoint that Sarajevans should consider, and that *Oslobodjenje* readers deserved to know what an elected member of the Bosnian presidency was saying. They suggested that the letter be accompanied by an editorial emphasizing the newspaper's own opposition to the plan that Abdić was endorsing. Kemal Kurspahić at first favored publicizing the letter but eventually deferred to Gordana and Rasim's strong feelings, and the letter was not printed. Other newspapers in the former Yugoslavia did report on the Abdić appeal, as did foreign news agencies, all of them seeing it as a legitimate story that could not be ignored.

Gordana and Rasim's objections to publishing the Abdić letter, in fact, had been based more on political considerations than on a dispassionate judgment of the letter's news value. They supported Izetbegović in his conflict with Abdić and did not want their newspaper to do anything that would work in Abdić's favor. Three months later, when Abdić launched a violent uprising against the Sarajevo government, Gordana and Rasim felt vindicated.

The Abdić affair illustrated Gordana's priorities: The Bosnian cause came before the narrower interests of her newspaper. Sometimes she lay awake at night, wondering if she, Kurspahić, Ćerimagić, and the other courageous and hardworking journalists at *Os-*

lobodjenje should devote their energies instead to working for Bosnia. They had shown what they could accomplish by keeping their newspaper publishing against all odds. Their professional achievement had caught the world's attention; perhaps they could do something equally dramatic if they were in the government, in place of the bumblers in whose hands it was faltering. "Why save the paper and lose the state?" she asked. "I would far sooner be a second-rate journalist at an unknown newspaper in a successful state," she told me, "than a top journalist at a famous newspaper in a state that doesn't function."

In comparison, Kemal Kurspahić took a more detached view of Bosnia's problems. A critical question facing Bosnian government leaders in the summer of 1993 was whether they would gain more territory by signing a bad peace plan or by fighting on with their underequipped army. Kemal didn't try to figure it out. "It's not my problem," he said, when I asked what he thought. "That's their business. My job is to put out a newspaper. I don't feel responsible for the state."

At the editorial board meeting where the Abdić letter was discussed, Gordana argued with Kemal, saying he was too idealistic in his thinking that the journalistic concerns of *Oslobodjenje* could be separated from the interests of the Bosnian state. "You would make a good editor of *The Washington Post*," she told him, "but this is Sarajevo."

Gordana Knežević's outspoken support for the Bosnian war effort, expressed in the pages of *Oslobodjenje*, was occasionally cited by critics as evidence of the newspaper's overly close ties to the Bosnian government. In fact, her feelings had less to do with any philosophical views she may have had about the role of a free press in a wartime democracy than with the circumstances of her own life and her attachment to Sarajevo. Her thinking, like that of other *Oslobodjenje* editors, had undoubtedly been influenced by the years she had spent working as a journalist during the Communist regime. But in Gordana's case this was not a critical factor. More important was the personal stake she had in the destiny of her city and country. She could not write objectively about Bosnia because she defined herself by its existence and depended on its surviving as a multiethnic state.

Kemal Kurspahić had sent his wife and eleven-year-old son out of Sarajevo in the fall of 1992, and by the following summer he was telling colleagues that he would be ready to resign his position and leave Sarajevo after taking the paper through its fiftieth anniversary at the end of August. If he were more able than Gordana to separate the business of his newspaper from the fate of the state, it was at least in part because he had also separated his own life from Bosnia's. In any case, as a Muslim, Kemal had a secure place in Sarajevo regardless of whether Bosnia became a Muslim republic.

Gordana had made no plans to flee. With her U.N. press accreditation, she had been able to leave Sarajevo regularly, but each trip outside only rooted her in the city more deeply. The world outside was the world of her children Igor and Olga, and of people who could befriend them and do something for her paper. But it was a world in which Gordana could never quite relax. Returning to Sarajevo after a trip to London, she told her reporter Džeilana Pećanin of a conversation she'd had with a foreign journalist. Why, he had asked her, didn't she leave to be with her children? Gordana told Džeilana she was angered by the question and answered that she was staying in Sarajevo for the *sake* of her children. "If I leave and go live with Igor and Olga in London, we would all be refugees," she had said. "By staying here, I don't undermine their identity. Igor will always know where he comes from, even if only my grave is here." As she related the conversation, tears came to Gordana's eyes. Džeilana, who had always been a bit intimidated by her editor's cool strength and discipline, realized it was the first time she had seen Gordana cry.

9

The Wounded City

After Ivo Knežević became information minister in the spring of 1993, the Bosnian government posted a guard outside his apartment building, but apart from that the appointment brought few benefits. His monthly government "salary" was twenty-five cents' worth of Bosnian dinars. Ivo occasionally got a few packs of cigarettes, but no extra food and no priority access to electrical power. The transformer serving the Knežević block was hit by a shell and then cannibalized for parts, and Ivo and Gordana went all summer without so much as a spark of electricity or a drop of running water. But Ivo had a job to go to each day and an important assignment—taking the Bosnian government's case to the world media. It kept his mind off his daughter, Olga, who had turned seven in the year since he had last seen her. She had written Ivo a letter in May, telling him of her plans for the summer. The family with whom she was staying in Zagreb was taking her to the Croatian coast for a few weeks. "I hope I will think of you," Olga wrote, crushing Ivo's heart with the tentativeness of her feeling.

With each passing month Sarajevo families were further strained. The woman looking after Igor in England wrote Gordana and Ivo to suggest that she legally adopt him so that he could become a British citizen and get a passport. The pain Ivo and Gordana felt at the thought of Igor becoming someone else's adopted son was made all the worse by the realization that it might be in his interests that it happen. Gordana was looking as well to find a family in the United States who could take custody of Boris, at least for the duration of the war. She and Ivo had concluded that it had been a mistake to keep Boris with them in Sarajevo.

With Ivo becoming a government minister and Gordana busy at the newspaper, Boris was left alone most days, and he began sneaking beyond his immediate neighborhood for the first time since the war started. At the beginning of the fighting, Gordana and Ivo had ordered him not to go past the Bosnian army barricade set up around the corner from their house. A whole year had gone by since Boris had been downtown. He had not seen the park on Djuro Djaković Street since the trees there had been cut down, or the Parliament Building across from the Holiday Inn since it had been turned into a charred ruin. But in the summer of 1993, he began spending more time with neighborhood friends, and bit by bit he ventured beyond the limits his parents had imposed.

One hot day a friend persuaded Boris to go swimming with him in the Bambaša River, a half-hour walk across town and just a few hundred yards short of frontline positions. Boris went and returned safely and a few days later did it again. Leaving his neighborhood for the first time, Boris was stunned by what he saw, surprised at his own fearlessness, and excited at every step. As he had with the death of his friend Kemo Merzić, he turned the experience into a short story. Six boys make the trek together, and Boris included himself as one of the characters:

> When they got there, Muamer thought it most fun to jump from the dam, and Tariq and Emir agreed, so Muaz, Adnan, and Boris continued farther down toward the beach and left the three at the dam. As they crossed the bridge to the other side of the river where the beach was, they all saw a shell crater on the other side, a bloody trail leading across the bridge and up into the hills with one big patch of blood around the middle. Nobody had bothered, or

wanted, to wipe that away, and when you looked at it, it gave you a rather mysterious, then scary, feeling—a feeling that you're never going to know who it was or if he lived or where he went. . . .

Boris got out of the water. He dropped himself onto the ground and put his head on a stone, using it as a pillow. His body stretched. There was no one around, and that was the reason they liked this place. It was nice and quiet, except for the distant noise coming from the dam where people were bathing.

Boris did not tell his parents about the first trip to the river, but after the second he could not keep the secret any longer. His parents were initially disbelieving and then furious that Boris had disregarded all he had been taught and knew to be prudent. Neither Gordana nor Ivo had any idea, however, what to do about the transgression. They were not about to whip Boris, and there were no privileges that could be taken away. They couldn't make him go to bed early; he did anyway. They couldn't ground him, because he had nowhere else to go. They couldn't punish him with extra work, because Boris already had the grueling job of hauling the family's water and cutting the firewood. In the end they just spoke sternly to him and made him promise not to do it again.

Mostly, Boris's swimming expedition made Gordana more determined than ever to get him out of Sarajevo. The escapade showed that he, like she and Ivo and everyone else in the city, was tired of being careful, of being confined to tight routines and sheltered spaces. The frustration of life under siege was steadily becoming unmanageable, and it was expressed in these impulsive acts of recklessness, as it was in spitefulness and violence. Sarajevo was close to breaking.

Lines of Stress

On the one-year anniversary of the day his wife was killed on their front doorstep, Fahro Memić and his son, Damir, went to visit her grave. Her death had brought Fahro closer to his son and made him more attentive to Damir's needs. He no longer volunteered for dangerous *Oslobodjenje* assignments, and he spent more time at home. Even on the weeks he was assigned to work around the clock as an editor at the *Oslobodjenje* production plant on the Nedjarići front line, Fahro would often hitch a midday ride home to prepare lunch for Damir.

On his weeks off Fahro managed a neighborhood bar called Mon Chéri. It was a sleek little place, with pink marble café tables, black chairs, and mirrors on the walls. The establishment had belonged to a friend of Fahro's who went to Germany when the war began, saying Fahro was free to do with it as he wished. By the summer of 1993, with the shelling reduced, cafés were reopening all around the city, and Fahro decided to get Mon Chéri going again in order to earn a little extra foreign currency.

The bar was on the ground floor of an apartment building that faced Sniper Alley, but Fahro placed some concrete slabs against the south side of the awning over the entrance and assured patrons they could come and go without fear of being shot. There was no electricity all summer, but Fahro hung a little fluorescent bulb on the wall of the bar and wired it to a car battery, so there was light at least for customers to see one another and for Fahro to pour drinks. Peering soberly over the top of his spectacles, however, he looked more like a newsroom copy editor than a barman.

Fahro sold whiskey, beer, and soda that came through black market channels from the Egyptian and Ukrainian UNPROFOR contingents in Sarajevo. A can of Heineken went for 12 German marks ($7.50) and a Coke for 10 marks (about $6.00); Fahro insisted his prices were the lowest in Sarajevo. He had only a handful of customers each day, but every drink he sold earned him a little extra money. "It's a simple question of survival," he told me, when I visited the bar one afternoon. "I have spent all my savings, and I have no other way to support my son. I'd just like to afford a kilogram of potatoes once in a while." But by the end of August the outlook was not good. A special U.N. commission had just arrived in Sarajevo to investigate corruption and black marketeering among the UNPROFOR units. If Fahro lost his suppliers, his business could be ruined.

The bar and caring for Damir took much of Fahro's attention. As a member of the *Oslobodjenje* editorial board, he supported a more compromising political line than the one held by Gordana Knežević and Rasim Ćerimagić. He was one of the editors who favored publication of the Fikret Abdić letter advising peace negotiations, and, in an August "In Focus" column of his own, Fahro argued it was time to recognize that "Bosnia as it used to be no longer exists" and that the republic's warring "peoples" should acknowledge their differences and "make up." Fahro wrote the column one night when he was the duty editor on the news desk, and he slipped it into the next day's paper without showing it to anyone.

The argument was not sharp and reflected little more than the wearied thinking of a man who wanted to get on with his own life, but it supported those who claimed the Bosnian conflict was a civil war, and Gordana among others was furious when she saw it. "We can't allow this," she told Kemal. Her objection to the column was so strong she briefly threatened to resign her editorial board position in protest of its publication. "This [column] contradicts everything that we stand for," she said, "and it's on our own front page!"

Gordana was also upset about Mon Chéri, fearing it might compromise the newspaper's relations with the U.N. command in Sarajevo. At an editorial board meeting the day after Fahro's "In Focus" column was published, *Oslobodjenje* business manager Emir Hrustanović reported that the U.N. officers who had been secretly supplying diesel oil to fuel the generators had cut off the deliveries and that the newspaper was running dangerously short again. Gordana had always had the responsibility of finding fuel for the paper through her U.N. and government contacts, and Hrustanović asked if she could do so again. No, she answered. "Let the one who is buying beer from UNPROFOR go find the diesel," she said. Fahro was sitting across the table, but Gordana did not look at him, nor he at her.

Other *Oslobodjenje* staffers were disgruntled over entirely separate issues. One group of reporters, claiming to be unhappy with the newspaper's tacit support for the Bosnian government, began writing for a magazine called *Blic* (Flash) that appeared for the first time in August. The debut issue included pieces that had been rejected by *Oslobodjenje* editors: the Fikret Abdić letter plus a story about the Bosnian government's alleged obstruction of an effort by the local Red Cross to arrange an evacuation of people wishing to leave Sarajevo. Gordana thought the *Oslobodjenje* editorial board should ask the reporters writing for *Blic* to choose between it and *Oslobodjenje*. Kemal was less concerned by the reporters' apparent disloyalty. "They're mostly unhappy because we're not giving them enough cigarettes," he said. *Blic* was being financed from outside Bosnia, Kemal pointed out, and the publisher was offering the *Oslobodjenje* reporters hard currency for their stories.

Several staff conflicts at *Oslobodjenje*, in fact, stemmed from professional jealousies and disagreements over money. Some veteran journalists resented the attention being given to younger reporters such as Vladimir Štaka, Senka Kurtović, and Džeilana Pećanin. The newspaper was being praised everywhere for its heroic publication efforts, and there were numerous opportunities to travel abroad to pick up awards on its behalf. Kurspahić and Knežević were the top two editors at the paper, and both spoke fluent English, so it was natural that they represent the paper internationally, but bitter arguments erupted over whether others should get a share of the travel opportunities.

Zlatko Dizdarević, who had been chief of the news desk in Nedjarići through the early months of the war, received an award in Paris given by Reporters without Borders, in part because he spoke French. When he was subsequently identified in France as the newspaper's *rédacteur en chef*, Dizdarević was accused by other *Oslobodjenje* journalists of having misrepresented his connection to the paper. Dizdarević had left his news desk position in July 1992 and had worked since then as executive director for foreign affairs, meaning he arranged outside assistance for the newspaper. The editor in chief was Kemal Kurspahić and no one else. Dizdarević argued in his own defense that a *rédacteur en chef* position in a French newspaper wasn't actually the top editorial job, but his argument was undercut when French reporters later used the same title in identifying Kemal Kurspahić.

1943–1993

A factor that held the newspaper staff together was their shared horror at the destruction of their own building. After incendiary shells had reduced the twin *Oslobodjenje* towers in Nedjarići to charred frames, the Serb gunners pounded them with explosive shells until the towers collapsed completely. Workers on the ground floor heard a roar and then a deep rumble, and they thought at first that they were being bombed. "There was a long, deafening sound of metal being crushed," said Senad Gubelić, an *Oslobodjenje* photographer on duty at the time. "Dust filled the air, and you couldn't see anything. People were choking and screaming and running to escape."

When it was over the towers had fallen into great piles of twisted aluminum and broken concrete slabs. Only the ten-story elevator shaft was left standing defiantly amid the rubble, a single column poking at the sky. Proud *Oslobodjenje* workers said their enterprise was giving "the finger" to the Serb nationalists entrenched a hundred yards behind.

The flattening of its grand and modern headquarters trivialized the other troubles *Oslobodjenje* faced during wartime. "Because of the building," Zlatko Dizdarević told me, "people don't want to speak too harshly about the paper, except to each other. It has to do with the dignity of the ruin, and with *Oslobodjenje*'s future."

In the summer of 1993, everyone at the paper tacitly agreed to put personal and professional conflicts aside and focus on the task of keeping *Oslobodjenje* alive through its fiftieth anniversary on August 30. Gordana and Zlatko told me (separately but in virtually the same words), "*Oslobodjenje* is bigger than any one of us." One variable, however, was out of the journalists' control: diesel oil for the generators. On several occasions during the summer, the stocks were down to a single day's supply, and Kemal Kurspahić more than once despaired of the paper's chance to publish continuously through to August 30. As a last resort he was prepared to print *Oslobodjenje* as a single sheet, in small quantities.

The parallels with 1943 were eerie: The closer *Oslobodjenje* got to its fiftieth anniversary, the more it was returning to the circumstances of its wartime origin. The paper had begun as a single sheet, produced on a mobile press by a section of propaganda specialists attached to the Sixth East Bosnian Brigade of the Partisan forces. The places of publication were never mentioned in the paper for fear of the sites being shelled. In 1993 the *Oslobodjenje* workers were professional journalists, computer operators, and pressmen. Two weeks before the anniversary, however, they were assigned military duties as well, just as the original *Oslobodjenje* workers had been given. The Bosnian government had finally persuaded the Ninth and Tenth Mountain Brigades to stop press-ganging civilian men for shovel duty in the trenches, but as part of the deal the government was requiring all able-bodied civilian men in Sarajevo to take regular turns digging on the front line. *Oslobodjenje*, as a principal employer, was obligated to send three men each night. The journalists and pressmen served in three-night shifts, gathering after dark in front of the building and then hiking to a nearby front line and digging until two or three in the morning within yards of Serb positions.

The 1943–1993 *Oslobodjenje* comparisons were highlighted at a downtown Sarajevo exhibit commemorating the newspaper's anniversary. The *Oslobodjenje* archivist had moved the files of the newspaper morgue into the bomb shelter during the first months of shelling, and he saved the August 30, 1943, issue. Yellowed and curling, it was laid out for display in a glass case at the exhibit. "Everything for the Front! Everything for the People's Liberation Army!" was the exhortation on the front page. The lead story reported that the German-

Oslobodjenje production editors worked and slept in unheated facilities, using computers powered by diesel generators.   (*OSLOBODJENJE*)

Italian alliance in Yugoslavia was "near to being broken." In the right column was an article announcing that the Seventeenth East Bosnian Brigade had been formed and was "destroying" Serbian Chetnik units in eastern Bosnia.

Both stories were accurate, and the developments were key. The fighting in Yugoslavia in August 1943 was separating from the larger Axis-Allied conflict and transforming into a civil war. World attention had turned to the Soviet offensive on the eastern front. The Axis forces were on the defensive. German troops in Yugoslavia were overstretched, and, within a month of *Oslobodjenje*'s appearance, Italian forces had surrendered. Within Yugoslavia the Ustashe, Partisans, and Chetniks were shifting war strategies in anticipation of an Allied victory. Tito's Partisans were destined to come out on top, and they knew it.

The August 30, 1993, issue was also triumphal, in its own way. The diesel oil and newsprint supplies held out, and *Oslobodjenje* reached its anniversary successfully. For that one day it resembled the papers of prewar times: twenty-four broadsheet pages, with the masthead printed in red ink, just as it used to be. The press run was three times larger than usual for wartime, and for the first time in months Sarajevans had a fair chance of finding the paper on sale at a street-corner kiosk. The anniversary issue included statements of support from President Izetbegović, U.S. Senator Joseph Biden, Susan Sontag, and others who had visited the newspaper's head-quarters, as well as a fair amount of self-congratulation, including a list of *Oslobodjenje* journalists who had won "life achievement" awards for their work through the years. Kemal Kurspahić wrote a special column noting the paper's ties to its founders' ideals. "If there is one unbroken thread linking *Oslobodjenje* through the years," he wrote, "from August 30, 1943, in Donja Trnova to August 30, 1993, in wartime Sarajevo, it is the struggle against fascism."

There was one problem with the 1943–1993 parallel, however: There were Croatian Ustashe and Serbian Chetnik forces again in 1993, but no multiethnic Partisan forces to challenge them—only an underequipped, Muslim-dominated Bosnian army. The front page of the 1993 anniversary edition, in contrast to the first issue, carried no reports of victory over the forces of nationalism. It was dominated instead by a large map of Bosnia, carefully drawn to show how the country was to be divided into separate Serb, Muslim, and Croat "republics" under the Milošević-Tudjman Plan. The *Oslobodjenje* workers who celebrated that day were not looking forward to a glori-ous future, only thanking their good fortune for having survived so far and wondering what lay ahead.

On the afternoon of August 30, the *Oslobodjenje* management threw a modest party on the ground floor of the Nedjarići ruin for the paper's employees and their guests. Even columnist Gojko Berić showed up, a bit nervously; the only other time he had left the safety of his apartment was to accept his newspaper's Best Journalist award a few weeks earlier. Small glasses of beer from Sarajevo's recently reopened brewery were offered, along with short sections of *burek*, a Bosnian meat pastry. Kemal Kurspahić called for a moment of silence in honor of *Oslobodjenje* journalists killed during the war, then gave a short speech. "Whatever maps they make," he said, referring to the partition plan, "whatever they decide to do with this unhappy coun-try, *Oslobodjenje* must remain the paper that nurtures the culture of a common life among people of goodwill who choose to live here to-gether."

The mood was not hopeful, however. Kurspahić noted to Gor-dana Knežević and other editors that no one from the Bosnian government was at the party or had sent congratulations, and he wondered aloud if that meant *Oslobodjenje* was seen by the ruling Muslim party as disloyal. The paper that had been born of the Partisan struggle against Serb and Croat nationalists and raised as an organ of Tito's Communist regime was standing almost alone in 1993. Gojko Berić, a Serb, expressed the prevailing sentiment: "We are the people who are nostalgic for the former times and very much afraid of the future."

That evening senior *Oslobodjenje* staff gathered at a private downtown dinner lounge. Reporters, editors, columnists, and special guests sat around the bar for a few rounds of whiskey, vodka, and brandy, courtesy of the newspaper management. After an hour they moved to the dining area, where a long table had been set with fine white china. Three trays of hot hors d'oeuvres were brought.

After that, however, no other food arrived. Dinner for the group would have cost hundreds of dollars, and the liquor tab had already broken the newspaper's anniversary entertainment budget. At first the would-be diners seemed not to notice, conversing over their empty plates as if in midfeast. Liquor was doing its work on empty stomachs, however, and after about an hour politeness gave way to nastiness. Manojlo Tomić, one of the paper's staff columnists, looked down the table at Kemal and surprised him with a question about the list of life achievement award winners published in the paper that day. Why, Tomić asked, had someone dropped the names of two award-winning Serbs who went to Belgrade at the beginning of the war? Were only "loyal" journalists to be remembered?

Kemal was caught off guard. He had seen the list before it was published and didn't remember anyone being crossed off. If what Tomić said was true, it would undermine the claims Kemal had always made that *Oslobodjenje* under his direction was fair-minded and liberal in outlook, without the prejudices associated with news media on the Serb and Croat sides. At first he denied any names had been dropped, but someone had a paper and showed him. The names of the two were indeed missing. Kemal could barely contain his rage. "Goddamn it!" he shouted. He gave his empty plate a furious shove and flung the silverware after it. His face, already red from drinking, turned crimson. Gordana, sitting at his side, had never seen him so angry: at Manojlo Tomić, for publicly embarrassing him during what should have been a joyous occasion, and at whoever had changed the list without his knowledge. "He'll be fired!" Kemal declared, without knowing who it was. "Either he's fired, or I'll quit!"

The evening was ruined. "This is the biggest scandal for *Oslobod-jenje* in the last twenty years," Zlatko Dizdarević told me afterward. Dizdarević blamed his old rivals Knežević and Kurspahić for the debacle. "This is the consequence of having a political line," he said gravely.

In fact, there was no scandal at all. The original list of award winners included people who had worked at weekly and monthly publications produced by the *Oslobodjenje* printing company. A night editor had decided the list was too long and limited it to journalists who had worked at the daily newspaper itself. Two Serbs who had gone to Belgrade had indeed been dropped from the list, but so had several Muslims who remained in Sarajevo. The anniversary celebration was spoiled not as a result of the *Oslobodjenje* editors going too far in their adherence to a political line but because seventeen months of living and working under war conditions had left everyone with badly frayed nerves.

Muslims and Others

Oslobodjenje staff members described the internal tensions that developed at the paper during wartime variously as personal, professional, or political. But never as ethnic. Although all nationalities were represented at the paper, no "Muslim" or "Croat" or "Serb" faction ever coalesced. Over and over *Oslobodjenje* demonstrated that its multiethnic character was genuine and that it was still possible for people of different national backgrounds to work together. This achievement was especially important given that Muslim nationalism was gaining ground in besieged Sarajevo and that the ruling Muslim party was beginning to mimic the Serb and Croat national parties in outlook and action.

Originally, the Muslim movement in Bosnia was qualitatively different from the more traditional Serb and Croat nationalisms, both of which assumed an ethnically distinct people with the right to a state all their own. The fact that "Serbs" and "Croats" in Bosnia did not necessarily have distinctive ancestries did not matter, because they acted as though they did. In contrast, the Bosnian Muslims had generally not portrayed themselves as an ethnic group or nation, being bound instead by their religion. "I have no national feelings at all," Alija Izetbegović once said. The Bosnian Muslims traditionally had asked not to have their own "national" state but only to be left to practice their faith in peace.

When Muslim political movements were organized in Bosnia, they were based either on the idea that Islam itself incorporated a political creed or, more often, on the argument that Bosnian Muslims needed to stand united against the Serb and Croat nationalists who laid claim to Muslim identity and tried to divide Bosnian territory. These two principles—one clerical, the other secular—were both represented in the Muslim SDA party, and competition between them had been present from the beginning of the Muslim movement in Bosnia. Clericalists advocated an Islamic political agenda, including the creation of Muslim social and political institutions, although most stopped short of advocating the establishment of an Islamic republic in Bosnia, knowing that the demographics made it politically inconceivable. Secular Muslim leaders argued that Muslim interests would be protected best under the model of a civil state, where all citizens had equal legal rights. Alija Izetbegović was somewhere in the middle. His "Islamic Declaration" showed that his sympathies were with the clericalists, but as leader of the Muslim party he had downplayed his religious orientation in order to win the support of secular Muslims, who in Bosnia vastly outnumbered those who were religiously inclined.

Among Yugoslavs who advocated a political culture that transcended national lines, the Bosnian Muslims were viewed relatively favorably, even affectionately. They made no irredentist claims and asserted that the Serb, Croat, and Muslim populations in Bosnia could coexist peacefully. Because their brand of Islam was relatively relaxed, the Muslims of Bosnia stood for moderation in a world of religious and national extremism. Many jokes about the Bosnian Muslims portrayed them as a somnolent and docile people, given to sensuality.

With the experience of wartime suffering, however, Bosnian Muslims began taking their group identity more seriously. They realized that their existence as a separate people in Bosnia was endangered by the Serb drive to remove all trace of Muslim habitation on "Serb" land. The Muslims suffered as individuals and families, with at least 100,000 civilians killed and a million displaced from their homes. But they also lost as a culture. Across Bosnia 1,000 mosques were destroyed, and Muslim cemeteries, libraries, and other cultural centers were razed. In the Drina valley counties of Foča, Rogatica, Višegrad, Vlasenica, Bratunac, and Zvornik—all of which had Muslim majorities before the war—Serb forces killed or expelled all but a handful of the Muslim residents, bringing to an end five centuries of Muslim life in the region.

Just as many European Jews did not feel their Jewishness fully until the Nazis set out to exterminate them, many Muslims began thinking about themselves collectively in Bosnia only when they saw Serbs persecuting, expelling, or killing Muslims on account of their name and ancestry alone. "We learned we were Muslim when our mothers were killed," the Bosnian writer Avdo Sidran said. Not surprisingly, Muslim political leaders began taking a harder political line, saying their people were suffering the consequences of having been naive over the years. They suggested that the Muslims' record of tolerance and gentleness had actually represented weakness and passivity, or at least that their Serb and Croat neighbors might have read it that way, thus being encouraged to move against them. By the fall of 1993, Muslim nationalism in Bosnia had moved closer in character to its Serb and Croat counterparts, with Muslim party leaders arguing that the Bosnian government should give precedence to Muslim national interests over the concerns of Serb and Croat citizens.

Such arguments were given a big boost when international mediators David Owen and Thorvald Stoltenberg promoted the Milošević-Tudjman proposal to partition Bosnia, creating a "union" of three ethnic republics. Owen and Stoltenberg had spoken continually of Muslims, Serbs, and Croats—rather than citizens of Bosnia—in the peace negotiations, and on July 31, 1993, Alija Izetbegović accepted their formulation and agreed to the proposal, at least in theory. Speaking from Geneva via Radio Sarajevo to listeners back home, Izetbegović sounded as if he saw himself no longer as the president of Bosnia but only as the leader of the Bosnian Muslim people. "We are trying to preserve a large piece of Bosnia for our nation," he told them. He said the Serb war aim in Bosnia had been "to exterminate the Muslim people" and that he had been forced to act to ensure his nation's physical survival.

With Izetbegović's tentative acceptance of the idea of a "Muslim" republic existing in a loose union with "Serb" and "Croat" republics, the goal of preserving a multiethnic Bosnian state appeared to have been abandoned, and Sarajevo's standing as a bastion of interfaith harmony and tolerance was put in jeopardy. Conservative Muslim leaders seemed unbothered. "We Muslims don't have much choice," said Selim Hadžibajrić, the Old Town politician. "The other sides [Serb and Croat] pushed us into a civil war. We are left alone, and now we must have our own state as well. Serbs and Croats who want to stay and live with us will be free to do so," he said, "but the question of civil authority must be left to the Muslims. We must be sure that we cannot be manipulated by Serbs and Croats again."

Muslim leaders, in fact, did little to encourage non-Muslims to remain in Sarajevo. Mustafa Cerić, the head of the Islamic community in Bosnia, went out of his way to slight Serbs in general. At a meeting with Russian journalists in the summer of 1993, he suggested that all Serbs in Bosnia shared responsibility for what the Serb army had done to the Bosnian Muslim community. During a three-day interreligious prayer and dialogue gathering a few weeks later, Cerić refused to participate in a Sunday mass at the Serbian Orthodox cathedral in Sarajevo. The city's Orthodox, Catholic, and Jewish leaders had prayed with him at the main mosque in Sarajevo two days earlier, and the four faiths were also present the next day at Jewish and Catholic services, but a colleague of Cerić announced that "prior engagements" prevented him from participating in the Orthodox services.

Muhammed Filipović, the opposition politician who led the breakaway secular branch of the Muslim party in Bosnia, condemned Cerić for "acting as a politician, not as a priest" in boycotting the Orthodox mass. "This is like spitting in the Serbs' eyes," Filipović said.

Cerić was unruffled by such criticism. With his black tunic, white cap, and neatly trimmed beard, he fit the image of a stern, dignified Muslim cleric. He prided himself on being the only Islamic leader in Bosnia educated both in the Middle East and in the West. For a decade he had been the imam at the main mosque in Chicago, and he spoke excellent English. But back in Sarajevo Cerić was ready by the fall of 1993 to give up on the idea of a civic culture transcending religious or national lines. "I no longer believe in European Humanism," he told the Spanish writer Juan Goytisolo. "We want a state, a country, in which we as Muslims have no need to apologize for our Islam," he said in an interview with my NPR colleague Sylvia Poggioli.

Such sentiments were not limited to the Muslim leadership, as Gordana Knežević discovered when she paid a visit to her friends Suada and Adnan, the daughter and son-in-law of Kana Kadić, Gordana's next-door neighbor. Adnan had asked Gordana for help in contacting a Bosnian army officer she knew, and one day she went by his apartment with the name and telephone number. An activist from the Muslim party was visiting, and Gordana stayed to hear what he had to say. "We Muslims have been alienated from our roots," he told her, "and now we must be brought back. And we won't be nice, polite European Muslims anymore; we'll be real Muslims." He favored the establishment of an Islamic authority in Sarajevo, with religious education introduced in city schools, beginning with kindergarten.

Gordana promptly got into an argument with the visitor. "I'm disappointed," she said. "This is exactly what the other side wanted. Milošević and Karadžić had the mosques bombed and thousands of Muslims killed just to get you to think this way, so as to end the possibility of living together. I'm sad that in your case they have achieved their goal." Suada and Adnan said nothing. Gordana suspected they were not far in their own thinking from the views of the Muslim activist, but she also knew that they liked and respected her as a friend and neighbor, and she was hoping to persuade them as much as the man to whom she directed her words.

The surge of Muslim nationalism in the summer and fall of 1993 threatened *Oslobodjenje,* and its editors recognized the danger they faced. "I'm afraid we're approaching the point where *Oslobodjenje,* by advocating a citizens' state, could be seen as a problem," Kemal Kurspahić told me. "If the government decides to be organized as a Muslim entity, they'll want a newspaper of their own."

Selim Hadžibajrić couldn't have agreed more. "*Oslobodjenje* has stayed as it was before the war," he said in the fall of 1993. "It's more like the old socialist Bosnia-Herzegovina. I would have to say that the Serb and Croat media have adjusted better to the new situation," he said. "They have turned around, while our media have not." Hadžibajrić said he was troubled by the high percentage of Serb and Croat journalists at the paper. "The composition of the newspaper staff," he complained, "has little to do with the situation on the ground. In Serbia, they have Serbs working, and in Croatia, they have Croats, but *Oslobodjenje* is still pushing for a multiethnic Bosnia. I would like to see them defending Muslim interests more."

A Victory for Citizens

The Milošević-Tudjman Plan to break Bosnia up into three ethnic minirepublics, as modified slightly by mediators Owen and Stoltenberg, gave the Muslims 31 percent of Bosnian territory, with the remainder being divided between the Serbs and Croats. Alija Izetbegović did not accept the territorial division but agreed to put the proposal before his Parliament for their review.

Because the plan called for the establishment of an explicitly Muslim republic, Izetbegović and other Bosnian leaders concluded that it should be considered first by a special all-Muslim assembly on September 27, 1993. The meeting was organized by Alija Isaković, the head of the Congress of Muslim Intellectuals in Sarajevo. "Now that multiethnic Bosnia has been destroyed," Isaković announced, "the Muslim state must create its own political and constitutional framework in the same way as the Bosnian Serbs and Croats have done."

The Muslim convention was held at the war-battered Holiday Inn, the only building still standing in Sarajevo that could accommodate the group. Among the Muslim leaders present were Bosnian army officers, politicians from the Muslim SDA party, Islamic priests, and representatives of Muslim cultural and humanitarian organizations. Non-Muslim officials were also permitted to attend the assembly, but only as observers. For the first time in modern Bosnian history, Serbs and Croats in Sarajevo found themselves without the right to vote on the question of Bosnia's future. The Muslim assembly was due to be followed by a session of the regular Bosnian Parliament, but the Parliament was dominated by the Muslim leaders who organized and participated in the special assembly, and it was expected to approve whatever decision the Muslim assembly reached.

Most *Oslobodjenje* journalists saw the establishment of an all-Muslim government body as an unwelcome development, but the newspaper maintained a low-key attitude toward the meeting. The lead commentary was written by the paper's senior columnist, Gojko Berić. Like other *Oslobodjenje* Serbs, he was dismayed at the organization of a Muslim state, but the tone of his editorial was impartial: "The great drama of saying good-bye to the [Bosnian] state begins in Sarajevo today," he wrote. "The Bosnian Muslims and those Serbs and Croats who have remained loyal are facing the fact that Bosnia-Herzegovina is beginning to disappear as a state." Berić was careful not to criticize the Muslim leadership for convening in special session. Partition, he said, had been forced on Bosnia, because "the leading powers did not want it to survive as a state." Given that the question to be decided was the "destiny of the Muslim nation," Berić wrote, the Muslim convention was "more competent" to consider the partition plan than the regular Bosnian Parliament. He said the Muslim delegates had the responsibility of articulating "the collective consciousness of the Bosnian Muslims." Foreign journalists were somewhat more alarmist in their assessment of the Muslim meeting, presenting it as clear evidence that Muslim nationalism had triumphed in Bosnia. Some prematurely declared that the special Muslim assembly had effectively replaced the Bosnian Parliament as the main legislative body in Bosnia.

In the end the Muslim assembly rejected the partition plan, largely on the ground that a tiny, landlocked Muslim republic surrounded by Serb and Croat enemies would not be a viable state. Among those on the losing side was Old Town politician Selim Hadžibajrić, and he left Sarajevo shortly thereafter and did not return. The hard-line Muslim nationalists who wanted to proceed immediately with the establishment of a Muslim republic realized they were not as strong as they had believed, even within the leadership of their own party. In the coming weeks the advocates of a unified, multiethnic Bosnian state showed they still had the upper hand. Having met once, the all-Muslim assembly immediately disbanded, and the Bosnian Parliament continued in its constitutionally prescribed legislative role. In October, Bosnia's collective presidency was reconstituted. Four of the seven permanent seats were given to non-Muslims, two Serbs and two Croats. A few days later the government itself was reorganized under a new prime minister, Haris Silajdžić, previously the foreign minister.

Silajdžić moved quickly to assert the government's authority. Interior Ministry policemen were finally authorized to arrest the renegade militia commanders Caco Topalović and Ćelo Delalić. Silajdžić himself went to Delalić and secured his surrender. Topalović resisted arrest, and a fierce shoot-out took place at his headquarters. Hostages were taken, and at least a dozen policemen were killed, as well as several of Caco's men, before he was finally captured. Hours later Caco was killed. The official accounts said he was shot dead while trying to escape, although witnesses reported seeing him severely beaten, and Sarajevo journalists who covered the incident suspected that he was killed by the Interior Ministry policemen themselves in retaliation for his murder of their colleagues.

The reconstitution of the collective presidency, the reorganization of the Bosnian government, and the crackdown on the Ninth and Tenth Mountain Brigade commanders came as welcome news to Sarajevans who feared their city was being taken over by Muslim extremists with their private militia. Caller after caller on radio talk shows praised the new appointments to the presidency. *Oslobodjenje* editors finally felt free to express their true feelings about Caco and

Ćelo and trumpeted their capture on the newspaper's front page, under the banner headline "Law in the Streets of Sarajevo."

Gordana Knežević was overjoyed by the developments. "These are defeats for the SDA," she told me. The party had come out as a loser in the reorganization of the collective presidency, and, with Caco and Ćelo gone, Gordana said, "the SDA has lost its army."

But hard-line Muslim nationalism as a political force in Sarajevo was by no means finished. It had emerged in the context of war, in response to the deliberate victimization of the Bosnian Muslim people by Serb nationalists. Because those conditions still existed, Muslim radicalism was sure to continue, and even to grow. The longer the siege and bombardment of Sarajevo dragged on, the more distant was the memory of the time before the war when residents of all backgrounds had lived in the city peacefully. What the people of Sarajevo had most in common during wartime was their suffering, not their traditions.

Sarajevo in the Dark

In October 1993 Sarajevo theater director Haris Pašović organized and hosted the Sarajevo International Film Festival to demonstrate resistance to what he called the "arts barbarism" of the besieging Serb forces and to show the world that urban culture and civilization were alive and well in the Bosnian capital. Through his international contacts Pašović secured videotapes of more than two dozen recently released films, and he arranged for such noted film actors as Vanessa Redgrave and Jeremy Irons to be present for the festival opening. Directors Roman Polanski and Bernardo Bertolucci taped special greetings to the people of Sarajevo and sent along clips from their most recent films. A catalog describing the festival features along with the times and places of their showing was prepared and distributed as an *Oslobodjenje* insert.

Džeilana Pećanin and Senka Kurtović, avid filmgoers in peacetime, excitedly huddled over the film schedule in the *Oslobodjenje* office the day it came out, putting checks by the selections they wanted to see; the Wim Wenders film *Until the End of the World* topped their list. Neither had been to a movie in the eighteen months since the war had started. They made plans to attend the opening program with Vladimir Štaka, Rasim Ćerimagić, and other *Oslobodjenje* staffers.

But the event was a fiasco from beginning to end. United Nations officials refused to allow the film stars to fly to Sarajevo aboard the aircraft that brought humanitarian aid from Ancona, Italy. Privately, U.N. officials said the British government had ordered them not to fly the actors to Sarajevo for fear they might speak out against Britain's Bosnia policy. The actors were carrying several films for the festival, and the films were stranded with them in Ancona. In addition, Serb forces severed the principal electricity line coming into Sarajevo just before the festival opened. The organizers had diesel generators to light the theater and run the film projectors, but they were not able to power the computers in which the film dubbing was prepared, and several films had to be shown without Serbo-Croatian subtitles.

Finally, the Serb army launched a furious artillery barrage, firing 1,500 shells onto the city on the day of the festival's opening. The combination of problems resulted in a total rearrangement of the film schedule, so that Sarajevans had no idea what films were being shown when. Frustrated filmgoers were almost as angry at Pašović as they were at the Serbs, the United Nations, or the British government. He had gotten their hopes up and then let them down. The idea of staging a film festival in besieged Sarajevo was admirable, but many Sarajevans considered it foolish, as though Pašović and others like him believed that by the force of will alone they could overcome the reality of war. Sarajevo was still fighting on, but blindly, like an injured soldier unaware of the seriousness of his battle wound.

"I wonder how much longer I can take this," Dželiana Pećanin said, after the film festival had been ruined and with it the chance to forget where she was for a few hours. Thinking a moment, she added, "The worst thing is, I think I can take it awhile." She feared that she had adjusted to the siege more than she wanted to, that she was settling into a long-term numbness and losing her capacity to feel pain, or hope.

Kemal Kurspahić was already gone. Shortly after the fiftieth anniversary celebration, he collected his wife and son, Mirza, in Zagreb and went on with them to the United States, where he settled down to write his war memoirs and serve as *Oslobodjenje's* Washington correspondent. Having personally guaranteed his staff at the outset of the war that his newspaper would publish as long as Sarajevo existed, Kemal angered many of his journalists by leaving while the struggle was continuing. But he felt that his work was finished in Sarajevo and that he could be more useful to the newspaper as an outside fundraiser.

After the anniversary celebration the production of the paper settled back into routine. The supply of diesel and newsprint was always inadequate, but somehow enough was found to keep the paper going. At the Nedjarići shelter the shift workers had become experts at their business. One evening when someone forgot to bring out the collection of stories from the downtown office, the editors in the shelter had to assemble the paper on their own, from wire dispatches, correspondents' reports, and stories they wrote themselves. They usually finished their work at about 4:00 A.M., then played cards or watched television for a couple of hours longer, taking advantage of the electricity generated for the printing operation. Once in bed they slept until noon or later.

The front lines were still barely a hundred yards away, and gunfire echoed around the building all day and night. For a half hour or so it might be quiet. Then the sudden, sharp crack of a sniper rifle would prompt another exchange of heavy machine-gun fire, producing a wild, rattling sound that reverberated through the building as if rocks were being shaken furiously in a huge wooden box. A few moments later would come the thunderous roar of an exploding artillery shell. But to the Nedjarići workers it was all no more than background noise, like the rumble of rush-hour traffic.

By November 1993 no regular electricity from the city grid was coming to the plant at all. The worst time for the workers was from 4:00 P.M., when it grew dark, to 7:00 P.M., when the diesel generator was switched on. In the time between there were no lights at all. The *Oslobodjenje* workers lay on their cots or sat in a corner of the cafeteria in total darkness. Dots of orange light hung and glided through the air, as burning cigarettes were drawn up to be inhaled, glowed brightly for a moment, and then arced back to their resting points. Feeling their way in the dark down the stairs to the shelter, the workers relied on memory and counted their steps: fourteen between the landings. Watch out for the eleventh step, because it was missing a section on the inside of the stairway and could trip you up.

After Kemal left for the States, Gordana took charge of the newspaper, though reluctantly; her own fighting spirit was weakening too. The combative patriotism she had felt just a few months earlier was dissipating, worn down by disillusionment in her government, by anxiety over her children, and by her own fatigue. I found her at home one November afternoon, huddled by her stove. Although it was not a chilly day, she was dressed in as many clothes as she could put on, and she was still shivering. "I feel like I'm cold on the inside," she said. "I can't seem to get warm." She was coughing deeply. A

Sarajevo doctor friend had given her antibiotics for her bronchitis, but they weren't curing it.

I also went to visit Nazif and Fata Merzić that day, in the apartment directly above Gordana and Ivo's. They said they still didn't think of the flat as their own, filled as it was by the possessions left behind by the Golijanins. Nazif had little to wear. "His clothes are all too big," he said. "I couldn't use any of his things, even if I wanted to." He would not refer to his former colleague Nikola by name.

Since their son, Kemo, had been killed, Nazif and Fata had not considered a return to Ilidža. "We don't think of the future anymore," Nazif said. "Everything is over for us."

10

A Loser's Peace

The shelling of Sarajevo in the first weeks of 1994 was as heavy as it had ever been, with U.N. military observers reporting hundreds of impacts in the city every day. On February 4 three mortar rounds fired from the vicinity of a Serb army base exploded in a crowd waiting for food in the government-controlled suburb of Dobrinja. Ten people, among them three children, were killed in the blasts, and twenty were injured. The next day sixty-eight Sarajevans died after a mortar shell crashed into the downtown market at the peak Saturday shopping hour, when people were packed elbow to elbow in the narrow passageways between the vendors' stalls. The burst of shrapnel left the marketplace awash in blood and bits of flesh. Journalists at the scene said it smelled like a butcher shop.

Outraged by the atrocities, NATO powers gave the Serb nationalist forces ten days to remove their heavy weaponry from around Sarajevo or face air strikes on their hilltop gun positions. The Serb leaders were initially defiant of the ultimatum, but an envoy of the Russian government, Vitaly

Churkin, persuaded them to comply at the last minute, and a massive Serb pullout began. By the end of the month most of the tanks and howitzers were gone, and the Serbs had agreed to allow U.N. soldiers to monitor any artillery pieces left in position. Under truce terms dictated by the new commander of U.N. forces in Bosnia, Lt. Gen. Sir Michael Rose, the Bosnian government army agreed not to take military advantage of the Serb withdrawal and to refrain from offensive actions in the local area.

Immediately following the Sarajevo ceasefire, U.S. officials brokered an agreement to settle the Muslim-Croat conflict in central Bosnia. On March 1, after three days of negotiations in Washington, representatives of the Bosnian Croat leadership and the Bosnian and Croatian governments agreed on the design of a joint Muslim-Croat federation in Bosnia, thus putting an end to talk of separate Muslim and Croat minirepublics. The Washington and Sarajevo truce accords were turning points in the Bosnian war; each agreement reinforced the other by contributing to a broader sense that the conflict was entering a conclusive stage. United States, European, and Russian officials devoted the months that followed to the negotiation of a peace plan that would have broad international support and a genuine chance of bringing the war to an end.

Safe in Sarajevo?

Sarajevans greeted the February ceasefire developments with skepticism and grumpiness. Many were disappointed that the Serb forces on the ridgetops had escaped attack from the NATO fighter jets; they had wanted the gunners to pay with their own lives for the damage, death, and pain they had inflicted. The city's residents were ready for peace, but many were angry and resentful that the diplomatic initiatives were so evenhanded in their treatment of the "warring sides." Fifteen-year-old Boris Knežević, in a February dispatch for the U.S. *Children's Express* news service, imagined the kind of agreement the world's diplomats could negotiate with the Serb leadership and then impose on the Bosnian government: "It is like a quarrel between two kids," Boris wrote. "[Only] one of the kids is right, but the parent, having too much on his mind and being too old to enter their little world, punishes them equally. They make peace, but one carries that stone of unfairness in his heart."

Boris, his parents, and everyone else in Sarajevo benefited, however, from a sudden and dramatic improvement in living conditions.

The break from shelling and sniping allowed utility crews to repair power lines, and electricity was soon restored across the city. Pumping stations began working again, and the Knežević family had running water in their apartment for the first time in more than a year. People went for walks downtown again and lingered in open spaces. On a Sunday afternoon in March, the Sarajevo soccer team played a multinational squad of U.N. soldiers in the wreckage of the Olympic Stadium, down the hill from the Kneževićs' apartment building. A trumpet band provided entertainment, and the stands were filled with thousands of cheering spectators. It was the first mass outdoor gathering in Sarajevo since the demonstration in front of the Parliament Building on April 6, 1992. Radovan Karadžić sent the United Nations' General Rose a written guarantee that Serb forces would not attack the stadium during the match.

Just two months earlier Karadžić had promised his Serb deputies in Pale that the war on Sarajevo would be intensified. "Sarajevans will not be counting the dead," Karadžić had said. "They will be counting the living." The threat to Sarajevo had not disappeared, but with the NATO ultimatum and the intervention of the Russian government, the world community had declared that the city should live, and the Serb nationalists had finally been forced to back down. On March 4, 1994, the fifteen members of the U.N. Security Council unanimously approved a resolution calling for complete freedom of movement for civilians in Sarajevo and the restoration of "normal life" to the city. If the Serb forces returned with their tanks and howitzers and resumed shelling the city, it would mean a confrontation with the entire international community.

Unlike the predominantly Muslim towns of Foča and Zvornik in eastern Bosnia or Kozarac and Prijedor in northern Bosnia, Sarajevo had not been overrun by the Serb army. Unlike the Croatian city of Vukovar, it had not been flattened. A U.N.-appointed special coordinator for Sarajevo arrived at the end of March with a team of international experts to begin planning the city's reconstruction. Tram lines were repaired, and the streetcars started rolling again. United Nations troops arranged the opening of a road across a Sarajevo airport runway and over nearby Mt. Igman to government-controlled territory, allowing limited traffic into and out of the city. The war was not over, but Sarajevans were getting a preview of postwar reality.

Freed from the immediate danger of death, injury, or starvation, Sarajevans stopped to assess what was left of their lives. For almost two years, they had been dreaming of the day they could again move freely in their city, but the peace they had envisioned was based on memories of happy prewar times, whereas the postwar reality was dead-end poverty and ruin. When the shelling and sniping stopped and the water and lights came back on, many Sarajevans found it hard to cope with the new varieties of stress they faced. They had mastered the wartime rules and learned the odds, and when the game changed the old habits and thinking were not easily shaken. Mental health clinics were inundated with new patients.

Some Sarajevans who had chosen to stay in the city even when they had opportunities to flee now made plans to grab the first bus out of town. Patriotism had made them stick it out as long as Sarajevo's survival was at stake, but they had promised themselves and their families that they would leave as soon as the war was finished. The residue of enmity, despair, and hopelessness that remained in the city after the guns were silenced was just what they had feared. The liberation of Sarajevo from German Nazi forces in April 1945 represented a stunning victory over the forces of fascism and was celebrated yearly thereafter as such. The end of the Serb nationalist forces' artillery bombardment of Sarajevo in the spring of 1994 did not even come close to delivering the same triumph.

There were Sarajevo residents, of course, who had nowhere to go and who refused to be discouraged about the rebuilding challenge in front of them. They cleared their streets of rubble, patched the walls of their apartment buildings, and volunteered to help reorganize their schools and workplaces. At *Oslobodjenje,* the diesel generators were shut down and moved aside as the presses began running again on normal electric power.

Having prevailed through the longest and most destructive siege of a major city since Leningrad, the newspaper seemed poised to prosper. *Oslobodjenje* had won international acclaim as a model of heroic endurance, it had a staff of war-hardened journalists, and its weekly European edition was turning a profit. But reconstruction would prove to be as slow and joyless for the newspaper as for Sarajevo itself. The triumph of the newspaper, like that of the city, was simply in its physical survival; the cost was too high to allow much glory.

The New Social Order

On March 31, 1994, about six weeks after the Sarajevo ceasefire took effect, Boris Knežević had a run-in with a street gang in his neighborhood. He had gone to deliver a music cassette to his best friend, Daut, who lived about a block away. At the entrance to Daut's apartment building, Boris suddenly found himself surrounded by about fifteen teenage boys. One of the group carried a broken crutch piece in his hand, and several of the others had sticks. Boris recognized them as a gang from Šip, a semirural suburb on the northern fringe of Sarajevo. The gang leader had a year earlier gotten into a fight with another of Boris's friends, Harun, the grandson of Kana, the Muslim woman who lived next door to the Knežević family. The gang leader had been itching ever since to get even with Harun, and beating up one of his friends would be a start. Boris tried to run, but one of the boys caught him and knocked him down.

Daut was waiting for Boris, and, when he saw the boys corner his friend in the building entryway, he went pounding on nearby apartment doors and screaming for help. The gang members had started hitting Boris with their makeshift clubs. He put his arms around his head in an effort to protect himself, but a boy landed several sharp blows on the left side of his face.

By the time Daut reached the scene with a woman from an upstairs apartment, the gang had gone. Daut found Boris crumpled on the floor, woozy and bleeding. The woman helped him up, covered his face with wet handkerchiefs, and called Ivo at his Information Ministry office to tell him what had happened. Ivo rushed over and took Boris immediately to Koševo Hospital to be examined. Although he had suffered no broken bones, he was badly cut and bruised on his face and shoulders, and his left eye was swollen shut. He didn't want to talk about what had happened. Ivo reported the beating to the Sarajevo police, but they told him there was nothing they could do.

Gordana told me of the attack on Boris about two months afterward, describing it as one of several "ugly incidents" that had occurred in Sarajevo since the ceasefire. Tensions that had been stifled during wartime came to the surface in the weeks after the shelling stopped, she explained, and one manifestation had been the appearance of teenage gangs. "They have been spreading real terror around Sarajevo," Gordana said. "We should have expected it, with these kids idle all this time and faced with such violence." It was like a scene from *A Clockwork Orange*. In just two years Sarajevo had been tossed from one epoch to another and back—caught in a time machine gone haywire. Once up-to-date and à la mode, Sarajevo slid into a state of medieval suffering and ended up having a postapocalyptic societal breakdown.

When Boris was beaten up, some people in the neighborhood wondered whether the gang, all Muslims, had gone after him because he was part Serb. Boris insisted that was not the case, however, and, considering that the gang members' original target, Harun, was as Muslim as they were, ethnic animosity was evidently a secondary factor at most. The Šip boys themselves later confirmed this. Harun's aunt, a high school teacher, spotted the gang members loitering outside her apartment building a few days after the attack on Boris, and she went to talk to them, bringing a pack of cigarettes along to get their attention.

"Tell me why you beat up Boris Knežević," she said.

"He's one of those 'cellar boys' who hide with their mommies in the basement," the gang leader told her. "We've been watching them since the war started. We don't like them. This was a way to teach them about life." Boris and his friends had long hair, played guitars, and listened to heavy metal music. They had been good students in their school days. The gang members came from working-class backgrounds, wore their hair short, and had scorned scholarly achievements and professional aspirations. The gang leader's father was a Bosnian army officer serving on the front line.

The war had inverted the social hierarchy in Sarajevo. Soldiers, policemen, and anyone else essential to the military effort, regardless of their origin, prevailed over the city's educated and monied elite. The shift of clout had been signaled in the summer of 1993, when profiteering army commanders managed to defy law enforcement officials for weeks, but it took the ceasefire to expose the transformation openly. New cars appeared on downtown streets, driven not by the people who had parked them in their garages two years earlier but by the well-connected army officers and black market traders who had bought them at bargain prices when the original owners fled.

Among those who had gone were the bulk of Sarajevo's professional class. Of Koševo Hospital's 8,000 staff members before the war, fewer than 3,000 were still working there by the spring of 1994. Ivo Knežević was one of only a handful of professors in his university faculty who remained in Sarajevo. When the ceasefire brought people onto the streets again, longtime Sarajevo residents were stunned at how many unfamiliar faces they encountered downtown. Thousands of apartments belonging to Serbs who had left at the beginning of the war had been given to arriving Muslim refugees from eastern Bosnia. The newcomers stood out as rural folk do in any big city, their faces rough and weathered and their step uncertain. Many of the Muslim women wore head scarves and the long, colorful skirts that were traditional dress in Bosnian towns and villages.

Oslobodjenje reporter Senka Kurtović didn't realize how many country people had come to Sarajevo until the streetcars started operating again, and their rough ways irritated her. "There are rules about how to behave on the trams, and these people don't know them," Senka said. "You don't spit, you don't push, and you don't shout; there is a proper way to get on and a way to get off; you should give up your seat if an elderly person needs it. But these refugees don't know any of these things. They don't even know the names of the stops."

The idea that the city had been taken over by bullies and bumpkins unnerved many Sarajevans, because for two years they had seen their struggle against the besieging Serb army largely as a fight to defend their city's cosmopolitan heritage against the assault of primitive nationalists. When the shooting stopped it turned out that Sarajevo's urban tradition had been undermined also from within.

The question of Sarajevo's character was further complicated as people who had fled the city began coming back. Those who had stayed throughout the war were less than welcoming of the others' return. Senka Kurtović described her feelings in an *Oslobodjenje* commentary: "They'll come back with a lot of money. They won't have been damaged mentally, and they'll have learned new customs. Compared to them, we'll all be second class." Like many Sarajevans, Senka just wished that the city could go back to the way it had been.

She was angry, but she also felt isolated, and that feeling deepened with the death of her mother. "I don't care about anyone else at all," she said in June 1994. "I figure: You survived and I survived, so we're fine on our own."

The influx of war refugees and the prospect of former residents coming back to Sarajevo raised key policy questions for the Bosnian government in the spring and summer of 1994. The government was committed to providing jobs and housing in Sarajevo for Muslims displaced from their homes in eastern Bosnia, but it also felt obligated to make room for returning Sarajevans who wanted to reclaim jobs and properties. Politically, the ruling Muslim party was inclined to attend first to the victims of Serb "ethnic cleansing" campaigns, especially because Muslim men from the "cleansed" areas were well represented in the ranks of the Bosnian army and constituted a militant political force. But if Sarajevo were to recover economically, there needed to be incentives for its displaced professional and managerial class to reestablish itself in the city. At the end of May the government proposed a law that would offer amnesty to young men who had left Sarajevo to avoid military service, an act that previously had been considered a criminal offense. Serbs who had gone to Pale or Belgrade would be excluded from the amnesty, although Serb men who had fled to neutral countries were to be covered.

"All of us who have spent the war here consider these people traitors," Deputy Prime Minister Edib Bukvić admitted. "But morality is one thing, and everyday life is another, and we must accept this fact. We simply have to allow these educated young people to come back here. Indeed, we must encourage them to come back, because we are a small country, and we need them." Bukvić said the government planned to "reward" those Sarajevans who had stayed in the city throughout the war, however, by giving them preference in the allocation of jobs and housing.

The government prepared its amnesty proposal largely at the urging of the Sarajevo representative of the Helsinki Citizens Assembly (HCA), an organization seeking to promote the values of civil society and democracy in post-Communist states in Eastern Europe. The HCA representative, Radha Kumar, felt the exclusion of many Serbs from the amnesty would make political reconciliation difficult if not impossible. She was also concerned that the government's planning was inadequate. "It's fine to encourage people to return," she said, "but there have to be guarantees of protection, freedom of expression, and possibilities for employment." She and other reform advocates worried that the government's plan to "reward" Sarajevans who had stayed in the city could open the door to legalized discrimination, and that under the postwar circumstances in the city any such bias could easily become ethnic in effect if not in design.

To many people in Sarajevo, however, the government's proposal went way too far. Among the angriest outbursts of criticism was from *Oslobodjenje* commentator Slavko Šantić, a Serb whose son had enlisted as a volunteer in the Bosnian army on April 6, 1992, and served ever since. In a column titled "Amnesty for Betrayal," Šantić blasted the government officials who backed the measure. "It would be more fair," he wrote, "if our fighters could for one minute feel the comfort and security that these people who were abroad have known for these two years. These people are traitors, and the authors of this law will have to face the rage of all those who will feel cheated by it."

With Sarajevo out of the line of gunfire, the focus of political debate was already shifting to questions of postwar life.

The Way Ahead

As an *Oslobodjenje* journalist, Šantić had been regularly censored during the war. No one ever accused him of making a Serb nationalist argument, but his criticism of high government officials had been so vituperative at times that his editors felt it was unprintable. The publication of his "Amnesty for Betrayal" column on page 2 did not signal a shift in *Oslobodjenje*'s political stance; several editors, in fact, found it distasteful. But with war pressures diminishing, the paper was beginning to accommodate a wider variety of opinions, sticking less rigidly to a single line, and showing its independence from the government.

In February the *Oslobodjenje* staff chose Mehmed Halilović, a veteran correspondent and commentator, to replace Kemal Kurspahić as editor in chief. A quiet and diligent journalist in his midfifties, Halilović had kept a low profile during wartime in Sarajevo, coming to the *Oslobodjenje* office only every few days, principally to deliver commentaries he had written at home. Many of the staff hoped he could be a source of new unity.

Gordana Knežević did not apply for the editor's position, although she had been Kemal's deputy during the paper's darkest days. In July 1993 Gordana had told me that she did not see herself playing a big role at *Oslobodjenje* once the war ended. "There will be a feeling," she had said, "that the people who ran the paper in wartime are an obstacle in peacetime." She remembered her mother telling her that after World War II the most heroic Partisan fighters generally found themselves ignored when positions in the new Yugoslav government were being allocated. "It seems," Gordana said, "that one kind of morale is important during war: you need strong people to do the work. But in peacetime, firmness is not so necessary, and strong moral principles can even get in the way of what is to be done."

I was surprised by her bitterness. "I'm going to go away from Bosnia after the war," Gordana had said. "I don't want to be around to see this ugly peace, with everybody kissing each other. I'll know I did my best and gave everything I had, so I can just forget it. My part will be finished."

After Boris was beaten up by the Šip gang, Gordana devoted her time and energy to finding a way to get him out of Sarajevo. The *Children's Express* news service in the United States requested U.N. press credentials for him; if he got a press card, he would be entitled to take a U.N. relief flight to Croatia or Italy. Gordana briefed Boris on what he might have to do. If he flew to Italy, she said, he would have to call family friends from the airport in Ancona and make further arrangements.

"But, Mom, I don't know how to use the telephone," Boris said. "I heard something about some cards you have to put in." He wondered how he could buy tickets for the bus and figure out which one to take. He even asked about the public lavatories. As a twelve-year-old in Cairo, Boris had mastered the urban public transport system. He had thought nothing of finding his own way across town to an unfamiliar movie theater or Pizza Hut to meet school friends, or of heading off to attend a soccer match on the opposite side of the city, a chaotic metropolis of 17 million inhabitants. But after being trapped for two years in besieged Sarajevo, Boris had lost all confidence in his ability to manage in the outside world.

Ivo Knežević sympathized with his son. "I feel the same way," he told me. "It seems to us like this war has gone on for twenty years, so we naturally assume that everything on the outside has changed, especially technology. We have this idea that everything has advanced beyond us." When Senka Kurtović had an opportunity to work for a month at the office in Slovenia where *Oslobodjenje*'s European edition was prepared, she was so nervous about the trip that she couldn't sleep the last two nights before she left. On the morning of her flight, she called her colleague Džeilana Pećanin at seven o'clock and begged her to accompany her to the airport. *Oslobodjenje* columnist Gojko Berić, who had gone more than a year without venturing past the front door of his apartment, demanded that the newspaper management send a younger staff member as his escort when he left Sarajevo. The editors refused, and Berić was able to steel himself for the trip only by drinking a half bottle of whiskey. He showed up for his U.N. flight dead drunk.

In May 1994 Boris Knežević was able to leave Sarajevo on a bus to Split with Gordana's father. Owing to delays and checkpoints, the trip took six days. From Split, Boris took a bus to Zagreb, where he met his eight-year-old sister, Olga, whom he had not seen in two years. They didn't recognize each other. Gordana followed her son out of Sarajevo at the end of the month. Two weeks later she sent him and his sister to spend the summer with their grandfather at his cabin on the Croatian coast, while she prepared to go to the United States for a four-month fellowship at Macalester College in St. Paul.

I returned to Sarajevo in June, just as Gordana left. I was staggered by the changes that had taken place in the six months since I had been there last. Traffic signals were functioning at downtown intersections again. What was more, drivers were actually heeding them, concerned more about getting a ticket for running a red light than about being shot by a Serb sniper while waiting for it to change. The Holiday Inn had reopened the café on the east side of the hotel, overlooking the Parliament Building, and waiters were serving breakfast on a balcony where it would have been unthinkable to set foot as long as the snipers were shooting. Espresso coffee and Austrian beer were available at the lobby bar, and I had hot running water in my hotel room for the first time ever.

Oslobodjenje had moved its downtown newsroom and was operating out of a suite of offices belonging to an architectural firm. With electricity available again, a dozen desk computers had been dug out of storage and hooked up. A new, creative spirit had taken hold at the paper. As the Oslobodjenje News Agency, the staff were producing a daily digest of Sarajevo news in English and Serbo-Croatian and wiring it to subscribers for as much as $500 a month. The service had been planned since Kemal Kurspahić edited the newspaper, but he could not get it started as long as there was no steady supply of electricity. The operation was earning the newspaper a good income, and, equally important, it was forcing *Oslobodjenje* journalists to be more responsible and enterprising, orienting their reporting to the needs and interests of the Western news organizations who were their principal clients.

Few other commercial firms in Sarajevo were as well positioned to thrive in the postwar period as *Oslobodjenje,* and the Bosnian government started to show interest in the newspaper's assets. The *Oslobodjenje* publishing company had been in the early stages of privatization when the war broke out, and its ownership was not yet clearly defined. In theory the paper was "social property," meaning it belonged at least partly to its employees, but it had not yet been converted to a stock company, so the employee share was not formalized. As Sarajevo prepared for economic reconstruction, the government announced that it considered "socially owned" firms state property, to be disposed of as state officials saw fit. "*Oslobodjenje* workers will have ownership rights if they come up with the money to buy the firm," Reconstruction Minister Munever Imamović told me. "If someone else has the capital to buy the newspaper [from the state], then that party will be the owner."

The *Oslobodjenje* staff were alarmed by the government declaration. Virtually all the newspaper's physical assets had been destroyed during the war, with the exception of its printing presses in the basement of its bombed-out offices in Nedjarići. What commercial value *Oslobodjenje* had in the summer of 1994 derived largely from the international reputation it had earned during the war period as a persevering and independent newspaper, and staff members were loath to let the ruling authorities cash in on that. Moreover, the Bosnian government was firmly in the hands of the ruling Muslim SDA party. *Oslobodjenje* thus faced the possibility of becoming a party organ again, just as it had been during the Communist period.

Concern about the looming prospect of Muslim party rule was one of the factors behind the paper's growing distance from the government in the spring and summer of 1994. The Muslim party had been entrenching itself throughout the war period, and by the spring of 1994 it thoroughly dominated the Bosnian government and public institutions. With peacetime approaching, advocates of liberal democratic values in Sarajevo increasingly began to disassociate themselves from the government.

The Social Democratic Party (SDP), for example, consisting mainly of reform-minded former Communists, had joined the government in the first months of the war but by the summer of 1994 was back in the opposition. Zlatko Lagumdžija, an SDP leader who had served as deputy prime minister in the wartime Bosnian government, said the shift was due. "When the war started," he told me, "there were just two political blocs; you were either for Bosnia or against Bosnia." Lagumdžija was injured in a mortar blast in early 1993 and was out of the country recuperating for several months. When he returned to Sarajevo in May 1994, with the war in Bosnia winding down, he did not want any connection with the ruling SDA party. "Until a few years ago," he said, "we had a totalitarian system in Bosnia, based on one-party rule. Now I see things headed in that direction again. Before, it was one party that claimed to rule on behalf of the working class. What we have now in Bosnia is one party ruling on behalf of one ethnic or national group. It's even more totalitarian, more unnatural."

Oslobodjenje's move toward and then away from the government mirrored the Social Democrats' shift. Mehmed Halilović had not shown the inspired leadership during the war that Kemal Kurspahić had demonstrated, nor did he have the uncompromising political commitment and combative drive of Gordana Knežević. But in the summer of 1994, he was preparing to fight for *Oslobodjenje's* independence. "I don't see any future for my newspaper as a servant of one party," Halilović told me. Within a month of our conversation, *Oslobodjenje* under his leadership had gotten itself into a bruising war of words with a government minister.

Another Phase of Struggle

With the ceasefire holding, hope rose that Sarajevo might actually recover its former social character and resume its democratic development. The revival of political opposition movements was a promising step, as were the signs that reconciliation might yet be possible. A Serbian correspondent from the Belgrade newspaper *Borba,* Dragan Banjac, spent a month in Sarajevo in April and May 1994. In the fall of 1992, during the height of the Serb nationalist bombardment of the city, a previous *Borba* correspondent had written of the deteriorating ethnic relations in the city, but Banjac's reports were far more upbeat and hopeful. He worked out of the *Oslobodjenje* office and before leaving posted a letter to the newspaper staff on the office wall:

> Colleagues and friends:
>   With you I have worked easily, and I have felt your human suffering and determination. I'm convinced that Bosnia will survive. I have no doubt you will preserve what are the best virtues of this place, unity (so needed in these times) and loyalty. Be proud of that, and if you notice that starting tomorrow you have a little less of your spirit, do not worry. It is because I have taken a part of it, secretly, back to Belgrade, where that "thing" is so needed right now.
>   —Dragan Banjac

Croatian journalists were also showing up in Sarajevo to report on the development of the Muslim-Croat federation agreement in Bosnia. Even a few Croats who had left Sarajevo during the war to side with the Croat nationalist movement in Herzegovina came back in the spring of 1994, though somewhat sheepishly. I was sitting in a café in the Baščaršija district of the Old Town when one such "disloyal" Sarajevo Croat walked in and greeted his old Muslim friends as though nothing had come between them in the months that he had been away. "We don't have to make up," he said. "We didn't really attack each other. We just got into a fight for no good reason."

In May *Oslobodjenje* reporter Džeilana Pećanin received a letter from her Serb friend Tanja, the soul-mate with whom Džeilana had practiced her English and watched her favorite film, *The Deer Hunter*, over and over, but who had then abandoned Sarajevo and broken Džeilana's heart.

The letter was dated March 24, 1994. Tanja told Džeilana that she had been miserable in Belgrade and that her mother had died of cancer. Then, switching to English, she apologized to her Muslim friend:

> You may not believe this, but it is true. I keep thinking and dreaming about you. I feel like I betrayed you by leaving Sarajevo. Of course, I had to go, but I remembered Michael's promise to Nick, not to leave him over there. I think now that we all have to continue living far from these unfortunate places. The question is where.

Džeilana immediately answered Tanja's letter, a bit cool in tone but thanking her for writing and holding out the promise that they could see each other somewhere again. The capacity of Sarajevans to forgive and forget was limited, and the last thing they were willing to hear was that their friends who had fled Sarajevo had suffered in some similar measure. "I will not allow anyone who has not been through this war to compare anything in their life with this," Senka Kurtović said when a friend in Herzegovina called to complain about her loneliness. But contact was being reestablished.

The critical question during the summer of 1994 was whether the nascent social and political revival in Sarajevo could offset the countervailing movement toward a more closed society. The two-year assault on Sarajevo by Serb nationalist forces had convinced many Muslims that coexistence was no longer as desirable as they had once thought. SDA hard-liners were arguing that Muslim interests should take precedence in Sarajevo, and their party position had never been stronger.

The advocates of a state based on civil rights had paradoxically been dealt a blow by the Muslim-Croat accord that opened a way to the ending of the Bosnian war. The federation constitution required that the presidency alternate between a Muslim and a Croat. Serbs who had remained loyal to the Bosnian government throughout the war were essentially excluded from political life, as the Muslim and Croat national parties held the keys to power. In Muslim-dominated

Sarajevo, the SDA was unstoppable. Gen. Jovan Divjak, the Serb deputy commander of the Bosnian army in Sarajevo, feared he would be forced to resign. "If people are not members of the SDA," he told a reporter, "they have no vote and no voice in the government, and that is humiliating."

The SDA clerical wing renewed its effort to impose Islamic practices on the population, although in secular Sarajevo religious extremism was kept firmly in check. Municipal authorities prohibited the sale of alcohol at cafés in the Baščaršija district, but made little effort to enforce the ban. The SDA-appointed general manager of Radio-Television Sarajevo sparked a controversy by outlawing leggings and short skirts on female employees. The limits of the crackdown were evident in the television programming, however. During my June visit R-TV Sarajevo broadcast the film *Basic Instinct,* starring Sharon Stone and Michael Douglas, with explicit sex and full nudity. The film was shown uncut at the peak family viewing hour, 8:00 P.M., immediately following the evening news. So much for Islamic fundamentalism in Sarajevo.

Mostly, the new strength of the Muslim nationalists was seen in their willingness to challenge Sarajevo's tradition of harmonious living. Džemaludin Latić, editor in chief of the pro-SDA weekly magazine *Ljiljan,* touched a nerve with a series of columns condemning interethnic, interfaith marriage as a "catastrophe." For Sarajevans who had been fighting to defend their cosmopolitan character against the Serb nationalist assault, the Latić broadside opened a new domestic battlefront.

As a Sarajevo institution that exemplified the ideal of "common life"—and as an enterprise with a higher than average rate of mixed marriages among its staff members—*Oslobodjenje* was immediately drawn into the polemic. The outspoken Slavko Šantić, muzzled by his editors during wartime but now free to criticize the government on almost any issue, wrote a column condemning Latić for his views.

Latić responded by attacking *Oslobodjenje* as a whole, "the newspaper which for more than half a century has been oppressing ethnic differences," an aim Latić evidently found objectionable. Although he attacked *Oslobodjenje* for its "UNPROFOR conception" and its promotion of "the myth of the superiority of European civilization," the newspaper's greatest fault in Latić's eyes was that its "insistence on mixed marriages . . . [promotes] the dangerous path of living together." Latić directly challenged the value of a political culture in which Muslims, Serbs, and Croats are treated equally. Non-Muslims who asked for such a state, he argued, were setting themselves up as "a privileged sect." As a Muslim, Latić asked why he should "apologize and abandon national issues, because of a few Serb and Croat patriots."

The battle was on. Šantić responded, in characteristically injudicious manner, by accusing Latić of promoting "fascism." The minister of culture in the Bosnian government, Enes Karić, jumped into the fray with a *Ljiljan* column of his own, calling *Oslobodjenje* "a paper of proven Communist-Chetnik reputation," apparently referring to its past as a Party organ and to the large number of Serbs still employed at the paper. Karić made clear he was not impressed by *Oslobodjenje*'s record of uninterrupted publication. "Why," he asked, "does *Oslobodjenje* have newsprint, and even imports it in wartime, while Sarajevo children don't have powdered milk?"

No more could anyone say *Oslobodjenje* was cozy with the Bosnian government, as had been charged through most of the war period; it was squarely in the opposition camp. From Washington Kemal Kurspahić fired off a riposte of his own, pointing out that he had in fact led the newspaper away from Communist rule. "The society advocated in the pages and in the ethnic composition of *Oslobodjenje*," the former editor argued, "is a society of human rights and liberties in which each individual is free to believe in what he wants, or not to believe; a society in which all religious and ethnic rights and traditions are guaranteed, but in company with the centuries-old atmosphere of tolerance and the culture of living together."

Kemal was worried, however, that his cause might already be lost. Serb journalists at the newspaper were increasingly anxious about their future in Sarajevo and, with the exception of Slavko Šantić, few had the strength or inclination to fight the SDA nationalists. Gordana Knežević had left the city and was focusing on her family problems. Veteran reporter Vlado Mrkić had virtually dropped out of sight. He filed a long story in May about a Serb woman in Sarajevo whose son had died fighting as a soldier in the Bosnian army. The woman called him a *shehid*, or holy war martyr, and had prayed for his soul at the local mosque as well as at her own Orthodox church. After that article, however, Mrkić slipped back into a deep and angry depression; he did not write again for *Oslobodjenje* for weeks.

In Zagreb Gordana Knežević went to a U.S. refugee resettlement office for information on applying for asylum status for herself and her children. The officer told Gordana that if they were Muslims he could get them classified as refugees without a problem, because

Muslims were officially recognized as the principal victims in the Bosnian war. He also told Gordana that he could help her if she testified that she had suffered mistreatment and discrimination as a Serb in Muslim-dominated Sarajevo. "I can't claim that," Gordana said, "because it's not true." She tried to explain that it was the Serb nationalists who were responsible for the physical and social ruin of Sarajevo, and also for her own feeling of insecurity, inside or outside the city.

"But I can't help you unless you say you're being persecuted," the refugee officer emphasized. Gordana told him to tear up the asylum applications. There was no special category for Sarajevans who felt their ideals had been smothered, first by war and then under a compromised peace. She felt lost. One son was in England, the other was in Croatia with her daughter, and Ivo was still in Sarajevo. When she flew out of Zagreb in June for Minnesota, Gordana had no idea when, how, or where she could get her family together again. She cried halfway across the Atlantic.

Vital Interests

The Serb nationalist forces did not conquer Sarajevo. The effort, through siege and bombardment, to force the city to surrender was unsuccessful. With their suffering moderated by the assistance of the United Nations and other international agencies, Sarajevans did not yield, and the city survived. But Radovan Karadžić and his followers weakened Sarajevo enough to change the balance of political forces in the city and strengthen the hard-line Muslims who had nationalist designs of their own. Those Sarajevans who were struggling for a civil state slowly gave up.

Many of them blamed "the West" for not supporting them. Among the few Western leaders who had recognized and articulated the international interest in Sarajevo was Czech president Václav Havel. He had spent years fighting to keep "European values" alive in a totalitarian Communist state, and he had a clear idea what they meant. Speaking at the Council of Europe in October 1993, Havel chided his fellow statesmen for "giving up on the idea of a civic society" in Bosnia and thus abandoning the "fundamental values upon which we would like to shape the future of our continent. We are cutting off the very branch we are sitting on," he said.

Most of the U.N. soldiers and Western diplomats who had represented the "international community" in Sarajevo and Bosnia had argued that the war amounted to little more than an ancient Balkan feud and should not be seen as a pressing international concern. The first U.N. commander in the former Yugoslavia, Lt. Gen. Satish Nambiar of India, left his command at the end of February 1993 advising the world to stay out of the Bosnian war. "There is no reason why men and women from faraway countries should shed their blood *on behalf of communities unwilling to come to terms with each other,*" he said [emphasis added].

Other U.N. officials echoed his view. "Dealing with Bosnia," Gen. Lewis MacKenzie told a U.S. congressional committee, "is a little bit like dealing with three serial killers. One has killed fifteen, one has killed ten, and one has killed five. Do we help the one that has only killed five?"

No one was more impassioned in denying that Bosnia was of world concern than Jose Cutileiro, the Portuguese foreign minister who coordinated the European Community's abortive attempt in 1992 to mediate the conflict. Writing in the *International Herald Tribune* in June 1993, Cutileiro sought to "put in perspective" the world's inability to stop the Bosnian war. "They have mostly themselves to blame," he wrote of the Bosnian Muslims, Serbs, and Croats. "International attention," he argued, had "bred in them delusions of centrality . . . [and] bloated their self-importance. Indeed, a pernicious side effect of international involvement in former Yugoslavia has been to make fighters for parochial interests appear as if they [are] champions of universal causes. They are not." Such comments blurred differences among the warring parties, especially between the Bosnian government and the Serb nationalists, the principal adversaries in the Bosnian war. In that regard, they were dishonest.

The Bosnian Serb leadership set out at the beginning of the Bosnian war to establish an ethnically pure state, and they never wavered in their determination. Their bottom line was expressed by their spokesman Jovan Zametica in March 1994, as diplomats were struggling to put together a final peace plan for Bosnia. "We remain flexible on territory," Zametica said. "But please don't force us to live together."

Four months later the Serb nationalists were demonstrating the seriousness of their intent, this time in Bijeljina, the town in the far northeast corner of Bosnia that had been under Serb control since the beginning of the war and where there was absolutely no military threat from the Bosnian army. Several thousand Muslims remained in Bijeljina in mid-1994, and they were among the most compliant of the non-Serbs still living in Serb-controlled Bosnian territory. Some had even changed their names to conceal their Muslim origins. Under the draft international peace plan then being circulated, Bijeljina would be assigned to the "Serb Republic," so there was no need for the Serbs to assert their claim to the territory.

In July 1994, however, Serb authorities began systematically expelling the remaining non-Serb residents from Bijeljina, family by family. The Muslims and Croats were stripped of their possessions and forced to sign over their property before leaving. Muslim women and children arriving in Tuzla, about twenty-five miles to the southwest, reported that Muslim men under sixty years of age had been sent to work in forced labor camps, a charge later confirmed by officials of the U.N. High Commissioner for Refugees (UNHCR). "The pace at which the authorities in Bijeljina are collecting people seems to indicate a new impetus to ridding the community of the last Muslims and Croats," UNHCR spokesman Peter Kessler said. He reported that the town authorities were so determined in their efforts that they had actually painted their trucks with U.N. markings and were telling Muslim residents that they were to be resettled in Sweden and Switzerland. "The local authorities," Kessler said, "are apparently prepared to use every possible ruse to get Muslims to identify themselves so they can be evicted." By October 1994, Serb forces had driven about 6,000 non-Serbs out of the Bijeljina area, according to the UNHCR.

The Bijeljina operation showed exactly what the Serb nationalists intended for their "Serb Republic": It was to be a state exclusively for Serbs. The Serb leaders had already demonstrated what they meant with their declaration of a separate "Serb Sarajevo" in 1992, by their expulsion of the Merzić family and other non-Serbs from the suburb of Ilidža, which was to be included in the "Serb" part of the city. The Serb understanding of ethnic partition in Bosnia and Sarajevo required the most thorough expulsion of minority populations in Europe since the Nazi extermination of non-Aryans. "We are aware that we have to go all the way," Radovan Karadžić said in October 1994. "The Serbian people are about to reach their centuries-old goal of creating a unified Serb state."

Momčilo Krajišnik, the Bosnian Serbs' "parliamentary" leader, was even more blunt. "The joint Serbian state must be formed with a firm, man's hand," he said. "It should be based on Serb nationalism, with all Orthodox and national traditions. Serbs are not forming some watered-down state with so-called civil rights."

To be sure, Muslim authorities had also expelled Serbs from some Muslim-controlled towns, generally under the pressure of Muslim refugees who had themselves been evicted from their homes by Serb forces. But this fact did not obscure key differences between the sides, a point made repeatedly by UNHCR officials. "While there have been some abuses against Serbs in Muslim and Croat areas," said Ron Redmond of the UNHCR's Geneva office, "they do not compare in scope with what we have seen happen in Serb-held areas against minorities." The 1992–1994 mass expulsion campaigns in Bosnia euphemistically known as "ethnic cleansing" operations originated with the Serb nationalists. Nothing in Bosnian Muslim history or in the Bosnian Muslim political program established a political precedent for the systematic expulsion of non-Muslim residents from Muslim-populated territory.

By the fall of 1994 Serbs in Sarajevo felt like second-class citizens and were being treated as such, but they were in far better shape than the few Muslims who remained in Banja Luka, the Serb stronghold in northwestern Bosnia, or in Bijeljina. The Bosnian minister of culture called *Oslobodjenje* journalist Slavko Šantić a Chetnik when Šantić dared to criticize ascendant Muslim nationalism in Sarajevo. But in Serb-held territory, there were no Muslim journalists.

The diminishing moral difference between the Muslim and Serb sides in the latter stages of the Bosnian war if anything underscored the world community's interest in settling the conflict. Arguably, Croat and Muslim nationalists were encouraged to pursue their own exclusivist programs when they realized that no one was willing to stand up to the Serb extremists. The Bosnian war suggests that when no distinctions are drawn between victims and aggressors, the victims can become aggressors themselves.

Sarajevo was the city that exemplified the spirit of pluralism and tolerance that has been the principal casualty of the Bosnian war. If there are moral champions in this story, they are those residents of Sarajevo who kept on defending their civic values even when the world was indifferent to their struggle. No group was truer to that cause than the people of *Oslobodjenje*, who thirty terrible months after the onset of siege were still publishing their newspaper every day and showing that right-minded Serbs, Muslims, and Croats could work together no matter the assault on their community.

When U.N. soldiers began repairing Sarajevo streetcar lines in late 1993, most people rejoiced. But Smajo, my grumpy driver, used to shake his bald head in disgust every time we passed one of the U.N. crews diligently at work along the road. "Idiots," he would mutter. Smajo kept in mind what others allowed themselves to forget, that Sarajevo's suffering stemmed entirely from its encirclement by a hostile army. To try to restore "normal life" in the city without first changing that basic fact of siege struck Smajo as an unbelievably stupid idea.

He was right, of course. The improvements that impressed me so much during my visit in June 1994 were reversed as soon as Serb army commanders decided that a return to normalcy in Sarajevo was not in their strategic interest. In July, the Serb leadership rejected the peace plan for Bosnia devised by the "contact group" of U.S., Russian, and European diplomats. The international community vowed to increase pressure on the Pale authorities until they accepted the peace plan, and Serbian President

Slobodan Milošević promised to support their efforts. But Radovan Karadžić and his cohorts figured their stranglehold on the Bosnian capital gave them all the leverage they needed to get their way.

In August 1994, Serb army commanders forced the closure of the Mt. Igman road into Sarajevo by withdrawing guarantees that the road would not be shelled. In the months that followed, they cut off the flow of gas, water, and electricity and blocked aid convoys into the city. Once again, Sarajevans were left cold and hungry. I returned in December to find conditions in the city as desperate as they had been two years earlier, or worse. Cleverly, the Bosnian Serb leaders were making a point: The more the international community pressured them to accept a peace plan they didn't like, the more tightly they would squeeze Sarajevo. Serb snipers on the south bank of the Miljacka River went back to work, this time targeting the streetcars that U.N. crews had just put back in operation. After dozens of tram passengers were killed or wounded, humbled U.N. officials agreed the system should be shut down. Sarajevo streetcars would run when Serb army commanders allowed them to run, and not a moment sooner.

Former U.S. President Jimmy Carter brokered a four-month truce that took effect January 1, 1995, and fighting across Bosnia diminished significantly during the winter months. But the lull did not facilitate new peace negotiations, as Carter had hoped, and it was unclear whether the "peace" that prevailed for a while stemmed from the negotiated ceasefire or from the fact that the Serb and government armies both needed a break from war and a chance to regroup. In March, government forces broke the truce preemptively with a series of attacks against strategic Serb positions in northern and central Bosnia.

Serbs retaliated in their customary way, by hitting their hostage city, Sarajevo. Serb army commanders announced they would no longer guarantee the safety of U.N. flights into the Sarajevo airport, and on April 8, U.N. officials were forced to halt the airlift of relief supplies indefinitely. Next, Serb troops raided the U.N.-supervised weapons collections areas where their artillery had been stored since the February 1994 NATO ultimatum. Taking back their tanks and mortars, the Serb soldiers aimed their guns again at Sarajevo and resumed firing.

The Bosnian government concluded that their capital city would be freed only when their own troops liberated it, and in June 1995 the Bosnian army launched an offensive to break the Sarajevo siege. Attacking in several directions at once, Bosnian troops managed to cut a few Serb supply lines and gain bits of territory on the city's periphery. But the Serb forces responded to the offensive by increasing their bombardment of the city to a level not seen since the early months of the war. In a new twist, Serb gunners attached 500-pound bombs to makeshift rockets and directed them at sites where they could do maximum damage. On June 28, one such rocket blasted into the Sarajevo radio and television building in the Alipašino Polje neighborhood, killing a Bosnian policeman, wounding dozens of journalists, and demolishing the offices of foreign news crews. "These indiscriminate, inaccurate devices are intended as much for terror as for their destructive value," a U.N. spokesman said. A half hour after the television center was hit, another rocket crashed into an apartment building across the street, wiping out three floors.

An *Oslobodjenje* reporter visited the bombed-out Alipašino building the next day and described the scene:

> One of the tenants, Josip Grbič, took us to the upper floors, noting that the whole building had been loosened from its foundation and that none of the apartments were safe any longer for habitation.
>
> "This flat in front of us," he said, "belonged to our neighbor Slavko. We don't know whether he's alive or not. Here is his shirt, you see. We know he came back from the battlefront yesterday. I'm very much afraid that he is lying under all this rubble." Slavko's body was found later.
>
> A blonde lady, weeping, told us she was worried as well about Hamed Živgovič, the father of two little boys who had been hurt and taken to the hospital. "Hamed was supposed to come back from the front line yesterday," she said, "but we don't know if he did. We hope not." Hamed's body was also found later.

To editors in the United States and Western Europe, the killing of Sarajevans was no longer noteworthy by the summer of 1995. But *Oslobodjenje*, the newspaper of record in a dying city, continued to note each massacre and the testimony of the anguished survivors, no matter that their stories were all the same.

"Another sad, sad Sunday in Sarajevo," began a typical article chronicling the casualties registered on June 25, 1995. Eleven people died that day, five of them children killed when a shell landed on their playground in the frontline suburb of Dobrinja. Seven children were wounded, their bodies torn by hot shrapnel. *Oslobodjenje* listed the children by name and age. "Everyone knows the doctors will do everything they can to save these little Sarajevans," the reporter wrote, "but still everyone is afraid for the children's lives. They belong to all of us. People are spreading a rumor that someone from the neighborhood informed [Serb gunners] where exactly the children were playing."

That Sarajevans actually believed there were traitors among them who were helping Serb commanders to target children was an indication of how traumatized the population had become. Such stories illustrated the loss of Sarajevo's soul, as reason gave way to paranoia. In this climate, Serbs who remained in the city faced growing suspicion and marginalization, and the sense of Muslim victimhood increased. When asked during an interview on Radio Sarajevo in July 1995 why the world was not acting to stop the killing in Bosnia, President Alija Izetbegović responded simply, "It is because we are Muslims."

The extent to which Bosnia was to be defined as a Muslim state had become a fiercely debated issue in Sarajevo. In February, five of the seven members of Bosnia's collective presidency publicly criticized the increasing association of the Bosnian army with Islam, evident in the use of Islamic symbols and quotations from the Koran among some army units. "We maintain that the army defending Bosnia-Herzegovina must be secular and multiethnic," the group wrote in an open letter. "Each weakening of multiculturalism diminishes the prospect for establishing a new, democratic society," they said. The two Serb and two Croat members of the Bosnian presidency signed the letter, as did one Muslim member. The criticism was addressed to Alija Izetbegović (officially the "president of the presidency") and Ejup Ganić , his vice president.

Oslobodjenje published the letter on its front page. The newspaper remained allied with the forces favoring a multiethnic state in Bosnia and regularly took positions opposing the Bosnian military. Even after tensions between the U.N. mission and the Bosnian government rose to perilous heights in 1995, *Oslobodjenje* reporter Vladimir Štaka continued to quote U.N. officers challenging claims of the Bosnian army. On those occasions, Vladimir could expect to get an admonishing fax from the army press center. The newspaper's mildly adversarial relationship with the government showed there was still room for debate and political disagreement in Sarajevo. *Oslobodjenje* had no counterpart in Pale, where Radovan Karadžić ran his "Serb Republic" as a police state.

The Serb nationalist leadership remained committed to a strict partition of Sarajevo along ethnic lines. As portrayed in the Serb media, the Muslims of Sarajevo were murderous fundamentalists and the notion of a multicultural society in Bosnia was repugnant. In their determination to undermine the possibility of interethnic life, Serb propagandists were not above telling lies. The most egregious example came in April 1995, when Serb television broadcasters fabricated a story about the death of a seventeen-year-old Sarajevo girl of partly Serb descent named Maja Djokić. Maja was killed by a Serb artillery shell one Sunday evening as she was walking home from volleyball practice. An onlooker, Aleksander Lucić (also of Serb ancestry), saw her fall and rushed to her rescue, but Maja was dead by the time he got her to the hospital.

Serb nationalists hated to admit that some Serbs chose voluntarily to remain in Sarajevo, supported the Bosnian cause, and felt more endangered by their Serb besiegers than by their Muslim neighbors. So they changed Maja's story. "The girl is not a victim of Serb shelling," a Pale broadcaster told his viewers, "but of Izetbegović's followers." The television announcer gave this version of Maja's death: "The Muslims caught this unfortunate girl as she was trying to escape to the Serb part of Sarajevo. On Friday night, they raped her, killed her, and threw her body out on the plaza in front of the [soccer] stadium. . . . UNPROFOR knows everything about this case but haven't said a word so far." Seeing the report on Serb television, U.N. officials were outraged. So was Mr. Lucić.

Forty months after the onset of war, Radovan Karadžić had not given up his intention to establish an exclusively "Serb" quarter in Sarajevo, adjacent to a "Muslim" section. "This is the most clear-cut solution," he told television interviewer David Frost in July 1995, "to transform the city of Sarajevo into two neighboring cities. . . . If we do not finish the job," he said, "then it's going to be like Lebanon and Beirut for many years."

With the Serb army holding Sarajevo in a death grip and Western governments unwilling to intervene, Sarajevans with the means and opportunity continued to flee the city. Many of those already outside gave up hopes of returning. Gordana Knežević remained in Zagreb, where she had been joined by her husband, Ivo, in September 1994, when her journalism fellowship in the United States ended. After working initially as a reporter for Agence-France/Presse, Gordana took a new job in March 1995 as a translator and Croatian field representative for an overseas branch of the AFL/CIO. "I had to leave journalism," she told me. "Working with trade unions like this is perfect for me, at least for now. I don't have to confront the news every day."

Gordana expected to return to Sarajevo in May 1995 to begin preparations for moving her family back to the city. She and Ivo hoped it would be possible for eight-year-old Olga to attend school in Sarajevo in the fall of 1995. But Gordana was thwarted in her travel plans by the renewed fighting around the city and by the cancellation of the U.N. airlift. A few weeks later, she and Ivo received the news that Muslim refugees had taken over their Sarajevo apartment. Gordana was philosophical about the loss. "I was upset for about a half an hour," she said, "and then I got over it. I only had to think about how many Sarajevo families had their homes destroyed during the war and had family members killed." She and Ivo settled into their Zagreb lives, unhappy but seeing no alternative.

Their son Boris spent a year as a tenth grader at a high school in Minneapolis, Minnesota. His academic performance did not match that of his brother Igor in England, owing in part to his tendency to read Hemingway novels in math class. But Boris excelled in his writing and literature classes, and his grades were good enough to win him an opportunity to spend the 1995–1996 school year at a suburban high school near Seattle.

Former editor-in-chief Kemal Kurspahić spent a year as a Niemann Fellow at Harvard University, then returned to Washington as *Oslobodjenje*'s U.S. correspondent, supported by a foundation grant. Reporter Džeilana Pećanin, came to the United States in January 1995 for a four-month journalism fellowship and then chose to stay in the country when it became clear that conditions in Sarajevo were only getting worse. Her mother had left Sarajevo in the meantime to join a sister in Macedonia. "I have no place to go back to," Džeilana said. Her *Oslobodjenje* friend and colleague Senka Kurtović also won a fellowship opportunity in the United States and left Sarajevo in July 1995.

Senka intended to return to Sarajevo at the end of her fellowship, but so had Džeilana. The situation in Bosnia in the summer of 1995 was so bleak that it was only reasonable to wonder whether it made sense to stay in Sarajevo indefinitely. The Serb army had captured the U.N.-declared "safe areas" of Srebrenica and Žepa, and in July General Ratko Mladić, the Serb army commander, boasted in an interview with the Belgrade magazine *Svet* that "By autumn we'll take Goržade, Bihać, and in the end Sarajevo, and we'll finish the war in Bosnia." Such words were dismissed as meaningless bluster by Bosnian leaders, but they nonetheless made many Sarajevans nervous about their future. Morale in the city had never been lower.

Vladimir Štaka was determined to stay in Sarajevo with his wife, Dubravka, and their two-year-old daughter, Maja. But their neighborhood was among those hardest hit by the shelling and sniping that returned to Sarajevo in the spring of 1995. By June, the three of them were sleeping in their bathroom each night. Vladimir and Dubravka worried that little Maja would grow up traumatized, and in July 1995 Dubravka and Maja left Sarajevo to join relatives in Croatia. Vladimir expected to follow in the fall, when they would all emigrate to Canada. Vladimir was probably the hardest working reporter on the *Oslobodjenje* staff, and editor-in-chief Mehmed Halilović was dismayed at the thought of losing him. "I tell him how sad I am," Mehmed told me in a telephone conversation from Sarajevo. "I have total confidence in him. But then I say, 'This is your choice. I wish you every success.'" Halilović himself had opportunities to leave, but was making no plans to do so.

Nor was Vlado Mrkić, the grizzled veteran reporter. He had not resumed regular writing for *Oslobodjenje* in the two years since he had quit from disillusionment and despair. But like Vladimir Štaka, Vlado Mrkić was one of those Serbs who remained loyal to Sarajevo. With *Oslobodjenje*'s blessing and support, Vlado had traveled several times to Hungary to meet his wife and sons, who were living in Belgrade, only to return days later to Sarajevo. His oldest daughter was following in his journalistic footsteps and had gone to work as a reporter for the lively newsmagazine *B-H Dani*.

In the summer of 1995, no one felt safe in Sarajevo. Dozens of shells were falling around the city center each day. Sidewalk cafés and open markets that had been packed with people in the summer of 1994 were all closed a year later. By 3:00 P.M., city streets were generally deserted, as Sarajevans hurried home to their basement shelters. Each day, a few people did not make it. More than 200 civilians were killed by Serb gunfire in June and July alone. One shell landed at the entrance to the *Oslobodjenje* building on Marshal Tito Street, killing two people on the spot and wounding several others. Another shell hit the upstairs office, blowing out windows and damaging equipment. For the fourth time since the war began, the newspaper staff had to move to a new location.

Food and supplies were also a serious problem. By blocking aid convoys, closing the Sarajevo airport, and firing at vehicles that dared to use the Mt. Igman road, Serb army commanders were apparently intending to starve Sarajevo into submission. By July 1995, U.N. relief agencies were delivering barely 10 percent of the humanitarian aid needed to serve the needs of the Sarajevo population. *Oslobodjenje* production managers again ran short of newsprint and had to cut the press run to a mere 1,500 copies, a new low. But the paper continued to appear each day. As of August 1995, its record of uninterrupted wartime publication remained intact, and the management was even planning to expand distribution of the newspaper. A central Bosnia edition was set to be printed daily in Zenica, and a daily European edition was to begin publishing in Germany. The newspaper that had been named the best in Yugoslavia six years earlier had proved to be as heroic, resourceful, and persevering as any newspaper anywhere and was known around the world as a symbol of the Sarajevo spirit.

SOURCES AND NOTES

My principal background sources for this book were the following:

Banac, Ivo. *The National Question in Yugoslavia: Origins, History, Politics.* Ithaca, NY: Cornell University Press, 1984.

Cohen, Lenard J. *Broken Bonds: The Disintegration of Yugoslavia.* Boulder, CO: Westview Press, 1993.

Dedijer, Vladimir. *Genocid Nad Muslimanima.* Sarajevo: Svjetlost, 1990.

Dedijer, Vladimir, et al. *History of Yugoslavia.* New York: McGraw-Hill, 1974.

Dragnich, Alex. *Serbs and Croats: The Struggle in Yugoslavia.* New York: Harcourt Brace Jovanovich, 1992.

Fine, John V. A. *The Late Medieval Balkans: A Critical Survey from the Late Twelfth Century to the Ottoman Conquest.* Ann Arbor: University of Michigan Press, 1987.

Glenny, Misha. *The Fall of Yugoslavia: The Third Balkan War.* New York: Penguin Books, 1993.

Jelavich, Barbara. *History of the Balkans*, vols. 1 and 2. New York: Cambridge University Press, 1983.

Magaš, Branka. *The Destruction of Yugoslavia.* London: Verso, 1993.

Norris, H. T. *Islam in the Balkans: Religion and Society Between Europe and the Arab World.* Columbia, SC: University of South Carolina Press, 1993.

Norwich, John Julius. *Byzantium: The Apogee.* New York: Alfred A. Knopf, 1991.

Pavlowitch, Stevan K. *The Improbable Survivor: Yugoslavia and Its Problems, 1918–1988.* Columbus, OH: Ohio State University Press, 1988.

Poulton, Hugh. *The Balkans: Minorities and States in Conflict.* London: Minority Rights Group, 1991.

Ramet, Sabrina. *Nationalism and Federalism in Yugoslavia, 1962–1991.* Bloomington: Indiana University Press, 1992.

Singleton, Fred. *A Short History of the Yugoslav Peoples.* New York: Cambridge University Press, 1985.

Thompson, Mark. *A Paper House: The Ending of Yugoslavia.* London: Vintage, 1992.

West, Rebecca. *Black Lamb and Grey Falcon: A Journey Through Yugoslavia.* New York: Viking Press, 1941.

Introduction: A War over Names

p. 3 more than 9,000 Sarajevans: The casualty figures came from the Bosnian government's Health Ministry, based on daily death and injury reports. Representatives of the Geneva-based International Committee of the Red Cross in Sarajevo said they considered these numbers broadly accurate.

p. 6 half of the city's 430,000 residents: Sarajevo actually comprises ten municipalities, with a total 1991 population of 525,000. But five of those municipalities—Hadžići, Trnovo, Pale, Ilijaš, and Vogošča—are rural or semirural. In tallying the "city" population, I count only the five core urban districts: Old Town, Center, New Town, New Sarajevo, and Ilidža. Muslims were the largest single group in each of those districts, ranging from 78.0 percent of Old Town to 36.0 percent in New Sarajevo. In the five districts combined, Muslims accounted for 49.4 percent.

1. Bloodlines

p. 24 almost no one goes to church: According to the 1990 *Encyclopaedia Britannica:* "Rates of religious practice are low throughout [Yugoslavia]. Only about ten percent of the population has an active commitment to religion." Poulton cites a 1985 poll showing that only 17 percent of the population in Bosnia-Herzegovina were even believers (p. 43).

Most of the ancestors: This paragraph draws on Banac, Jelavich, Norris, and Sima Ćirković's chapter "The South Slavs Between the Byzantine and Frankish Empires" in Dedijer et al.

p. 35 Serb animosity toward Muslims: The quotations from Serb nationalist politicians in the 1920s are taken from Banac.

p. 37 Cvetković reportedly said: Stjepan Kljuić, former head of the Croat national party in Bosnia-Herzegovina, gave me this quotation. *Oslobodjenje* journalist Tihomir Loza cites Cvetković saying this in the June 1993 edition of *Balkan War Report,* published in London.

p. 38 A Partisan historian observed: Vladimir Dedijer, designated by Tito the Partisans' official historian, made this observation in Dedijer et al., p. 697.

In a declaration that echoed: The Chetnik leaders are quoted in Dedijer, *Genocid Nad Muslimanima.*

p. 39 Bosnian Muslims died in greater numbers: This assertion is supported by the demographic analyses of Bogoljub Kočević (1985) and Vladimir Zerjavić (1989).

p. 41 In a survey taken in 1990: The survey results appear in Cohen, p. 173.

2. A Time of Change

p. 47 Bosnia's population at the time: This breakdown does not reflect the number of Bosnians who were the products of mixed marriages or had mixed ethnic backgrounds. Bosnian citizens were free to declare any nationality they wished. A child of a Serb father and a Muslim mother could declare his or her nationality as Serb, Muslim, or Yugoslav. It would not be uncommon for one child of such a marriage to declare a Serb nationality and a sister or brother to choose to be a Muslim. It was in this sense that a census in Bosnia was in some respects like an election; citizens could "vote" for whichever nationality they preferred.

p. 55 wild and unfounded stories: The Yugoslav Forum for Human Rights found that only 9.6 percent of rapes in Kosovo between 1982 and 1986 were committed by Albanian men against Serb women.

p. 60 Serbs in Bosnia were never able to show: In an April 24, 1994, article in *The Washington Post* "Outlook" section, the former U.S. ambassador to Yugoslavia, Warren Zimmerman, wrote: "During my time as U.S. Ambassador to Yugoslavia, Milošević told me several times before the war that Serbs had no grievance in Bosnia." Similarly, Bosnian Serb leaders did not attempt to persuade the international community that the Serb people in Bosnia were badly treated by the Muslim-dominated Bosnian government in 1991. The Serbs' concerns were presented instead as fears stemming from World War II experiences.

p. 63 The call was finally accepted by Radovan Karadžić: The Karadžić section is based on interviews in Sarajevo with Ismet Cerić, Zdravko Grebo, Avdo Sidran, Gavrilo Grahovac, Marko Vesović, Judge Vasvija Vidović, Ahmet Pašalić, and others who knew Karadžić well.

4. Humiliation

p. 117 MacKenzie wrote friends and family: MacKenzie tells the day-by-day story of his Sarajevo tenure in his memoir, *Peacekeeper: The Road to Sarajevo* (Toronto: Douglas & McIntyre).

5. Hatred

p. 135 A U.N. team of experts concluded: A team of experts investigated rape allegations in the former Yugoslavia on a visit to the region from January 12 to 23, 1993. Their report appears as Appendix 2 of the third situation report of the U.N. Commission to Investigate the Human Rights Situation in the Former Yugoslavia, published February 12, 1993, in Geneva.

   The report of the European Commission mission into the treatment of Muslim women in the former Yugoslavia was published in Brussels on February 2, 1993.

p. 148 Perhaps in Bosnia men should be warned: The quotation from "A Letter from 1920" is from Ivo Andrić, *The Damned Yard and Other Stories,* ed. Celia Hawkesworth (London: Forest Books, 1992).

p. 149 Of all the things that man raises: The "Bridges" essay was published in English in *Books in Bosnia and Herzegovina,* vol. 3, no. 4 (Sarajevo: Association of Writers of Bosnia and Herzegovina, 1984).

8. War, *Oslobodjenje,* and Democracy

p. 200 Old Town Municipal Council President Selim Hadžibajrić: Each municipality in Bosnia had its own legislative body and executive leadership. Beginning with the collapse of Communist authority in 1990, the municipal councils became increasingly powerful.

ACKNOWLEDGMENTS

I could not have written this book without the full support and cooperation of my employer, National Public Radio, where I have worked for twelve years. Bill Buzenberg, vice president for news and information, encouraged me to take time off from my reporting duties to write this book and showed enthusiasm for the project at every step. Senior Foreign Editor Elizabeth Becker indulged me when I asked for an extra week of leave time, and then another, and then another. European Editors Julie McCarthy and Bob Duncan did not complain when my absence meant that important stories went uncovered. Rob Robinson and Kee Malesky of the NPR Reference Library and Katherine Miller in the London Bureau were generous in their research assistance. To the staff of *Oslobodjenje*, I owe respect as well as gratitude. Their courage inspired me, and their hospitality comforted me.

In war zones and in book writing, journalists depend on one another. Mary Battiata of *The Washington Post* and Chuck Lane of *The New Republic* kept me company, helped me work, and sharpened my thinking. I am indebted to them in particular. In Berlin and Sarajevo, I also benefited from the counsel and friendship of Ed Serotta, David Rieff, Ed Vulliamy, Neenah Ellis, Senada Kreso, Dželiana Pećanin, Vlado Štaka, Nedžad Imamović, Miroslav Tadić, Kemal Kurspahić, and Gordana Knežević, among other colleagues. Tina Rosenberg, Dan Gjelten, Lynda Gorov, and Cadi Simon gave helpful comments on my manuscript. Gail Ross looked after my interests, personal as well as professional. Aaron Asher had faith in an unpublished author and gave me the chance to write this book. Joy Johannessen got me started, and Wendy Wolf saw me through with patience, good humor, insightful criticism, and just enough firmness to keep me going.

INDEX

Page numbers in italics refer to photographs.

ABOUT THE AUTHOR

Tom Gjelten is a foreign affairs correspondent for National Public Radio. He was based in Berlin as NPR's correspondent for Central and Eastern Europe from 1990 to 1993. His coverage of the conflict in the former Yugoslavia earned Gjelten a Robert F. Kennedy Award, the 1991 Lowell Thomas Award from the Overseas Press Club, and the 1992 George Polk Award for Radio Reporting. Before his Berlin posting, Gjelten was NPR's Latin American correspondent, based in Mexico City. Gjelten has also written for *The New Republic* and other periodicals. This is his first book. He lives in Washington, D.C.